Praise for

TUTANKHAMUN

'An authoritative history . . . A thoughtful new account of
Tutankhamun's life and afterlife'
The Times

'Highly readable . . . the importance of discovering
the truth – rather than the myths, rumours and scandals
of the past century – comes to the fore'
Mail on Sunday

'Tyldesley pieces together as clear a picture as possible of
the pharaoh's life, death and afterlife, using expert insight
and a wealth of evidence to illuminate a compelling
character and his universe'
Book of the Month, *BBC History Revealed*

'A spirited and interesting account that sifts through the
surviving evidence and seeks to combat the widely held
belief that Tutankhamun was an insignificant king'
Minerva

Joyce Tyldesley was born in Bolton, Lancashire. She studied archaeology at Liverpool and Oxford Universities, before writing a series of academic yet accessible books on ancient Egypt, including several books for children. Her 2008 book *Cleopatra: Egypt's Last Queen* was a Radio 4 Book of the Week. Her 2012 book *Tutankhamen's Curse* (published as *Tutankhamen* in the USA), won the Felicia A. Holton Book Award of the Archaeological Institute of America. Joyce currently holds a chair in Egyptology at the University of Manchester.

Also by Professor Joyce Tyldesley

Professor Joyce Tyldesley

TUTANKHAMUN
PHARAOH · ICON · ENIGMA

Lost for three thousand years, misunderstood for a century

HEADLINE

First published in 2022 by
HEADLINE PUBLISHING GROUP

First published in paperback in 2023 by
HEADLINE PUBLISHING GROUP

2

Maps on pages xi and xiii and the family tree on page xix
© Martin Lubikowski, ML Design.
The cross section through the Valley of the Kings featured on page xiii is
a redrawing of Steve Cross's plan.

Please refer to page 294 for picture credits.

Cataloguing in Publication Data is available from the British Library

ISBN: 978 1 4722 8986 5

Designed and typeset by EM&EN
Printed and bound in Great Britain by Clays Ltd, Elcograf S.p.A.

HEADLINE PUBLISHING GROUP
An Hachette UK Company
Carmelite House
50 Victoria Embankment
London EC4Y 0DZ

www.headline.co.uk
www.hachette.co.uk

Contents

Acknowledgements

Many people have helped and encouraged me to write this book. In particular, I would like to thank Dr Paul Bahn, Dr Robert Connolly, Professor Fayza Haikal, Dr Meguid el Nahas, Dr Nicky Nielsen and James Wills. I am particularly grateful to Professor Steven Snape, who provided many of the hieroglyphic translations used within this book.

At Headline I would like to thank Georgina Polhill, Fiona Crosby, Iain MacGregor, Holly Purdham and Mark Handsley: all showed great patience as successive bouts of ill-health threatened the completion of this project. Finally, I would like to thank the online Egyptology students of Manchester University for their many years of loyal support and thought-provoking discussion.

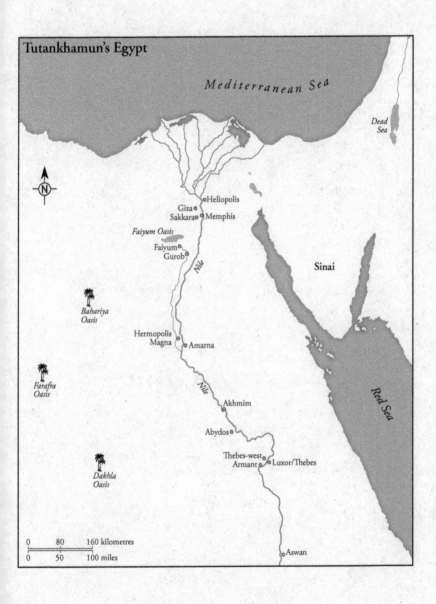

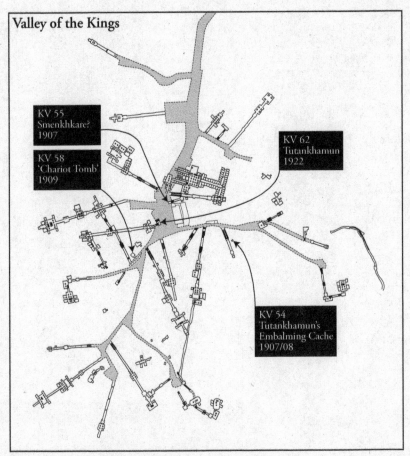

Valley of the Kings

KV 55
Smenkhkare?
1907

KV 58
'Chariot Tomb'
1909

KV 62
Tutankhamun
1922

KV 54
Tutankhamun's
Embalming Cache
1907/08

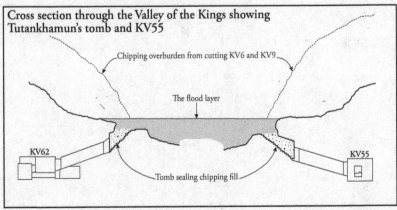

Cross section through the Valley of the Kings showing Tutankhamun's tomb and KV55

Chipping overburden from cutting KV6 and KV9

The flood layer

KV62

KV55

Tomb sealing chipping fill

Tutankhamun in Context

It is not possible to study Tutankhamun – or, indeed, any pharaoh – without some understanding of the history, geography and traditions of ancient Egypt. This preliminary section provides the key information that will underpin our in-depth investigation of Tutankhamun's life and death.

The time that we call the Dynastic Age – the time when Egypt was ruled by a king (known today as the 'pharaoh') – started in approximately 3100 BCE with the unification of the independent city states dotted along the Nile Valley and Delta, and ended in 30 BCE with the suicide of Cleopatra VII and Egypt's absorption into the Roman Empire. Over 3,000 years the dynastic Egyptians developed a highly efficient civil service, prodigious building skills, spectacular two- and three-dimensional art, a pantheon of gods and goddesses, and a sophisticated theology of death which included the preservation of the corpse in a bandaged, still lifelike form. For much of this time Egypt was the wealthiest and most powerful nation in the eastern Mediterranean world.

To the casual tourist, dynastic Egypt can appear perfect, coherent and unchanging from start to finish. A visit to one of the many elite cemeteries will reveal near-identical figures happily performing near-identical actions on stone walls; a visit to an ancient temple will reveal three-dimensional stone kings standing tall, proud and indistinguishable to worship the gods and goddesses revered by generations of ancestors. The date of these monuments seems almost immaterial. Are they 4,000 years old, or a mere 3,000 years? It doesn't really matter, as they are essentially the same. This comforting sense of visiting a place both isolated from the outside world and untouched by time is of course an illusion: the selective and seductive vision offered by artists determined to display the best and most traditional aspects of their land.

A closer examination of the written and archaeological evidence makes it clear that life did indeed change over the years, with the introduction of new peoples, new technologies, new beliefs and new fashions. For the most part these changes occurred gradually. But there are periods when sudden change – invasion or civil war, for example – caused a jolt. In 1352 BCE the coronation of the 'heretic king' Akhenaten heralded one such jolt: an unprecedented theological change which attacked many centuries of religious certainty and caused the court to take up a new way of life and death in a new royal city. It was into this atmosphere of religious uncertainty that Tutankhamun was born.

Egypt's priests were all too aware of the passage of time. They were charged with making regular – often hourly – offerings to the gods on behalf of the king. These offerings would please the gods, who, as a thank you, would allow Egypt and the king to flourish. Accurate timekeeping was therefore a matter of great importance. The priests monitored the movements of the sun and the stars to calculate the hours, and they maintained the King List – a lengthy record of royal names and reign lengths stretching back to the mythical era when gods rather than kings ruled Egypt – to record the passing years. These years were counted as repeating cycles of reigns, with every new king restarting the cycle with a new Year 1.

Tutankhamun dated events with reference to his own reign: Year 3 of the reign of Tutankhamun, Year 4 of the reign of Tutankhamun, and so on. Egyptologists often use this ancient system; not to baffle the non-specialist, but because it is extremely accurate. We are able to be very precise when we say that a particular wine jar was sealed in Tutankhamun's Year 9, but we struggle to tie his Year 9 into our own linear calendar. Was the wine jar sealed in 1328 or 1327 BCE?

An additional layer of complexity is introduced when a king changes his name. Akhenaten came to the throne as Amenhotep, and his successor, Tutankhamun, came to the throne as Tutankhaten; both changed their name for religious reasons soon after their accession.

To make the vast King List manageable, late-dynastic historians separated their monarchs into 'dynasties': successive lines of kings who were connected but not necessarily blood relatives. These dynasties have in more recent times been grouped into times of centralised rule (Kingdoms) interspersed with times of decentralised or foreign control (Intermediate Periods):

Early Dynastic Period (3100–2686 BCE): Dynasties 1–2

Old Kingdom (2686–2160 BCE): Dynasties 3–8

First Intermediate Period (2160–2055 BCE): Dynasties 9–11 (part)

Middle Kingdom (2055–1650 BCE): Dynasties 11 (part)–13

Second Intermediate Period (1650–1550 BCE): Dynasties 14–17

New Kingdom (1550–1069 BCE): Dynasties 18–20

Third Intermediate Period (1069–664 BCE): Dynasties 21–25

Late Period (664–332 BCE): Dynasties 26–31

Macedonian and Ptolemaic Period (332–30 BCE)

This is a far from perfect classification which ignores the rich complexities of Egypt's long history. The divisions between the Kingdoms and the Periods are by no means as clear-cut as the system suggests. But it is a classification that has become deeply embedded in Egyptological thinking, and it cannot be avoided. Tutankhamun therefore belongs to the late 18th Dynasty. Under a different, equally problematic dating system he rules Egypt during the Late Bronze Age.

The kings and queens of the late 18th Dynasty, Tutankhamun's family and contemporaries, are:

Tuthmosis IV (reigned 1400–1390 BCE) and Queen Nefertari

Amenhotep III (reigned 1390–1352 BCE) and Queen Tiy

Amenhotep IV/Akhenaten (reigned 1352–1336 BCE) and Queen Nefertiti

Smenkhkare (reigned 1338–1336 BCE) and Queen Meritaten

Tutankhaten/Tutankhamun (reigned 1336–1327 BCE) and Queen Ankhesenpaaten/Ankhesenamun

Ay (reigned 1327–1323 BCE) and Queen Tiye

Horemheb (reigned 1323–1295 BCE) and Queen Mutnodjmet

Smenkhkare's brief reign overlaps with Akhenaten's reign: it seems that they were co-regents, with Smenkhkare either enjoying a brief solo reign or dying before he could achieve independent rule. Queens Tiy (consort of Amenhotep III) and Tiye (consort of Ay) have the same name: I have used variant spellings to distinguish the two. Ay was not born royal, but may have been linked to the royal family by his sister (who was, perhaps, Queen Tiy) and his daughter (who was, perhaps, Queen Nefertiti). Horemheb, too, was a commoner, but his wife, Mutnodjmet, may have been Nefertiti's identically

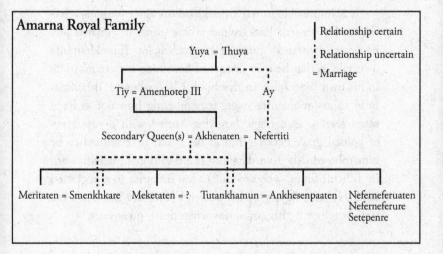

named sister. His reign marks the end of the 18th Dynasty. The next king, his friend and colleague Ramesses I (reigned 1295–1294 BCE), is classified as the first king of the 19th Dynasty. He was succeeded by his son Seti I (reigned 1294–1279 BCE) and his grandson Ramesses II (reigned 1279–1213 BCE), popularly known today as 'Ramesses the Great'. The earlier Ramesside kings are therefore more closely connected to the Amarna kings than they would perhaps like us to know.

Tutankhamun's family includes some of the best-known characters from the ancient world. Akhenaten and Nefertiti in particular have fascinated historians for over a century; he for his unique religious convictions and she initially for her great beauty and more recently for her perceived political power. Each has left art so striking that it is instantly recognisable 3,000 years after their deaths. The time during which the 'heretic' Akhenaten ruled Egypt from his isolated purpose-built city has been given its own modern name: the Amarna Age.

It is impossible to tell Tutankhamun's story without referring to his Amarna background. These stories of Amarna life, however, constantly threaten to overwhelm Tutankhamun's own tale so that he is in danger of becoming a mere footnote in his own biography. In this book I have allowed Tutankhamun to assume centre stage, remembering him not as he is often seen – as a tragic boy-king buried with a vast array of golden grave goods – but as he would have wished to be remembered. My Tutankhamun is a traditional pharaoh born in difficult times, who sets out to restore order to a neglected land. He rules Egypt for ten peaceful years and is well on the way to achieving his ambitions when death intervenes.

Tutankhamun's Egypt

Tutankhamun inherited a land of two very different halves, united by a dependence on 'the River'. The River entered Egypt at the southern border town of Aswan and flowed northwards for 600 miles before splitting into multiple branches and emptying into the Mediterranean Sea. It is difficult to overestimate its importance. The River brought water and prosperity to an otherwise arid region, allowing the people to fish, hunt, raise animals and grow food, flax and papyrus. It served as a highway, a laundry and a sewer, and it provided the thick mud needed to create pottery and an endless supply of bricks. Today the River is better known as the Nile.

Northern Egypt, or Lower Egypt, was the wide, flat Nile Delta: a moist expanse of fields, canals and papyrus marshes whose extensive coastline and Sinai land bridge allowed links to the wider Mediterranean world. The principal city, Ineb-Hedj, or 'White Walls' (better known today as Memphis), occupied a strategically important location at the junction of Upper and Lower Egypt, near modern Cairo. Memphis was founded at the time of unification and remained important throughout the Dynastic Age. During the New Kingdom it was a significant international trading centre, with ships from the Eastern Mediterranean arriving via the Pelusiac branch of the Nile to unload copper, wood and resin and pick up Egyptian grain, glass and gold. The bureaucrats who lived and worked in Memphis built impressive stone tombs in the nearby Sakkara cemetery, which housed Egypt's earliest pyramids. The chief god of Memphis was the shrouded craftsman-creator Ptah. In its heyday, Ptah's temple complex was a magnificent sight, with major and minor temples, lesser shrines, monumental gateways, processional avenues and sacred lakes. Today, most of ancient Memphis has vanished.

Southern Egypt, or Lower Egypt, was the long, narrow Nile Valley. This was a hotter, drier land focused on the River. Mudbrick houses for the living were built on the edge of the fertile soil bordering the River – the Black Land – and stone houses for the dead were built in the vast, inhospitable desert – the Red Land – that lay beyond. The principal city, Waset, known to the locals as simply 'the City' (and better known today as either ancient Thebes or modern Luxor), owed its high status to the local rulers who united Egypt after both the First and Second Intermediate Periods and who subsequently used their wealth to develop their home town and promote their local gods. Much of 18th Dynasty Thebes was built on the east bank of the Nile, around and between the temple complexes at Karnak and Luxor. Today this ancient city is almost entirely lost beneath the modern town of Luxor. The chief god of Thebes was Amun, 'The Hidden One', who had merged with the sun god to form the composite deity Amun-Ra. He was worshipped in his extensive Karnak temple complex and, modestly veiled to protect his secret persona, made regular journeys through the streets, travelling south to the Luxor temple in celebration of the annual Opet Festival, or sailing across the River to visit the royal mortuary temples that fringed the desert edge.

Situated on the east bank of the Nile, halfway between Thebes and Memphis, Akhetaten, or 'Horizon of the Aten', was the brand-new royal city built on virgin land by Tutankhamun's predecessor, Akhenaten. Today, Akhetaten is better known as Amarna or el-Amarna. The Amarna preserved in Akhenaten's art is a garden city filled with palaces, solar temples and trees: a city of sunlight and happy people. The Amarna preserved by archaeology is an altogether darker place: a city where children labour on building sites, the poor go hungry and the elite are forced to abandon their traditional expectation of a life after death. Tutankhamun was born at Amarna: that is where his story starts.

Tombs and mummy numbers

For many centuries the kings of the Old and Middle Kingdoms built magnificent pyramids in the desert cemeteries of northern Egypt. The 18th Dynasty kings broke this tradition and started to cut their tombs into the rock of the remote Valley of the Kings on the west bank of the Nile, opposite the city of Thebes. Their tombs have each been allocated a sequential KV number. Tombs in the Western Valley, an offshoot of the main or Eastern Valley of the Kings, are given interchangeable WV or KV numbers, so that the tomb of Amenhotep III may be designated either KV22 or WV22. Just twenty-five of the KV tombs are royal tombs. Others were built for Egypt's non-royal elite, while some are not even tombs. The same system is applied throughout the vast Theban necropolis, with tombs in the Deir el-Bahri bay being given specific DB numbers and other tombs receiving more general TT (Theban Tomb) numbers.

In 1922 Tutankhamun's tomb was given the next number in the sequence, becoming KV62. Two tombs have been discovered since: KV63 (discovered in 2005) is a storage chamber or mummification workshop and KV64 (discovered in 2011) originally belonged to an unknown 18th Dynasty female but had been robbed and usurped during the 22nd Dynasty.

The tomb number may be used to identify any anonymous mummy found within that particular tomb. So, for example, the Valley of the Kings workshop-tomb KV55 has yielded the much-discussed anonymous male known simply as mummy KV55, while the cache tomb KV35, the original tomb of Amenhotep II, has yielded, amongst others, the female mummies known as KV35EL (the 'Elder Lady') and KV35YL (the 'Younger Lady'). All three of these mummies feature in Tutankhamun's story.

Tutankhamun's tomb is comprised of four chambers, a short passageway and a flight of steps. The names used to describe the chambers – Antechamber, Annexe, Burial Chamber and Treasury (originally named the Storeroom) – are not the names that Tutankhamun would have recognised but potentially misleading modern names applied by the excavators.

The grave goods, or groups of grave goods, were each allocated a reference number before being removed from the tomb. Some grave goods have also been given a modern name, which in many cases also has the potential to mislead: a distinctive

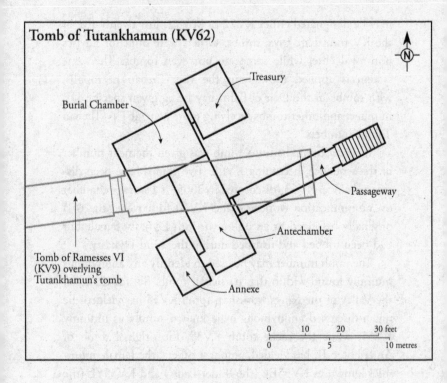

Tomb of Tutankhamun (KV62)

Treasury

Burial Chamber

Passageway

Antechamber

Tomb of Ramesses VI
(KV9) overlying
Tutankhamun's tomb

Annexe

0   10   20   30 feet

0   5   10 metres

inlaid ebony chair with a curved seat (no. 351), for example, is known today as the 'ecclesiastical throne' simply because it reminded Howard Carter of the seats used by modern bishops, while a two-handled lotus-shaped alabaster vessel has become the 'wishing cup' (no. 14) because its inscription expresses a longing for a peaceful afterlife: 'May your spirit live, may you spend millions of years, you who love Thebes, sitting with your face to the north wind, your eyes beholding happiness'. The reference numbers were allocated to the grave goods as the excavation team worked their way through the tomb as follows:

1–3: Outside the tomb and staircase

4: First doorway

5–12: Passageway

13: Second doorway

14–170: Antechamber

171: Annexe blocking

172–260: Burial Chamber (Tutankhamun's mummy is no. 256)

261–336: Treasury

337–620: Annexe

These reference numbers will be used to denote specific artefacts throughout this book.

After conservation work in the Valley of the Kings, the vast majority of the grave goods were transferred to the Cairo Museum, with botanical material going to the Cairo Agricultural Museum. In 2020–21 they were gradually relocated to the Grand Egyptian Museum at Giza. Most of the 18th Dynasty royal mummies are now housed in the National Museum of Egyptian Civilization. Tutankhamun, however, still lies in his tomb in the Valley of the Kings.

Prologue

(At Least) Two Tales of One King

Tutankhamun knew that death did not have to be the end of his life. As a dead king, he had several exciting options. He might merge with the bandaged god Osiris, to rule over the deceased who performed agricultural work in the Field of Reeds. Or he might join the crew of Ra's solar boat, to fight the night demons who threatened to stop the sun from rising. He might even become a star, eternally twinkling in the deep blue sky. But he also knew that these futures were far from guaranteed. In order to achieve any afterlife, Tutankhamun had to be remembered. If he were to be forgotten – if all trace of him were erased from the living world – he would die the second death from which there could be no return. This was a fate too horrible to leave to chance. Throughout his reign Tutankhamun worked to impose his presence on his land so that his story might be remembered by generations to come. Ten years, however, was not enough. Tutankhamun died unexpectedly young with his ambitions unfulfilled. It was not prudent planning but a succession of unforeseen events plus an unexpected cloudburst that allowed him to become Egypt's best-remembered king.

Tutankhamun has left not one but two very different stories, separated by more than 3,000 years. The first, told in the first and longer part of this book, is the story that he himself would recognise; the biography of the living king, his death and burial. It is, unfortunately, a story severely short on detail. Lacking any official record of his reign and missing the eyewitness accounts that would add some personality to the peoples of the ancient past, Egyptologists have been forced to play detective. Tutankhamun's life has been reconstructed as a series of disjointed events using clues gleaned from archaeology, art and random monumental inscriptions. Information gaps have been plugged with informed speculation and, occasionally, wishful thinking. As new evidence has become available, this fragmented data has been reappraised and rearranged to produce a new version of the same history. Having taught Egyptology at different levels for many years, I know that some readers will find this lack of a clear storyline frustrating, seeing the discussion of minute detail as nothing more than academic nit-picking. To these readers, I can only apologise. This book is written for those who see Egyptian history as an intellectual challenge and who relish the opportunity to sift through the evidence, spot significant clues and use them to reconstruct their own version of the past. For these readers the uncertainty – the sense of a story on the verge of being revealed – contributes to the joy of studying the ancient world.

It is obvious that older accounts of Tutankhamun's life – accounts written before the discovery of his tomb and the unwrapping of his mummy – will be out of date and misleading. It is far less obvious that the 'biographies' written in the more recent past might tell very different stories. While one Egyptologist might believe that Tutankhamun was the son of the mighty pharaoh Amenhotep III, another might convincingly argue that he was the son of the heretic king Akhenaten and a third might, with compelling supporting evidence, class him as the son of Akhenaten's shadowy co-regent, Smenkhkare. Meanwhile Tutankhamun's mother might with equal validity be selected from a list including, but not confined to, Queens Tiy and Nefertiti, Princesses Meritaten and Meketaten, the secondary Queen Kiya or the foreign-born Tadukhepa, who, having been sent to Egypt to marry Amenhotep III, outlived her fiancé and married his son. To add an additional layer of complexity, some have suggested that either Nefertiti or Kiya may actually be Tadukhepa. This lack of certainty over key events continues throughout Tutankhamun's life – what was his path to the throne? Did he rule at Amarna? Did he fight in battle? Did he limp? – to his death, which has been variously attributed to tuberculosis, malaria, murder, battlefield wounds, a high-speed chariot accident or trampling by a hippo.

My own approach to Tutankhamun's story is loosely based on the principle of Occam's Razor: 'entities must not be multiplied beyond necessity', or, other things being equal, the simplest explanation is usually the correct one. Faced with two or more competing theories, I will tend to accept the most straightforward. I have applied this approach throughout this book, but have highlighted areas where others legitimately take a different view and have occasionally asked questions that, at the moment, do not have answers.

Scanty and disjointed as it may be, the evidence makes one thing clear. Tutankhamun was a far from typical king. Born at Amarna – the isolated city built by Akhenaten – he was raised to worship just one god: the sun disc known as the Aten. Throughout Tutankhamun's childhood the Aten poured its life-giving light over Egypt's king, empowering him to rule as a semi-divine being. The traditional state gods, relegated to the shadows, could only watch. The elite, those who surrounded the king, were forced to watch too, as slowly, inexorably, royal power dwindled both within Egypt's borders and throughout the empire beyond. Akhenaten's death brought his religious experiment to an abrupt end. He had not done enough to persuade his court that the Aten offered the path to true enlightenment. And so, with the help of his advisors, Tutankhamun dedicated his reign to the restoration of the glorious pre-Amarna days: days that he was too young to have experienced.

Ten years after inheriting his tarnished throne much had been accomplished, and, with Amarna abandoned, the pantheon re-established, the royal necropolis reopened and the army on the verge of achieving the victories that would secure his empire, it seemed that Tutankhamun was destined to become one of the great pharaohs. Then an ill-advised expedition brought everything to an abrupt end. As Egypt mourned her lost king, the royal family shattered under the pressure of finding a suitable successor. The age of the sun kings had ended: the age of the warrior kings was about to begin.

Tutankhamun's other story, told in the second and shorter part of this book, is the far better-documented history of the discovery and excavation of his tomb, and of the reinvention of the king that followed his resurrection. In November 1922 a team of British Egyptologists, financed by Lord Carnarvon and directed by Howard Carter, determined to discover the barely remembered 18th Dynasty king Tutankhamun. They were expecting to find an elderly courtier who, having gained his crown by marrying into the royal family, died soon after of old age. Instead, to their great surprise, they discovered a 'boy-king' lying in a nest of golden coffins surrounded by an astonishing array of 5,398 grave goods. Their excavation sparked an unprecedented global public interest in Tutankhamun and his elaborate preparations for death that, boosted by occasional touring exhibitions of real and replica grave goods, has continued to this day.

Prologue

In its traditional telling this discovery is an epic tale of adventure, sudden death and glinting gold, which features the archaeologist as a hero battling to reveal the past to an admiring world. But not everyone regarded the excavation as a triumph. Already in the 1920s, many were starting to question the archaeologists' easy assumption of their God-given right to visit a foreign land and rip a young man – not just any young man, but a king – not only from his grave but also from the bandages that guaranteed his afterlife. Meanwhile, excluded from the excavation, the Egyptian people could only watch as Western culture first absorbed Tutankhamun as one of its own and then started to squabble about what it had done. As arguments broke out over the ownership of Tutankhamun and his grave goods – did he belong to the world, to the Egyptian people or to Lord Carnarvon? – the press started to question the wisdom of excavating what they had identified as a 'cursed tomb'. This was surely a dangerous interference with the occult from which no good could come.

Unfortunately, Carter died before he could complete the formal, academic publication of the tomb and its contents, leaving just three popular books plus a host of journal and newspaper reports of varying accuracy to tell the story of his great adventure. Tutankhamun's grave goods are housed in the Cairo Museum and, as I write, are in the process of being transferred to the new Grand Egyptian Museum near the Giza pyramids, where they will be displayed in splendid, state-of-the-art galleries. Thirty years ago, when I started to write about ancient Egypt, this would have made them inaccessible to most of the world. In those pre-Internet days resources were confined to museums and specialist libraries, so that the study of ancient Egypt was effectively restricted to those lucky enough to live near resources or rich enough to visit them.

Prologue

Today, the Internet increasingly allows everyone to visit museums and libraries, to examine specific artefacts and to research archived material. The Griffith Institute at Oxford University has set a splendid example here, by making the Tutankhamun excavation records – the Howard Carter archive (notes, cards, photographs and lantern slides), Arthur Mace's diaries, notes taken by Alfred Lucas and Harry Burton's Tutankhamun photograph – freely available in the online exhibition *Tutankhamun: Anatomy of an Excavation*.[1] My hope is that readers inspired by Tutankhamun's story will access this archive, examine the photographs and use the original records to conduct their own armchair re-excavation of his tomb. To help with this private research I have provided Carter's reference numbers for the significant grave goods discussed throughout this book. These numbers are indicated thus (no. 541).

The death of a young person is always a shock, even if that death occurred thousands of years ago. We want to know what happened: how could things have gone so wrong? It is therefore not surprising that, while Tutankhamun's grave goods remain substantially uninvestigated and unpublished, his body has been subjected to four major medical investigations. In 1925, a team led by the anatomist Professor Douglas Derry conducted the initial unwrapping and autopsy of his mummy, but was unable to X-ray the remains. In 1968, Tutankhamun was re-examined and X-rayed by a team from Liverpool University led by the anatomist Professor Ronald Harrison. A decade later, Dr James Harris, a dentist from the University of Michigan, led a third examination, focusing on the king's head and teeth.

The most recent phase of investigation, conducted by the Supreme Council of Antiquities (now the Ministry of Antiquities) under the leadership of the Egyptologist and Secretary

Prologue

General of the Supreme Council of Antiquities, Dr Zahi Hawass, was the first re-examination for which permission was granted to remove the king's body from his tomb, allowing the team to work away from the curious gaze of tourists. Their work started in 2005 with a virtual autopsy using state-of-the-art scanning technology and progressed to DNA sampling and an attempt to define Tutankhamun's family tree. The results of their investigations have been disseminated and discussed, with the DNA evidence in particular sparking heated debate amongst Egyptologists and scientists. Despite the dramatic headlines – 'King Tut, Queen Nefertiti and their Incestuous Family Tree' being one of the more restrained examples – many experts believe that we are not yet close to proving Tutankhamun's birth family.[2] Due to its contentious nature, I have presented the DNA evidence for Tutankhamun's family separately as the epilogue to Chapter 10.

Many books have been written about Tutankhamun, his life, his death and his afterlife. Is there really room for more? I firmly believe that there is. Of course, as the author of two Tutankhamun-themed books, I am bound to think so. But, examining the evidence objectively, it is clear that his is a still-evolving tale; evolving both in terms of the archaeological and textual evidence which continues to emerge, and in terms of the cultural lens through which we view this evidence. A decade ago I wrote about Tutankhamun, focusing on the excavation of his tomb and the development of the 'Tutankhamun's curse' myth. Now I am able to present evidence that allows me to focus far more on Tutankhamun's life and times. I still tell the story of his afterlife – his life post-excavation – but while I have included enough material to fully explain the history of the discovery for those unfamiliar with it (with apologies to readers who feel that this story has already received sufficient attention from me and other authors), the details of the actual discovery have been reduced, as they are less relevant to the king himself.

Not everyone agrees that Tutankhamun is worth this degree of detailed scrutiny. However, the objection often raised by professional Egyptologists, that Tutankhamun is an insignificant king unworthy of this attention – that he is somehow stealing the spotlight that should be focused on higher-achieving kings, and in so doing falsely persuading the general public of his importance – rather misses the point. Like it or not, 'King Tut' is an ancient world celebrity and, as with all celebrities, the modern world is eager to read more about him. If those who know most about ancient Egypt draw away from Tutankhamun with a fastidious shudder, the books will be written anyway, by those who know far less.

I question the assumption that Tutankhamun is insignificant, either in life or in death. Tutankhamun started his reign as a boy under the control of his advisors and family members and ended it as the most influential man in the Bronze Age Mediterranean world. He vanished for 3,000 years, then reappeared as an ancient world ambassador, inspiring the modern world to learn more about Egypt's glorious past. The occasional touring exhibitions of his grave goods and associated artefacts (real and replica) have generated much-needed income for Egypt and have boosted the vitally important tourist industry: an industry that in pre-Covid 2019 generated over $13 billion.[3] There are many professional Egyptologists working in museums and universities in the UK today who will admit to having been inspired by the 1972 Tutankhamun touring exhibition and the high-quality publications and documentaries that accompanied it. I know this because I am one of them.

Prologue

Tutankhamun has, more than any other Egyptian king, achieved the often-expressed hope of being remembered forever. My own hope is that he is remembered as accurately and as thoroughly as he deserves to be.

PART ONE

THEBES 1336 BCE

1

The Prince's Tale

Tutankhaten's Family and Early Life

In a lengthy poem, carved on the wall of a private tomb, the 'heretic king' Akhenaten addresses and explains his god:[1]

The earth becomes bright when you rise on the horizon and shine as the Aten in the daytime. You dispel the darkness when you cast your rays. The Two Lands are a celebration of light, awake and standing upright now you have roused them. Their bodies are cleansed and clothed as they raise their arms in adoration of your rising.

Now the whole land begins to work. All the flocks are content with their pasture, trees and plants grow. Birds fly up from their nests, their wings stretched in praise of your Ka. All the flocks gambol on their legs and everything that flies and perches lives when you rise for them. Ships sail to the north and to the south, and every road is open at your rising. The fish in the river leap before you, for your rays are in the middle of the sea.

Fifty years after Tutankhamun's death, the commoner-born king Seti I carved a copy of the King List onto the wall of his Abydos temple, ensuring that he would be eternally associated with his illustrious 'ancestors'. It should be an easy matter for us to visit Abydos, consult Seti's list, identify Tutankhamun and establish the pattern of late 18th Dynasty rule. Unfortunately, Egyptology is rarely that simple. Seti, regarding Tutankhamun and his immediate family as undesirable heretics, had them ruthlessly excised from Egypt's history. His list of kings jumps from the respected Amenhotep III to the equally respected Horemheb, omitting all reigns in between. So strong was the magical power of the hieroglyphic script, it was as though these reigns had never been. No one, however, could wipe all trace of the kings – Akhenaten, Smenkhkare, Tutankhamun and Ay – from their land. Denied official recognition, Tutankhamun's tale survived, without a continuous narrative, in fragments of archaeology, art and monumental inscriptions scattered throughout Egypt. To reconstruct his life and death, we need to gather this evidence and piece it together.

When, in 1352 BCE, Amenhotep III died after thirty-eight peaceful and largely uneventful years on the throne, his son Amenhotep inherited his crown, becoming Neferkheperure Waenre (*The transformations of Ra are perfect, the unique one of Ra*) Amenhotep IV. Young Amenhotep was the second-choice heir; his elder brother, Tuthmosis, had been groomed for kingship but had died sometime during their father's third decade of rule. The evidence for Tuthmosis's life as crown prince is limited. However, a small schist statuette allows us to glimpse him, semi-prostrate and dressed in the kilt, side-lock hairstyle and leopard-skin cloak of a priest, as he ritually grinds grain for the great Ptah of Memphis. Inscriptions engraved around the figure introduce him as '. . . the King's Son, the Priest Tuthmosis . . . I am the servant of this noble god; his miller . . .' The limestone sarcophagus of his pet cat, Ta-Miu (The Cat), confirms his full and final titulary as 'Crown Prince, Overseer of the Priests of Upper and Lower Egypt, High Priest of Ptah in Memphis and Priest of Ptah'. Finally, a second schist statuette shows him as a bandaged mummy, lying on a bier.[2]

Tuthmosis's tomb has never been found, and we can say no more about him.

Amenhotep IV started his reign as an entirely typical 18th Dynasty king, crowned by the god Amun-Ra and ruling from the twin administrative centres of Memphis in the north and Thebes in the south. As the workmen started to cut his tomb in the Western Valley, the offshoot of the Valley of the Kings where his father now lay, building work continued in and around the Karnak temple complex of Amun-Ra. Here Amenhotep demonstrated his intention to preserve *maat* – the ideal state of affairs – by completing his father's unfinished projects. Within three years of his coronation, however, Amenhotep had turned his back on the traditional pantheon and dedicated his life to the service of one god: an ancient but hitherto insignificant solar being known as 'the Disc', or 'the Aten'. Amenhotep (*Amun is satisfied*) had become Akhenaten (*Living Spirit of the Aten*). To please his god, Akhenaten founded a royal city on virgin land, part way between Thebes and Memphis. He named his city Akhetaten (*Horizon of the Aten*); today it is better known as Amarna or el-Amarna. The period of no more than twenty years when Egypt was ruled from Amarna is known as the Amarna Age or Amarna Period.

Egyptologists have a tendency to isolate and magnify this brief period, zooming in on the new city and its unique religion and seeing it as something very different to the periods that had gone before and those that were still to come. This was indeed a very different time, and this difference directly affected both the elite who surrounded Akhenaten and the ordinary people who were compelled to move to Amarna city to work for the king and his god. However, for the vast majority of the population, the peasants living in the hamlets and villages of the Nile Valley and Delta, life throughout the Amarna Age continued very much as it had before.

Akhenaten's city, like his religion, proved unsustainable. Both were quickly abandoned after his death. While the mud-brick domestic architecture – the houses, palaces and offices – degraded to form a valuable fertile soil which would in modern times be spread across the fields, wrecking the archaeological stratigraphy, thousands of inscribed stone blocks from the Amarna temples were salvaged and incorporated in the sacred buildings of the neighbouring city of Hermopolis Magna (modern el-Ashmunein). This recycling was far from unusual; it was far easier to quarry old buildings than to cut and transport new stone, and throughout the Dynastic Age older blocks were routinely incorporated into newer buildings with their already inscribed faces turned inwards. It is on one of these recycled and badly damaged temple blocks that we find our first mentions of a prince named Tutankhaten (*Living Image of the Aten*), who is described as 'the King's Son of his body, his beloved'.[3] Within a few years of this carving, Tutankhaten would change his name and his religious allegiance to become Tutankhamun (*Living Image of Amun*). He would be the one to end the Amarna experiment.

Egypt's kings celebrated their greatest triumphs in stone. Epic battles, lucrative trading expeditions, unparalleled building works, generous acts of devotion to the gods: all these and more were commemorated in the extensive hieroglyphic inscriptions and extravagant illustrations carved and painted on multiple temple walls. Akhenaten therefore celebrated his new city in a series of inscriptions and associated statues cut into the cliffs on both banks of the Nile around Amarna. His 'Boundary Stelae' tell the story of the founding of his city, define its limits and even include a brief mention of his growing family of daughters:[4]

> *The Aten gives life eternally and my heart rejoices in the king's wife together with her children, which causes the king's wife Neferneferuaten Nefertiti to reach old age in these millions of years . . . she being in the care of Pharaoh, and which causes the king's daughter Meritaten and the king's daughter Meketaten to reach old age, they being in the care of the king's wife, their mother, for ever . . .*

That is as personal as his inscriptions get, however. Eighteenth-Dynasty kings did not share more intimate details of their private lives on their public monuments, and the births of their children went unannounced. We learn about the six daughters who would eventually be born to Akhenaten and his consort, Nefertiti, because, in increasing numbers, they appear with their parents in the images and statue groups that filled Amarna city. This official art makes it clear that Akhenaten was surrounded by women who supported him in all his endeavours. But sons – potential future kings – were excluded from official art and are to all intents and purposes invisible to us. All too often, our first sighting of an Egyptian prince occurs when he steps out of the shadows to assume the role of crown prince, or king-in-waiting. This is what happened to the young Akhenaten. While his four sisters stand beside their parents in decades' worth of official art, he is represented in a few scenes with his father which were probably carved after the old king's death, plus one wine jar label which mentions 'the estate of the King's true son Amenhotep'. Tutankhaten's sudden, unexplained appearance at Amarna at an age when he might have become the officially recognised heir to the throne is far from unusual.

If we want to learn more about the young prince's birth we have to leave Amarna and travel south, to Thebes. Here, hidden from view on the west bank of the Nile, is the remote royal necropolis known as the Valley of the Kings. Although Tutankhamun's small tomb was famously packed with a vast quantity of 'wonderful things' – sacred and magical artefacts to help the dead king to achieve his afterlife, family heirlooms, personal belongings and more practical, daily-life objects which would allow him to live comfortably beyond death – it was, in one important respect, a great disappointment. It yielded no informative writings. As his was the first substantially intact royal tomb to be discovered in the Valley, the excavators had been uncertain what to expect, but they had hoped to find a written account of Tutankhamun's reign, details of his private life and, perhaps, an explanation of Akhenaten's heretic regime. Unfortunately, there were no personal or unique documents, no diplomatic correspondence and no information that would allow the creation of a family tree. Most disappointing of all, a 'box of papyri', which the archaeologists had optimistically dubbed 'Tutankhamun's library', proved to be a collection of discoloured linen loincloths.

The tomb did, however, hold indirect clues to Tutankhamun's age and identity. Included amongst the golden grave goods was an assortment of plain wine jars. Some had been smashed by the priests who packed the tomb and by the various gangs of robbers who had tried to empty it, but many were complete and labelled with details of vintage, vineyard, vintner, wine type and – crucially – regnal year. From these labels we learn that in Year 9 a chief vintner named Sennefer, working at the vineyard known as 'House of Tutankhamun ruler of Upper Egyptian Heliopolis [Thebes], life! prosperity! health! From the Western River', instructed his workers to fill a wine jar with a beverage described, rather unhelpfully, as 'wine' (no. 541). Sennefer has given us Tutankhamun's highest confirmed regnal year. We can reasonably assume that a jar containing 'wine of good quality', dated to Year 10 of an unnamed king, was also filled during Tutankhamun's reign, but an equally anonymous Year 31 jar of simple 'wine' must have been sealed during the unusually long reign of Amenhotep III.[5]

Lying in the burial chamber at the heart of his tomb, protected by successive layers of linen bandages and shrouds, three nested golden coffins, a stone sarcophagus and four gilded wooden shrines, Tutankhamun's body preserved the forensic evidence which would reveal his age at death. Teeth – their presence or absence – can be hugely helpful in determining age at death, as tooth development is less likely to be affected by factors such as malnutrition and illness which can have an impact on skeletal development. During the 1925 autopsy, however, the anatomist Douglas Derry found that Tutankhamun's mouth had been accidentally glued shut by the resins and unguents poured over the mummy's head during the funeral ritual. This made his teeth inaccessible. To avoid damaging Tutankhamun's face by forcing his mouth open, Derry cut into his head, beneath the chin. This damage was subsequently repaired with resin and is today invisible to the naked eye. Derry could now see that Tutankhamun's right upper and lower wisdom teeth 'had just erupted into the gum and reached to about half the height of the 2nd molar. Those on the left side could not be seen easily, but they appeared to be in the same stage of eruption.'[6] This dental evidence, combined with a visual examination of the ephyphises (the growth plates at the end of the long bones), led him to suggest that Tutankhamun had died at between seventeen and nineteen years of age, a diagnosis which has subsequently been confirmed by consideration of the eruption of his third molars using X-rays and CT scans.

If the teenage Tutankhamun had ruled Egypt for no less than ten years, he must have inherited his throne as a child of roughly eight years of age. Akhenaten himself enjoyed seventeen years on the throne; his reign length is evidenced by two jar labels, one of which has its original 'Year 17: honey' label superseded by the 'Year 1: wine' label of the anonymous next king.[7] As there is no evidence for an extensive gap between Akhenaten's death and Tutankhaten/Tutankhamun's accession, we can conclude that Tutankhamun was probably born during Akhenaten's Year 9 and, as Akhenaten had already moved his family to Amarna by this time, we can deduce that he was born at Amarna.

More evidence for the child-king can be gathered by rummaging through the boxes and chests that filled the outer chambers of his tomb. Tutankhamun was buried with a wide assortment of clothing made from hand-spun linen so fine that archaeologists have struggled to replicate its quality. There were sleeved and sleeveless tunics, shawls, sashes and belts, gloves, head coverings and socks with a separate big toe to allow him to wear his toe-post sandals. Leather accessories included shoes, sandals and the sadly misidentified library-loincloths (at least 145 of them; the more damaged examples were deemed impossible to conserve and were thrown away). There was even what seemed to be a 'mannequin': a wooden, armless and legless model of the crowned king which Howard Carter assumed was used to display his clothes and jewellery (no. 116). This was not a wardrobe designed specifically for the grave: textile analysis has revealed the minute signs of wear and washing which confirm that these clothes were actually worn by the living king.

A quick glance at any decorated 18th Dynasty elite tomb wall will show adults dressed in sparkling white linen and children of all classes naked and near-bald. This is how many of us picture life in ancient Egypt. Tutankhamun's garments, however, reveal an altogether more elaborate and colourful world: a world where royal tunics might be so heavy with fringing, tapestry, appliqué, embroidery, beading and sequin-like spangles that they could not have been worn on a daily basis. The archaeologists who emptied the tomb were confused and leapt to the conclusion – perhaps inevitable for a group of early twentieth-century Western men – that some of the more elaborate costumes must have been female garments. So a 'ceremonial robe' – a simple rectangle of fringed cloth with a round neck hole, decorated all over with blue and green glass beads and sequins of beaten gold (no. 21d) – was officially classified on Carter's record card thus:

> *This pattern garment should belong to a woman. It may, like some others in the box have been a child's garment. The King as a child might conceivably have been dressed as a girl on some occasions – cp. modern circumcision custom, or boy wearing girl's clothes to avoid evil eye.*

The tiny robe, measuring an estimated 80 x 50 cm, may be compared to a man's 'shirt', also recovered from the tomb, which measured 138 x 103 cm. It was, as the excavators noted, just one of several child-sized garments stored in the elaborately decorated 'Painted Box' in the Antechamber (no. 21). To Carter's great surprise, these were the garments of a child-king:[8]

> *Our first idea was that the king might have kept stored away the clothes he wore as a boy; but later, on one of the belts, and on the sequins of one of the robes, we found the royal*

cartouche. He must, then, have worn them after he became
king, from which it would seem to follow that he was quite
a young boy when he succeeded to the throne.

As it seems unlikely that the fully grown Tutankhamun would
have wished to squeeze into miniature garments, we must
question why his childhood wardrobe was packed for the
afterlife. Here we can draw a useful comparison with the linen
clothing used to dress the statues of the gods in the temples
each day. These garments were understood to absorb a form of
divinity from the statues, and this made them immensely valuable. It seems that the clothes worn by kings, too, absorbed an
aura of 'royalness' and semi-divinity that made them impossible to discard.

Tutankhamun took his childhood jewellery to his tomb as
well. His treasures included earrings that, during his lifetime,
were worn by women and children but not adult men. The
wide (7.5 mm) piercing in Tutankhamun's empty left earlobe
is presumably the legacy of a childhood spent wearing ear
studs. We can reasonably assume that there would have been a
matching hole in his right earlobe, but this was lost during the
autopsy. The ears on Tutankhamun's innermost coffin, and on
his gold mask, were also pierced for earrings, but these holes
were subsequently covered with small gold discs, possibly to
indicate that the king had outgrown childish jewellery. Meanwhile an empty box whose label was translated by Carter as
'the King's side-lock (?) as a boy' suggested that Tutankhamun
may have saved the elaborate plait that elite children wore on
the side of their otherwise shaven head (either no. 575 or no.
494).[9] Sadly, Carter's translation is inaccurate and the word
that he translated as 'side-lock' is more likely to refer to a
linen bag.

As to Carter's tentative thoughts of an elaborate circumcision ceremony – a rite of passage marking the transition from child to man, perhaps – there is no evidence that this was common practice in dynastic Egypt. Occasional texts and images suggest that some men were circumcised, but many mummies, including royal mummies, are not. Several years after the 'ceremonial robe' was discovered, Derry was able to examine Tutankhamun's shaved genitals as part of his autopsy. He found, somewhat to his surprise, that while the king's scrotum had been flattened against his perineum, his penis, 5 cm in length, had been bound and glued with resin to give a permanent, almost 90-degree erection. This would have encouraged Tutankhamun's eternal sexuality and fertility – an important aspect of the Egyptian male afterlife – while linking him to the mummified Osiris, a god so fertile that he fathered his son Horus after his own death. Derry was unable to determine if Tutankhamun had been circumcised.

As so often happens with Tutankhamun-related items, his penis went on to develop its own mini-mythology. Photographs confirm that, detached from the body but with the scrotum attached, it was present when Tutankhamun's autopsied body was laid on a tray of sand and replaced in his sarcophagus. But then it vanished. For a long time it was accepted that the penis had been stolen, probably during the Second World War when security was lax in the Valley of the Kings. This led to accusations of gross negligence, much speculation as to its whereabouts (foreign servicemen made a useful scapegoat), and many unfortunate puns citing lost 'crown jewels'. In 1968, Harrison discovered the missing member lurking in the loose cotton wool beneath the sand tray and, rather than attempt to reattach it, replaced it in the sand. Lost again, the penis was rediscovered during the most recent examination of the king's body.

The evidence from the tomb allows us to conjure up the shade of a little boy standing in the heat of the Amarna sun, dressed in elaborate but uncomfortably heavy garments and wearing the ear studs and side-lock which indicate that, although he is about to become a divine being, he is still very much a child. A highly stylised image of this same child can be seen on an inlaid gold perfume box discovered in the Burial Chamber, the most sacred part of the tomb (no. 240bis).[10] The box is shaped as a double cartouche – the hieroglyphic device representing a loop of rope that encircled the throne-name and birth-name of the king – standing on a pedestal, and each cartouche is topped by a solar disc and double plumes (the lid). As it is decorated front and back, there are four cartouches, each presenting Tutankhamun's throne-name: Nebkheperure (*Lord of Manifestations of Ra*). In its usual writing the 'Kheperu' element of his name would be represented by the scarab beetle plus three lines. Here, however, the beetle has been replaced by a squatting figure of Tutankhamun himself. The four images are subtly different, and it has been suggested that the changing colours of their faces, which vary from light to dark, may represent the king at four different stages of his existence: boy-king, adult king, dead king and reborn king. But the fact that two of the Tutankhamuns wear an elaborately plaited side-lock (the other two wear crowns) confuses this sequence and it may be that we are looking at just two stages – Tutankhamun equated with the living king (Horus) and the dead king (Osiris). However we interpret these images, it is clear that they are not true portraits as we understand the word today.

Young kings do not take their thrones by force: they inherit them. Tutankhamun's tomb confirms that he was born the son or grandson of a king but, frustratingly, does not tell us who this king might be. The most obvious candidate for the role of Tutankhamun's father has to be Akhenaten, the ruling king at the time of Tutankhamun's birth. However, Tutankhamun has left two random pieces of evidence that encourage us to doubt this paternity. The first is the dedication on the handle of a wooden astronomical instrument that names the 'father of his father' as Tuthmosis IV.[11] Tuthmosis IV was the father of Amenhotep III, and the grandfather of Akhenaten. The second is an inscription on the base of one of the 'Prudhoe Lions': a pair of 18th Dynasty red-granite recumbent lions originally commissioned by Amenhotep III for his Nubian Soleb temple, and later re-inscribed by Tutankhamun.[12] Here Tutankhamun describes himself as 'He who renewed the monument for his father, the King of Upper and Lower Egypt, Lord of the Two Lands, Nebmaatre, image of Re, Son of Re, Amenhotep Ruler of Thebes.'

Tutankhamun seems to be claiming Amenhotep III as his father: this would make him Akhenaten's younger brother. At first sight this seems impossible, as we know that Akhenaten ruled for seventeen years. However, Amenhotep III could perhaps have left an eight-year-old son to rule after his older son, Akhenaten, if he himself had been alive within Akhenaten's reign. Are we looking at a lengthy Amenhotep III–Akhenaten co-regency, with each king using his own year dates so that Akhenaten's Year 1 would have also been Amenhotep's Year 29? As co-regencies are rare in the 18th Dynasty, and as it is unlikely that nine years of joint rule would have gone entirely unrecorded, this seems highly unlikely.

Happily, but confusingly, we do not need to read Tutankhamun's statements literally. The Egyptian language was highly flexible and, just as we may today use the English words 'brother' and 'sister' to describe both actual siblings and friends, so the Egyptian word for 'father' could be used to describe a range of connected males: an actual father, a grandfather, a great-grandfather or a more generalised ancestor, while 'son' might also be used to indicate a son-in-law or a grandson. Tutankhamun is not claiming to be the actual son of Amenhotep III, but is deliberately aligning himself with his distinguished grandfather and his equally distinguished great-grandfather and, in so doing, distancing himself from his less than distinguished father.

As Akhenaten, like all of Egypt's kings, had many wives, so Tutankhamun has many potential mothers. If all went according to plan, his mother would be his father's consort, the Great Royal Wife Nefertiti. As she was the wife in the nuclear royal family (the king, his consort and their children), it was accepted that Nefertiti's son would inherit his father's throne. If Nefertiti failed to produce an heir, however, Akhenaten would look to his harem to find his successor. This was a far from unusual occurrence. Akhenaten's own father, Amenhotep III, had been the son of a harem queen named Mutemwia, while his father, Tuthmosis IV, had been the son of a harem queen named Tia.

While we know that Nefertiti bore six living daughters, there is no evidence that she ever bore a son or sons. That, of course, does not mean that she did not; we have already seen that royal sons had the potential to remain invisible throughout their fathers' reigns. We can roughly calculate the births of Nefertiti's six daughters from their appearances in their father's art. This is a far from perfect system – there are many reasons why a daughter might be excluded from the official family group – but it allows us to re-create the growing family of girls with a reasonable degree of confidence:[13]

— Meritaten Meritaten (*Beloved of the Aten*): born at
Thebes no later than Akhenaten's regnal Year 1, proba-
bly before Akhenaten became king.
— Meketaten (*Protected by the Aten*): born at Thebes proba-
bly in Year 4.
— Ankhesenpaaten (*Living through the Aten*): born before the
end of Year 7.
— Neferneferuaten-the-Younger (*Exquisite Beauty of the
Aten*): born at Amarna, probably by Year 8.
— Neferneferure (*Exquisite Beauty of Ra*): born at Amarna
before Year 10.
— Setepenre (*Chosen of Ra*): born at Amarna before Year 10

We know that Nefertiti was consort from the start of
Akhenaten's reign to her last attested mention in Year 16,
but we do not know how long they had been married before
Akhenaten became king. It is entirely possible that she produced one or more sons, and perhaps her eldest daughter,
before she became queen. According to our calculation, however, these sons would be too old to be Tutankhamun. We can
see that Nefertiti did not produce a daughter each year. There
are likely to be perfectly natural reasons for the gaps – failed
pregnancies, infant mortality or Akhenaten being distracted
by the women of the harem, perhaps – but it may be that
these were the years in which she gave birth to sons. If, as we
suspect, Tutankhamun was born during Akhenaten's Year 9,
Nefertiti could easily have been his mother.

The Amarna royal tomb – a super-sized tomb built by
Akhenaten as an eternal home for selected members of his
family – offers a possible glimpse of the infant Tutankhamun.
Situated in an ancient dried river bed (known today as the
Royal Wadi) cutting through the cliffs that formed Amarna's

eastern boundary, the tomb was never finished. Nevertheless, archaeological evidence – broken grave goods and damaged wall art – indicates that it was used for more than one burial before Amarna was abandoned. Akhenaten's own burial suite lay at the end of a long descending corridor, at the heart of the tomb. Two additional suites were, as Akhenaten himself tells us, designed for his consort and his eldest daughter: 'Let a tomb be made for me in the eastern mountain [of Akhetaten]. Let my burial be made in it . . . Let the burial of the Great King's Wife Nefertiti be made in it . . . Let the burial of the King's Daughter Meritaten be made in it . . .'[14]

Unfortunately, by the time it was discovered in the 1880s the tomb had been robbed multiple times, and any mummies were long gone. The carved and painted walls had suffered extensive damage but many scenes survived to show, as we would expect, Akhenaten and his family being blessed by the Aten's life-giving rays. The burial suite originally intended for Meritaten consists of three rooms, today designated Alpha, Beta and Gamma. In Room Alpha (Wall F), sitting incongruously beside unremarkable scenes set in the Great Aten Temple, we see an intimate, unexplained vignette.[15] Two registers, one above the other, tell a single, poignant story. The upper scene, set at the palace, shows Akhenaten and Nefertiti – unnamed, but identified by their distinctive crowns – standing beneath the sun disc. The couple are bowed in grief; their right arms are raised to their heads in mourning and Akhenaten clutches Nefertiti's left arm in a gesture of support. They are mourning before something or someone who has vanished from the scene. Outside the room female attendants are wailing, and a group of male dignitaries raise their arms in sorrow. A woman standing directly outside the room is holding a baby of uncertain gender in her arms, while an attendant standing in the doorway holds a fan, the symbol of royalty, over the infant. It looks as if the infant, the woman and the fan bearer are exiting the chamber. In the second scene we are shown the body of a woman lying on a bed. Akhenaten and Nefertiti are again mourning and there are smaller-sized figures (their daughters?) grieving. Outside the room female attendants weep and one, apparently overcome by emotion, is supported by two men. Damage to the wall makes it impossible to determine whether a baby was originally included in the scene.

It seems that a woman at the heart of the royal family has died and is being mourned by the king, queen and some of the princesses. It may be that the woman overcome by grief outside the room is the nurse who cared for the dead woman when she was a baby. If we push our interpretation further, linking the death to the appearance of the baby whose royal status is signalled by the fan, we can suggest that the woman has died in childbirth. This would explain the presence of the male dignitaries who have, perhaps, gathered to record a royal birth. However, we do need to be cautious. The baby may simply be one of Nefertiti's daughters in the arms of her nurse; it may even be, as the burial chamber was a place of rebirth, a representation of the deceased woman after death.

Who is the dead woman? We know that she is not Nefertiti, and she cannot be either Meritaten or Ankhesenpaaten as they outlived their father. It is possible that she is Meketaten, but this is unlikely as her death is recorded elsewhere in the Meritaten suite, in Room Gamma (Wall A). Meketaten's death scene is extensively damaged. Her body and most of the royal couple are missing, and the inscription carved above the dead princess is now largely obscured but, as it was recorded at the turn of the century, we know that it originally read 'King's Daughter of his body, his beloved, Meketaten, born of the

Great Royal Wife Nefertiti, may she live for ever and eternally'. Once again we see Akhenaten and Nefertiti standing beside a bier and, once again, outside the room we see a nurse carrying a baby. She is followed by two female attendants who carry fans. Although she can have been little more than twelve years old, the suggestion is that Meketaten has died in childbirth, although, again, we need to be careful in linking the deceased to the baby. A subsequent scene in the same room (Wall B) shows the dead Meketaten, or perhaps her statue, standing within a bower whose papyrus columns are entwined with convolvulus and lotus blossom. Meketaten wears a long robe, a short wig and a perfume cone. She faces her grieving parents and three of her sisters, who raise their arms in an attitude of mourning. Beneath the mourners there are tables laden with food, drink and flowers. Meketaten's bower is reminiscent of the birth bowers used by women in labour; it is, perhaps, intended to signify her own rebirth.[16]

Meketaten, who was probably born in Year 4, could not have given birth to Tutankhamun, who was probably born in Year 9. However, assuming that she is not Meketaten, the anonymous dead woman in Room Alpha could have been Tutankhamun's mother. Who is she? There are several possibilities: the three younger princesses, the queen mother, Tiy, one of Akhenaten's sisters or a favoured harem queen. If we are correct in our assumption that the woman died in childbirth, the three princesses (too young) and the queen mother (too old) can be ruled out. We are therefore looking at either one of Akhenaten's sisters or a harem queen who could, of course, in a land of consanguineous royal marriages, be one and the same person. There are a lot of 'ifs' and 'buts' in this reasoning, but we leave the royal tomb with the possibility that the scene in Room Alpha shows the birth of Tutankhamun (therefore breaking the rule that male children do not feature in official scenes) and the death of his mother, who is not Nefertiti.

Under normal circumstances – when the succession went as planned – we know nothing of the shadowy queens who lived, bore royal children and died within the harem walls. However, Amarna has yielded a surprising amount of evidence for the 'wife and great beloved of the king of Upper and Lower Egypt', Kiya. Kiya's origins are never explained, but her unique prominence tempts us to speculate that she is a woman of high birth, possibly the renamed Tadukhepa or, more likely, one of Akhenaten's renamed sisters. Kiya's portrait has survived on stone blocks recovered from Hermopolis, enabling us to recognise her rounded face, curled, bobbed 'Nubian-style' wig and large, circular earrings or ear studs. Earrings are not, of course, genetic, yet so closely have they become associated with Kiya that there is a tendency to classify any anonymous Amarna woman wearing large earrings as her. It is a measure of Kiya's great importance that she is allowed to accompany Akhenaten as he makes offerings and presides over official ceremonies, though she never appears if Nefertiti is present and it is clear that she does not outrank the Consort. Like Nefertiti, Kiya's intimate connection to the king enables her to worship the Aten directly, and this allows her to assume the significant, and we can guess lucrative, position of priestess in her own 'sunshade': a shrine dedicated to solar worship, set in a walled garden with trees and a pool outside the main city.[17] Also, like Nefertiti, Kiya bears Akhenaten's children. Continuing the tradition of invisible princes, we have images of her with an unnamed daughter but no son. A woman of such great importance would surely be given an appropriately high-status burial. Could the woman dying in Room Alpha be Kiya?

To collect our next piece of evidence for Tutankhamun's early life we need to sail north from Amarna, to the already ancient cemetery of Sakkara, burial place of the elite who lived and worked in Memphis. Here, in 1996, a team led by the French Egyptologist Alain Zivie discovered the tomb of the lady Maia cut into the limestone cliff.[18] The tomb had been thoroughly robbed in antiquity. It yielded neither Maia's mummy nor her grave goods, and a heap of partially burned mummified cats found in one of the chambers was a relic of the time, hundreds of years after Maia's death, when the tomb was repurposed as a catacomb for the burial of animals dedicated to the cat-headed goddess Bastet. Happily, the original inscribed and decorated walls were still intact, and these tell an interesting story.

Dressed in a simple sheath dress and fashionably long wig, Maia is at first sight indistinguishable from the many hundreds of 18th Dynasty wives who shared their husbands' tombs. She is, however, very different to these women: she has earned the right to her own large tomb. Freed from the dominating presence of a husband whose achievements will always take precedence over her own, she is able to speak about her life at some length on her tomb walls. It is here that we learn how she has had the great honour of being both 'Wet Nurse to the King' and 'Educator of the God's Body'; a scrap of broken pottery adds the further information that she was the 'Great One of the Harem'. The king in question is Tutankhamun. Within her tomb, we can see the nurse and her charge together. Maia, young, slender and enigmatic beneath her heavy wig, sits on a throne with a heavy-looking Tutankhamun across her lap. This is the pose traditionally used when depicting royal nurses and their charges. Tutankhamun, a miniature adult rather than a baby, wears the king's Blue Crown. Maia raises a hand in homage to her king.

Who is Maia? Once again we are faced with a tomb owner whose family goes unmentioned. All that we can say with certainty is that if we are correct in our translation of the title *mnat* as 'wet nurse', she must have given birth to at least one child before caring for Tutankhamun. During the 18th Dynasty the role of *mnat* was an honourable one awarded to elite women, who would be remembered with fondness by their royal charges. Sitre, nurse to the female pharaoh Hatshepsut, was rewarded with a life-sized statue and the honour of a tomb in the Theban necropolis. Tiye, wife of the prominent Amarna courtier Ay, started her career as nurse to Nefertiti and ended it as queen consort of Egypt. However, we should not be over-confident that *mnat*, a feminine title which incorporates the hieroglyphic sign representing either a breast or a nursing woman, always means wet nurse as opposed to the more general nursery nurse, foster mother or even tutor. We can compare its use to that of the male title *mnay*, which also incorporates the sign of a breast, and can consider with some confusion the tomb autobiography of the (male) courtier Ahmose-Pennekhbet who, earlier in the 18th Dynasty, claims to have raised Hatshepsut's daughter Neferure 'when she was a child who was at the breast'. The confusion continues as the slightly older Neferure moves first into the care of the (male) courtier Senenmut, who becomes her 'great nurse', and then into the care of Senimen, another 'royal nurse'.[19] Whatever her actual duties, Maia must have been a member of the Amarna elite, either the wife of a courtier or, maybe, one of Akhenaten's lesser harem queens. Speculation that she may have been Akhenaten's eldest daughter, Meritaten, is based on nothing more than the fact that the two women look alike (as, indeed, do most 18th Dynasty elite women depicted on tomb walls) and have – to modern ears – similar-sounding names.

As he passes from Maia's care the young Tutankhamun passes from our view. We can imagine him following Neferure's educational path – specialist instruction by a series of elite teachers – and it is possible that he was for a time the pupil of the vizier Aper-El whose Sakkara tomb, a neighbour to Maia's tomb, accords him the titles of 'father of the god' and 'director of the foster fathers and mothers of the children of the king'.[20] Another possible mentor is the anonymous 'Overseer of Tutors', whose tomb was built in the southern city of Akhmim during Tutankhamun's reign.[21]

We have no details of the subjects taught by these experts but, given the enormous emphasis placed on the role of the scribe throughout the dynastic age – 'There's nothing better than books . . . [Scribedom] is the greatest of callings' – it seems inconceivable that Tutankhamun was not, at a minimum, taught to read and write the hieroglyphic and hieratic scripts.[22] He may not have needed to be a scholar in life – he could, if necessary, order others to read and write for him – but he would need to be fully literate in the afterlife when, like all dead kings, he might be called upon to act as scribe to the sun god Ra. To help him accomplish this duty he was buried with a large quantity of stationery: seventeen scribal palettes (brush, pen and ink holders) and associated paraphernalia including a pen case, two writing horns, one curious item identified as a burnisher used to smooth papyrus, a sandstone eraser, black, white, yellow, red and blue pigments, plus, of course, papyrus to write on.[23] While some of his palettes were models made specifically for the tomb – funerary spells would allow these to function after the funeral – others show signs of use. These include a child-sized gilded palette bearing the early form of his name: Tutankhaten (no. 271e).

What other evidence for his early years can we glean from Tutankhamun's tomb? A shortage of instruments – just two military trumpets (nos 50gg and 175), two sistra or sacred rattles (nos 75 and 76) and a pair of ritual clappers (a form of castanet) (no. 620.13) – perhaps suggests that music did not play an important role in his life. Board games, however, probably did. His tomb has yielded six game boards with enough gaming pieces, knucklebones and casting sticks to allow Tutankhamun to play both *senet* (similar to backgammon) and twenty squares (similar to snakes and ladders). Games were immensely popular throughout the Dynastic Age. They were played by old and young, men and women, the elite who invested in beautiful, inlaid game sets and the peasants who played with pebbles and temporary boards scratched into the ground. Board games could be pure entertainment, but could also serve as a portal that allowed the dead to communicate – and play games – with the living. Within Tutankhamun's tomb a game of *senet* played against an invisible opponent might symbolise the struggle of the soul to reach the security of eternal life.

Reminding us that not all his tutors would have been scholars, Tutankhamun's grave goods include six dismantled chariots and an arsenal of bows, arrows, swords, knives, slings, throwsticks and clubs. Carved a century before Tutankhamun ascended his throne, a scene in the Theban tomb of Min shows a young prince – Tutankhamun's probable great-great-grandfather Amenhotep II – learning how to handle these weapons. Following his tutor's instructions, 'Stretch your bow up to your ear. Make strong . . . [fit] the arrow . . .', Amenhotep shoots into a large rectangular target and his arrows stick in place.[24] Young Amenhotep would grow up to become a multi-talented athlete who excelled in running, rowing, riding and, of course, archery:[25]

> *He drew three hundred mighty bows . . . He found that four targets of Asiatic copper, one palm in thickness, had been set up for him. Twenty cubits separated each post from the next. His Majesty appeared in a chariot like Montu in all his power. He seized his bow and took in his fist four arrows at a time . . . His arrows stuck out of the back of each target and he then hit the next post. This was a feat never done before.*

Amenhotep's pride in his own almost superhuman achievements is more than simple boasting. He is citing his physical prowess as proof of his fitness to rule. The health of the king was closely connected to the health of Egypt, a connection that inspired the royal artists to depict their monarchs as prime physical specimens capable, if necessary, of wielding clubs, swords and spears to fight off the enemies who constantly threatened the stability of their land.

Not only were Egypt's kings scholars and sportsmen, they were priests, too. The career of Akhenaten's prematurely deceased elder brother, Tuthmosis, High Priest of Ptah in Memphis, confirms that heirs to the throne were expected to spend time attached to one or more of the great state temples. Here they would study the rituals and administrative routines of the cults. This was a matter of supreme importance: as the only living person able to communicate effectively with the pantheon, the king took personal responsibility for the regular offerings demanded by the gods. By keeping the gods happy, he kept Egypt secure and, of course, himself safe on the throne. If we look at the scenes carved on the state temple walls we see a reciprocal system in action. Kings present gifts to the gods and

gates and buttresses, and surrounded by gardens, the North Riverside Palace was plastered, tiled and painted with bright scenes and artificial wood panelling. The family regularly left the palace to travel by chariot along the long, straight Royal Road running parallel to the River; a journey that provided the people of Amarna with a reminder of the divine processions that had once paraded through the streets of Thebes. They might stop in the city centre to make an offering in the Great Aten Temple or perform an official duty in the warren of administrative buildings known today as the Palace, or they might continue southwards, passing beyond the city to visit the remote Maru Aten sunshade temple. Images in the elite Amarna tombs show the royal family hard at work: they offer to their god, stand on a balcony to throw gold to their faithful followers and, perhaps worn out by their labours, sit down to enjoy a meal, caressed by the sun's rays. We cannot know if Tutankhamun participated in any of these more public rituals, but we can be fairly certain that he enjoyed clean clothes, perfumes and cosmetics, plentiful food and drink, and access to bathroom facilities (a shower and an unplumbed toilet being the height of Amarna luxury). And, should the worst happen, he knew that he would be mummified and buried in an appropriate rock-cut tomb in the Royal Wadi.

At the base of the social pyramid the public cemeteries used by at least 10,000 non-elite Amarna residents offer a stark contrast to the Royal Wadi and the private rock-cut tombs.[27] Here, the majority of the bodies were buried, unmummified but wrapped in linen and matting, in single or shared pit graves with minimal grave goods. The graves were marked by heaped stones or, occasionally, by a simple mudbrick superstructure. Poor though these graves were, they were robbed extensively in antiquity and their bones, stones and grave goods scattered across the desert floor. Bone analysis has shown that the majority of these 'ordinary' people died as infants or what we would classify as young adults, between three and twenty-five years of age. There were very few burials of the over-fifties, either because relatively few older people moved to Amarna, or because most people never reached that great age. The people buried in the public cemeteries were short in stature – an indication of poor nutrition, perhaps – and many had suffered stress damage which may have been caused by moving heavy weights and carrying water for long distances. Under normal circumstances no one would have the strength to lift a stone building block. Akhenaten, however, speeded up the building process by employing small-scale blocks known as *talatat*, a name derived from the Arabic word for three, which reflects the fact that the blocks are three handspans long. At Thebes, Akhenaten's blocks measured 52 × 26 × 24 cm; at Amarna, they were even smaller, allowing easier transport and on-site handling. The Amarna sun temples, built of *talatat* blocks with a mudbrick rather than a stone core, were not well constructed, and the carved and painted plaster that covered their walls concealed shoddy workmanship beneath. Akhenaten's architects were aware of this, and a restoration programme was already under way when Akhenaten died.[28]

Sandwiched between the royal family and the urban proletariat, Amarna's elite were well fed and healthy, yet they had their own problems. Denied direct access to the one acceptable god, they were forced to worship using their king and his consort as intermediaries. The wisest amongst them did this in a very obvious way. Their luxurious villas included conspicuous images of the royal family – carved stone slabs (stelae) or small statues – which functioned as altars for private worship, while their tombs, cut high in the cliffs to the east of the city, were decorated with scenes featuring the royal family so that the deceased became secondary characters in their own afterlives. Denied access to Osiris and the Field of Reeds, Akhenaten's courtiers knew that they would dwell in these tombs, surrounded by images of Akhenaten, his god and his family, until the end of time. We cannot know what they thought of this situation; there are no written documents to suggest that anyone was anything other than delighted to be living at Amarna. But if we look closely at the scenes on the elite tomb walls we can see that Akhenaten is perhaps not as secure as he would have us believe, as he constantly surrounds himself with bodyguards. Mahu, chief of the Medjay (police) and 'General of the Army of the Lord of the Two Lands', was an important Amarna figure who was rewarded for his loyalty with a gift of gold and a rock-cut tomb. Here we can see Mahu in action as he and his soldiers run alongside the royal chariot. The danger in this scene, however, comes from within the chariot. Akhenaten is holding the reins of the two lively horses, but his attention is entirely focused on Nefertiti, whom he appears to be kissing. With her parents distracted, the young Meritaten is beating the horses with a stick.[29]

In the second month of Year 12, Akhenaten hosted a splendid but unexplained (at least to us) festival. Amarna, a city normally isolated from the outside world, was for a short time filled with exotic visitors summoned from all corners of the empire to pay homage to Akhenaten and his god. Meryre II, a courtier whose title 'Overseer of the Royal Quarters and the Apartments of the King's Great Wife' demonstrates his close relationship with Queen Nefertiti, recorded the celebrations in a large scene on the east wall of his Amarna tomb chapel.[30]

As we might expect, Akhenaten and Nefertiti dominate events; far larger than everyone else, they sit side by side on a canopied platform and, although the queen appears only as an outline drawn around the figure of her husband (a device possibly employed to express the unity of the king and queen), it seems that they are holding hands. Their six daughters stand behind them, supervised by their nurses. From the comfort of his shaded throne Akhenaten inspects 'the chiefs of all lands', a crowd of ambassadors and representatives from Nubia, Libya, the Mediterranean islands and the Near East who are forced to stand in the hot sun and bow before him. He graciously accepts a vast amount of 'tribute', including horses, chariots, weapons, gold, ivory, ostrich eggs and feathers, and male and female slaves. Tutankhaten is, as we would expect, absent from the scene.

This is the last time that we see the official royal family – king, consort and all six princesses – together. Year 12 was a time of plague in the Near East and it may be that Akhenaten's international festival was a super-spreader event that brought more than tribute to Amarna. We know that the second-born princess, Meketaten, died soon after the celebration, possibly as early as Year 13, and, as her three youngest sisters, Neferneferuaten, Neferneferure and baby Setepenre, were from this time on omitted from official scenes, it seems likely that they too were dead. Kiya not only vanished, she was partially erased from Amarna history. Several of her images were clumsily altered so that they depicted Princess Meritaten, and her inscriptions on the Maru Aten sunshade temple wall were overwritten so that they, too, referenced Akhenaten's oldest daughter. This seems a curious way of treating a favoured wife. It only makes sense when we realise that the alterations are not intended to be read as sign of royal displeasure. In fact, they are not intended to be noticed at all. They are a practical if unsubtle response to the fact that Kiya's vital religious role has passed to Meritaten.

Tempting though it is, we cannot assume that every royal woman who has dropped out of sight has died. Nefertiti's temporary 'disapearence' provides us with a useful reminder of the archaeologist's mantra 'absence of evidence is not evidence of absence'. For many years it was accepted that Nefertiti vanished from Amarna soon after Meketaten's death, prompting Egyptologists to develop elaborate stories to explain her fate. My own interpretation of the (lack of) evidence was a simple one: 'The obvious inference is that she too is dead, possibly another victim of the plague which seems to have claimed so many members of her family.'[31] Others suggested that she had been banished to a remote Amarna palace after challenging her husband's extreme religious views; or that she had been exiled to Thebes for promoting her own extreme religious views.[32] In 2012, the publication of a graffito dated to Akhenaten's Year 16 put an abrupt end to all speculation. The graffito names the 'Great King's Wife, his beloved, mistress of the Two Lands, Neferneferuaten Nefertiti', confirming that the consort was alive and performing her normal duties shortly before Akhenaten's death.[33]

The devastating loss of his mother, a favourite wife and four of his daughters seems to have prompted Akhenaten to plan for the future. Tutankhaten's sudden appearance at Amarna indicates a change of status that has allowed him to step out of the shadows and become, for the first time, a 'visible' member of the royal family. The career of the young Ramesses II, a well-documented king who ruled almost six decades after Tutankhamun, offers an interesting parallel here. At no more than ten years old, after a childhood hidden from public gaze, Ramesses was officially recognised as his father's 'Eldest Son', or crown prince, even though, as he was Seti's only son, this must surely have been a formality:[34]

> It was Menmaatre [his father, Seti I] who brought me up. The Lord-of-All himself advanced me while I was a child until I became ruler. Even when I was in the egg he assigned the land to me. The officials kissed the ground before me when I was installed as the Eldest Son and as delegate on the throne of Geb. I reported on the affairs of the Two Lands as commander of the infantry and of the chariotry.

In a separate inscription, his admiring courtiers confirm this change of status and add more details of Ramesses's life as heir apparent:[35]

> You made decisions while you were in the egg in your role as child of the Heir-Apparent. The affairs of the Two Lands were told to you while you were still a side-lock-wearing child. No monument happened unless it was in your charge. You acted as chief of the army when you were a youngster in his tenth year.

If we strip away the exaggeration, we see that Ramesses has been promoted to become his father's apprentice. He learns his trade by spending time with the army, supervising public works and, we assume, working with other branches of the civil service and priesthood. The young Tutankhaten, it seems, has received a similar promotion. He is now in the line of succession.

Tutankhaten is not, however, the only royal person to emerge in the later part of Akhenaten's reign. Indeed, he is not even the most important person to emerge. That accolade must be shared by the mysterious 'Ankhkheperure Smenkhkare

(*Living form of Ra, the soul of Ra is made firm*)' and the even more mysterious 'Ankhkheperure Neferneferuaten (*Living form of Ra, Exquisite Beauty of the Aten*)'. As both these characters play an important, though brief, role in Tutankhaten's journey to the throne, we need to investigate them further.

There is no doubt that Smenkhkare and Neferneferuaten existed; their names are found, written in cartouches, in several Amarna contexts and even within Tutankhamun's tomb. But they are unexplained and we cannot be sure if we are looking at one or more previously unseen people or, indeed, at people whom we have previously met, now using a new name. It was once believed that both could be Nefertiti, who was changing her name as she advanced from conventional queen consort first to become co-ruler alongside her husband (Neferneferuaten) and then, following Akhenaten's death, to become solo female king (Smenkhkare).[36] However, we now know that Nefertiti was still queen consort, and still using her original name, shortly before Akhenaten's death. For her then to 'inherit' her husband's crown would have been an unprecedented coup, and one which would have been difficult to justify given that it would have displaced Tutankhaten and her two surviving royal-born daughters, Meritaten and Ankhesenpaaten, from the succession. Although the idea that Nefertiti ruled Egypt as a female king has recently gained popular support, there is not one shred of evidence to prove that this actually happened.

To solve the mystery of Smenkhkare we need to return to the Amarna tomb of Meryre II. Here, on the north wall, we see a badly damaged scene roughed out in paint.[37] A king and queen stand tall beneath the rays of the Aten as they reward the miniature Meryre with golden necklaces. This is a typical Amarna ceremony and at first glance the couple look very much like Akhenaten and Nefertiti, although the queen is not wearing Nefertiti's trademark tall, flat-topped crown. The names that originally identified the king have been hacked off the wall but, happily, both names had been copied by nine-teenth-century visitors before the modern thieves struck, so we can be confident that we are looking at the 'King of Upper and Lower Egypt, Ankhkheperure, son of Re, Smenkhkare-djeserkheperu' and the 'King's Great Wife Meritaten, may she live forever continually'. The scene is undated, but the fact that it is incomplete indicates that it was started after the neighbouring Year 12 tribute scene. Smenkhkare is now king of Egypt, with Akhenaten's eldest daughter, Meritaten, beside him as his consort.

Is Smenkhkare ruling alone? Or does he briefly share a co-regency with Akhenaten? Occasional uncaptioned images showing two crowned individuals have been found at Amarna, but we can only guess at their identities and roles. To find firm evidence of kings Akhenaten and Smenkhkare together we have to return to the Valley of the Kings. Tutankhamun was buried with over 350 litres of precious oils and unguents stored in more than eighty stone vessels, some bearing the names of earlier kings stretching back over a century to the reign of Tuth-mosis III. These oils were immensely valuable, and this made them a prime target for the thieves who attacked the tomb in antiquity. Happily for us, the robbers decanted the oils into larger vessels, leaving the emptied jars behind. One globular calcite jar bears an inscription: two double cartouches, incised and painted blue (no. 405). This inscription had, however, been partially erased before the burial. Carter read the names as Amenhotep III and Akhenaten; they have since been accepted as Akhenaten followed by Smenkhkare.[38] The two names do not prove a co-regency, but they do hint at a close connection.

Once again we are forced to reconstruct the past on the basis of incomplete evidence. Following the principal of the simplest explanation being the most likely, we can suggest that Smenkhkare was a son born to Akhenaten and one of his higher-ranking wives. He was the brother or half-brother of Tutankhaten, and the brother or half-brother and husband of Meritaten, the oldest and most important of the Amarna princesses. Smenkhkare's promotion to the role of crown prince allowed Tutankhaten to – temporarily, it would have been assumed – step forward as heir to the throne. A son born to Smenkhkare and Meritaten, or indeed any son born to Smenkhkare, would have replaced Tutankhaten in the succession, but this never happened. Smenkhkare briefly succeeded Akhenaten but died young, his short reign leaving few traces in the archaeological record. As his highest regnal year date is a wine label dated to Year 1, it is possible that he died in the same year as his father. Smenkhkare's death stripped Meritaten of her consort's role and placed the young Tutankhaten onto the throne.

Neferneferuaten is an altogether more nebulous figure. Although her name is non-gender-specific, it is occasionally linked to the epithet 'effective for her husband', so we know that we are looking for a woman.[39] She uses a double cartouche, but so does Nefertiti. At Amarna, it seems, the double cartouche may indicate either a king or his consort. So who is she? There were already two Neferneferuatens in the royal family, one being Akhenaten's fourth daughter (presumed dead after Year 12) and the other being the consort Neferneferuaten Nefertiti, who had added a second element to her name at the time of Akhenaten's religious conversion. We know that Nefertiti's role, however, had not changed by Year 16. If we are looking for a royal woman who grows in importance towards the end of Akhenaten's reign, we should focus our attention on Meritaten. Meritaten, the eldest daughter of Akhenaten and newly widowed consort of Smenkhkare, has an impeccable royal pedigree and, most unusually, her political importance is confirmed by evidence originating far from Egypt.

In 1887, a peasant woman digging for fertile soil in the ruined Amarna buildings uncovered hundreds of sun-dried clay tablets stamped with curious signs. Egyptologists, unfamiliar with cuneiform 'wedge' script and the ancient Babylonian language, dismissed the tablets as naive forgeries. By the time it was recognised that they were actually valuable antiquities the collection had been dispersed and many letters lost; there are fewer than 400 in museums and private collections worldwide today. We now know that these 'Amarna Letters' are the remnants of the archive storing the diplomatic correspondence between the king of Egypt and fellow kings and vassals in the Near East. Most are, as we would expect, letters written to Egypt, but a few are copies of letters sent from Egypt. Spanning a period of approximately thirty years from the end of the reign of Amenhotep III to the end of the Amarna Period, they provide tantalising glimpses of the characters who ruled the great Bronze Age states. Consorts are not routinely included in this correspondence and Nefertiti goes unmentioned. Queen Tiy is mentioned, and the correspondence makes it clear that she is regarded as a significant influential figure in Akhenaten's life. Meritaten is not only mentioned, Burna-Buryas of Babylon sends her a valuable present: '. . . concerning your daughter Mayati, having heard [about her] I send to her as greeting-gift a necklace of cricket [-shaped] gems of lapis lazuli, 1,048 their number'.[40]

It is easy to reconstruct an impressive curriculum vitae for Meritaten. Serving as king's eldest daughter to Akhenaten, she is the princess who is most prominent in official Amarna art. She assists her mother in the female-orientated rituals of Aten worship before inheriting her own sunshade temple where she performs her own rites. As consort to the short-lived Smenkhkare, she then becomes queen of Egypt, a role that brings her to the attention of rulers across the ancient Near East. Finally, as an experienced queen, she serves as regent to the young Tutankhaten, who is by now married to her sister Ankhesenpaaten. It was a long-established tradition that an infant king would be guided by the widowed consort, who was usually his mother or stepmother. For Meritaten to guide Tutankhaten in the earlier years of his reign would therefore seem an entirely natural development. We might have expected the adult Tutankhamun to acknowledge this support and, on one of his monuments – his mortuary temple perhaps – to name his birth mother, too. The fact that he does not get around to doing this is a good indication that he that he never expected to die so young.

This reconstruction of royal family relationships opens up another possibility. Could Meritaten and Smenkhkare be Tutankhamun's parents? This would allow the succession to flow as it should, seamlessly from great-grandfather to grandfather, father and son (from Amenhotep III to Akhenaten, Smenkhkare and Tutankhaten). As we have no idea when or where either Meritaten or Smenkhkare was born, it is indeed theoretically possible for them to be the parents of a child born in Akhenaten's Years 6–9. We will revisit this idea in Chapter 6.

As a prince, possibly just one of many princes who might one day become king, Tutankhaten spent much of his childhood hidden from our view. He did not feature in the official art and private altars that decorated Amarna and we do not see him riding in the royal chariot or eating a meal with the king and queen. His destiny was as yet undecided. But he would have been taught that he carried a latent divinity that separated him from the common people. Should he survive his father and ascend to the throne, this divinity would be activated by his coronation. Some time after Year 12 he experienced a significant change of status that allowed him to step out of the shadows and become, for the first time, a 'visible' member of the royal family. Tutankhaten was now directly in the line of succession.

2

The King's Tale

Tutankhamun the Restorer

In a text written to impress his gods, King Tutankhamun boasts of the heroic efforts that he has made to restore his damaged land:[1]

He has restored what was ruined, as monuments of eternity. He has repelled wrongdoing throughout the Two Lands and established maat.

After a brief period of confusion we regain historical certainty when, in approximately 1336 BCE, the young Tutankhaten ascends the throne of Egypt supported by the dowager queen, Meritaten, his sister-wife, Ankhesenpaaten, and, perhaps, if she is still alive, Nefertiti. His advisors, all Amarna survivors, include the 'God's Father Ay', the Chief of the Treasury, Maya, and the two viziers, Pentu and Usermont. Generalissimo Horemheb is not only commander-in-chief of the army, but 'King's Deputy in the entire land' and 'Noble of Upper and Lower Egypt'. This was very much a family affair. Ay was the husband of Nefertiti's wet nurse, Tiye, and there is strong circumstantial evidence – including his use of the title 'God's Father', which was formerly held by Yuya, father of Queen Tiy – to suggest that he was both Tiy's brother and Nefertiti's father. Generalissimo Horemheb was married to a woman named Mutnodjmet, who may have been Nefertiti's identically named younger sister and therefore Ay's daughter. Both Ay and Horemheb would eventually succeed to the throne.

Like all kings before him, the new pharaoh selected a set of five formal names, each preceded by a title that would serve as a short mission statement for his reign. Just two names – the final two – would be written in a cartouche.

— Horus Name: Image of births

— Two Ladies Name: Beautiful of laws who quells the Two Lands/who makes content all the gods

— Golden Horus Name: Elevated of appearances for the god/his father Ra

— Prenomen or throne name: King of Upper and Lower Egypt Nebkheperure (*Lord of Manifestations of Ra*)

— Nomen or personal name: Son of Ra Tutankhaten (*Living Image of the Aten*). This would soon be changed to Tutankhamun (*Living Image of Amun*)

His penultimate name, Nebkheperure, is the name by which his people knew him.

His coronation transformed Tutankhaten from an extremely important little boy to a semi-divine being so far removed from his people that they could not look directly at his face. It was a major, life-changing ritual, yet we know virtually nothing about it. While there are temple scenes showing various kings being crowned by gods, only Horemheb has left a description, part of a longer biography, of his own Theban ceremony. This, inscribed on the back of a damaged grey-granite double statue of the king and his consort, Mutnodjet, is not as specific as we would wish:[2]

Then did he proceed to the King's house, when he [Amen] had placed him [Horemheb] before himself, to the Per-Wer [great shrine] of his noble daughter the Great-of-Magic

[Werek Hekau], her arms in greeting and she embraced his
beauty and fixed herself on his forehead. All of the Ennead,
the Per-Neser [House of Flame] exulted at his appearance
. . . [Saying] 'Behold, Amen has come to the palace, his son
in front of him, to the Palace order to establish his crown
upon his head.'

The human-headed snake goddess Weret Hekau can be equated with the uraeus goddess Wadjet of Buto: the snake that rears on the pharaoh's brow. She was believed to have suckled the king, and in so doing prepared him for his coronation.

Comparisons with other reigns suggest that Tutankhamun's accession might have been celebrated with a relatively simple crowning ceremony in a palace setting, followed by a year-long series of rituals performed in temples throughout Egypt.[3] But he acceded to his throne in abnormal times, and it is possible that his celebration was both shorter and entirely Amarna-based. Just one fragmentary statue hints that he may have been crowned at Thebes. The Metropolitan Museum of Art in New York houses a beautifully carved indurated limestone head of Tutankhamun. The king appears very young with rounded cheeks, a well-defined mouth and an unfortunately broken nose. The head was once part of a bigger piece depicting the king standing before a much larger, seated god. While the god's right hand still rests on the back of Tutankhamun's Blue Crown in New York, his lower body has been identified in a storage area at Karnak and his upper body is currently missing.[4] Given this provenance, it seems reasonable to assume that the vanished god is Amun-Ra of Thebes. Egyptologists have variously interpreted the statue as the god actually crowning the young king, or the god more generally extending his protection to the new king.

The ritual may have vanished, but some of the coronation regalia has survived. There are no crowns – remarkably, we have no crown belonging to any pharaoh or consort from Dynastic Egypt – but Tutankhamun's tomb has yielded two sets of the crook and flail, the symbols of authority carried by all Egyptian kings from the divine Osiris onwards. One set is child-sized and is inscribed for Tutankhaten (nos 269d and 269f); the other set is adult-sized and inscribed for Tutankhamun (nos 269h and 269e).[5] Their bands of blue glass, obsidian and gold make these beautiful objects in their own right; their symbolism makes them extraordinarily powerful objects.

Equally powerful is a child-sized tunic decorated front and back with embroidery and gold sequins, with a repeating pattern of *heb sed* hieroglyphs (no. 44t). The *Sed* Festival was a celebration designed to renew and reinforce the king's divine right to rule. In theory it was celebrated after thirty years on the throne and roughly every three years thereafter but, as thirty years was an almost unimaginably long time, kings happily bent the rules to enjoy premature celebrations. Amenhotep III, one of the few who did rule for more than thirty years, celebrated three legitimate jubilees at Thebes (Years 30, 34 and 37). Akhenaten celebrated a Sed Festival at Thebes just three years after his accession, using the occasion to dedicate himself, his family and his people to the service of a new god. Tutankhaten would not have been born by Akhenaten's Year 3; his tunic must therefore have been worn at a later, Amarna-based celebration – Akhenaten's Year 12 festival, perhaps? – or at a ritual conducted as part of his own coronation.

Chairs were a sign of wealth and authority in a land where wood was scarce and the majority of the population, lacking both chairs and tables, routinely sat or squatted on the ground.

Royal chairs, or thrones, carried additional mythological significance; they were closely linked to the goddess Isis, wife and protector of the god Osiris, who wore the hieroglyphic symbol of the throne as her headdress. As Egypt's written words (hieroglyphs) were pictures, Egypt's pictures could be considered as words so that any image of a king sitting on his throne may be 'read' as a king being supported by the divine consort, Isis. We can therefore add all six of the chairs found in Tutankhamun's tomb to his list of ceremonial accessories. One of these, an uninscribed ebony-armed chair decorated with ivory inlays and gold leaf, stands just 71 cm high and was presumably used by the king as a child (no. 39). Another, the adult-sized inlaid and inscribed ebony and ivory chair which Carter misleadingly named the 'ecclesiastical throne' (no. 351), straddles the time when the king changed his name. While the design of this chair is a standard one used by the elite throughout the New Kingdom, its back panel is decorated with a row of cobras with sun discs on their heads and a large vulture with outspread wings, and these design elements confirm that this is a seat made for royalty. Most of the chair's inscriptions name the owner as Tutankhaten, but two replacement ebony inlays reference the 'perfect god' (a traditional pre-Amarna title) Tutankhamun, suggesting that the chair was created for Tutankhaten, then repaired when he was ruling as Tutankhamun. A carved ivory gaming-box recovered from the Annexe reinforces this feeling of a king who has inherited conflicting religious loyalties (no. 585r):[6]

> *May He live, the Good God, Image of Ra, son of Amen* [sic] *upon his throne, lord of strength who seizes all lands, the King of Upper and Lower Egypt, Nebkheperure, given life and health for ever.*

May He live, the Good God, son of Amen, son of Aten in heaven, the King of Upper and Lower Egypt Nebkheperure, Son of Ra, Tutankhamen, Ruler-of-Thebes, may He live for ever.

The sculptor Tuthmosis had made a great success of Amarna life. The manager of an extensive workshop, he had been responsible for many of the stone statues that decorated Amarna city. His rewards had included a luxurious villa in a prestigious suburb, a private well and grain store, an expensive chariot and two equally expensive horses to pull it. If we visit his well-appointed compound we can find evidence – a wine jar fragment dated to Year 1 of an anonymous king and a broken faience ring bearing the name 'Nebkheperure' – to confirm that he was still in residence and presumably still churning out royal statues at the start of Tutankhaten's reign.[7] But almost immediately there came the decision to reverse Akhenaten's religious experiment. The Aten was to be demoted, the old gods were to be reinstated and the court was to return to Thebes. To emphasise this momentous U-turn, the king was changing his name to Tutankhamun (*Living Image of Amun*), and the queen was changing hers to Ankhesenamun (*Living through Amun*).

When it became clear that this decision would never be reversed, those who served the royal family, and those who served those who served the royal family, had no choice but to pack up their belongings and relocate. Amarna, without the royal family, had nothing to offer them. Slowly but surely the population dwindled from an estimated 50,000, and the mudbrick city started to crumble. Only the Workmen's Village and the Stone Village – the homes of Amarna's tomb builders and others engaged in desert-based activities – survived to be reoccupied and even expanded before being abandoned during Horemheb's reign. Tuthmosis the sculptor locked up his villa and sailed north, to a new life at Memphis and, eventually, burial in the Sakkara necropolis.[8] He left behind a cupboard packed with stone sculptures and plaster heads representing Akhenaten's now-discredited court. Included amongst these was the world-famous bust of Nefertiti wearing her diagnostic Blue Crown, which is currently displayed in Berlin's Neues Museum.[9]

We don't have a precise date for this momentous change, but the fact that only one mention of 'King Tutankhaten' has been discovered outside his tomb – a small stela which originally showed the crowned king making an offering to Amun-Ra, 'king of the gods', and his consort, Mut, 'Lady of Heaven; Mistress of the Gods' – indicates that it occurred soon after his accession.[10] It must have happened before – probably several years before – the otherwise unknown scribe Tjai scribbled a graffito recording his visit to the Sakkara Step Pyramid on the third day of the fourth month of summer, in the fourth year of King 'Tutankhamun'.[11]

As the living departed it was time for the dead, too, to desert Amarna. Most of the rock-cut tombs carved for the elite were substantially unfinished and it seems that only one, the tomb of Huya, Steward of Queen Tiy, had actually been used. In contrast the Royal Wadi housed, at a minimum, the burials of Akhenaten, Smenkhkare, Meketaten, Kiya, Tiy, Neferneferuaten, Neferneferure and Setepenre. We don't know when Nefertiti died, but a single broken *shabti* (funerary figure) hints that she too may have been interred at Amarna.[12] The relocation of the court would leave these burials unprotected and highly vulnerable to thieves. The Wadi would have to be guarded night and day and, even then, could there be any guarantee that it would not be robbed? Who would guard the guards?

The decision was taken to move the royal burials to the security of the Valley of the Kings. This must have presented someone with a logistical and security nightmare. The sealed tombs and tomb chambers had to be opened and the mummies and their grave goods carried, or dragged on sledges, across 11 km of desert and cultivated land to the boat that would take them upstream to Thebes. Here the more desirable grave goods were diverted to Tutankhamun's own growing funerary provision. The mummies faced a second, lengthy desert journey, eventually arriving at a temporary workshop in the small private tomb that we know as KV55. Here they were processed – stripped, we can assume, of all but their most personal valuables and rewrapped – before being allocated to an appropriate resting place. Queen Tiy is the easiest of these mummies to trace. We know that she spent some time in KV55 before being re-interred in the Western Valley tomb where her husband already lay. The large box-like golden shrine that once surrounded her sarcophagus was, with some considerable difficulty, we can imagine, transferred to Thebes, only to be abandoned in KV55 when its size made it too cumbersome to move on.

The new king had decided that Egypt must be restored. A large red-granite stela discovered in the pillared (hypostyle) hall of the Karnak temple of Amun-Ra, but probably originating in a more public location within or just outside the temple precincts, explains his policy in some detail. The double image carved at the top of the stela originally showed twin Tutankhamuns presenting offerings to Amun-Ra and Mut, while Ankhesenamun stands supportively behind him. Today she has almost entirely vanished. The two scenes are similar but not mirror images: one Tutankhamun wears the Blue Crown and offers flowers, while the other wears a *nemes* (a headcloth which covers the crown, back of the head and nape of the neck, and has a large flap of cloth descending behind each ear to the shoulder) and offers a libation. Like many of Tutankhamun's works, the Karnak stela was usurped by Horemheb, who crudely carved his own name over that of the original owner. Tutankhamun's text is still clear but the date has been damaged, so that we only know that it was carved in the 'fourth month of inundation, day 19':[13]

> . . . He has restored what was ruined, as monuments of eternity. He has repelled wrongdoing throughout the Two Lands and established maat . . .
>
> Now when His Majesty arose as king, the temples and cities of the gods and goddesses, from Elephantine to the marshes of the Delta, had become ruins. Their shrines had fallen into decay and become mounds overgrown with weeds. Their sanctuaries were as if they had never existed, their temples were a footpath. The land was in confusion, and the gods abandoned this land. If [an army] was sent to Djahy to expand Egypt's borders, they did not meet with success. If one prayed to a god with a request, he would not come at all. If one prayed to a goddess in the same way, she would not come at all . . .
>
> After some days had passed, [His Majesty] appeared on the throne of his father; he ruled the Shores of Horus. The Black Land and the Red Land were under his dominion, and every land bowed down before his might . . .
>
> Then His Majesty took counsel with his heart, searching out every excellent deed, seeking benefactions for his father Amun . . .

The stela tells us that Tutankhamun was living in a northern palace built by his ancestor Tuthmosis I when he consolidated his plan to restore the traditional gods. The recovery of several disparate stone architectural fragments in and around Memphis, all now badly damaged, many re-carved by later kings and some incorporated into later buildings, but each apparently having once borne Tutankhamun's name or image, strongly suggests that he commissioned his own building(s) in this area. However, there is not enough evidence to confirm what, exactly, he built.

The stela then explains that Tutankhamun's divine father, Amun-Ra, is to receive a statue made from electrum, lapis lazuli, turquoise 'and every precious stone', and a new processional boat that will allow him to 'sail' out from his temple, carried on the shoulders of his priests. Ptah of Memphis will receive a similar but slightly less splendid donation, and other, unnamed gods will receive statues. There will be new shrines, and generous new endowments will ensure that the daily temple rituals can be performed correctly. The temples will be staffed by high-born priests and female singers and dancers 'who have been maidservants in the king's house'. Male and female slaves 'from the tribute of his Person's capturing' will labour in the temple workshops. This last phrase suggests that Tutankhamun had access to prisoners of war but this is not necessarily the case, as kings who never fought used the identical phrase.

It was not unknown for a new pharaoh to make grand claims of restoring *maat* – the correct state of affairs – to a chaotic and godless land. These claims can usually be dismissed as propaganda, particularly when there is no evidence to suggest that Egypt was in anything resembling a state of chaos. The 18th Dynasty female pharaoh Hatshepsut, for example, apparently felt no shame in claiming to have 'raised up what was dismembered, from the first time when the Asiatics were in Avaris of the North Land', even though 'the Asiatics' had actually been expelled from Egypt many years before she came to the throne.[14] She, as king, felt fully justified in claiming the achievements of her predecessors as her own. However, knowing that Egypt outside Amarna had indeed been neglected, and that Amun-Ra and his family had been ruthlessly persecuted by Akhenaten, it is tempting to read Tutankhamun's statement as a genuine attempt to right the wrongs caused by the Amarna Age.

This does not mean that we should accept his words too literally. Tutankhamun had been born at Amarna and raised in the cult of the Aten; he had known no other way of life and worshipped no other gods. His decision to end the Amarna experiment was made for him by advisors who felt no personal devotion to the Aten – who maybe even blamed the Aten for Egypt's obvious decline – and who regarded Amarna as an unsuitable city from which to govern an empire. Their decision to promote Tutankhamun as a traditional New Kingdom pharaoh – a brave warrior, conscientious priest and wise administrator – may have been a devout attempt to restore *maat*, but is equally likely to have been a cynical attempt to re-boot the monarchy and set the new king (and themselves) apart from his immediate predecessors without actually blaming them for the chaos that now threatened to overwhelm Egypt.

Had Tutankhamun lived a long life this 'restoration' plan would probably have succeeded. But it would take more than ten years to fully restore *maat*. Five years after Tutankhamun's death Horemheb, now himself king of Egypt, found it necessary to issue a decree outlining a programme of internal reforms designed to protect state and temple assets. During his reign we see an abandonment of the reticence that has until now protected us from the harsher realities of New Kingdom life. For the first time the harsh penalties for the anti-social behaviour that has been plaguing Egypt are spelt out:[15]

> [If someone] steals a boat which belongs to any soldier or any person in the entire land, let the law be applied to him by cutting off his nose and sending him to Tjaru.
>
> But as for any mayor or any priest about whom one hears that he sits to administer justice in the court which has been set up for administering justice, and yet he acts falsely with a worthy case, it shall be against him as a great crime, deserving of death.

Outside Egypt, there was a lot of work to be done if Tutankhamun was to regain his rightful place as leader of the eastern Mediterranean world. Akhenaten had inherited a mighty empire. Beyond the southern border, Nubia was fully absorbed within the Egyptian imperial administration and contributed valuable revenues to the Egyptian treasury. In the north, an active network of vassals and allies stretched across the Near East in modern Israel/Palestine, Lebanon, Jordan and Syria. We know that Amarna did not flourish in isolation; there were imports of food, flax and other necessities from within Egypt, and the *Amarna Letters* testify to a lively diplomatic correspondence and gift exchange with rulers beyond Egypt's borders. Yet Akhenaten seems to have treated the world outside his city with an indifference bordering on contempt, turning a blind eye to the shifts in power that were starting to destabilise the Near East. Abdi-Astarti of Qiltu (location uncertain) was not the only vassal to plead in vain for help when under attack:[16]

Say to the king, my lord: Message of Abdi-Astarti, servant of the king. I fall at the feet of the king, my lord, 7 times the feet of the king, my lord and 7 times, here and now, both on the stomach and on the back. May the king, my lord, be informed that the war against me is severe, and may it seem good to the king, my lord, to send a magnate to protect me. Moreover, the king, my lord, has sent orders to me and I am heeding them. I heed all the orders of the king, my lord. I herewith . . . send on 10 women . . .

The story of Aziru of Amurru (modern Lebanon), which can be traced through the *Amarna Letters*, testifies to the political uncertainty of the times. Although an Egyptian vassal, Aziru had invaded neighbouring territories, and Rib-Hadda of Byblos had been forced to write to Akhenaten, pleading for protection. Rib-Hadda was eventually exiled and killed, and Akhenaten summoned Aziru to Amarna to explain his deeds. Meanwhile, in what is today Turkey, the growing Hittite empire was starting to test its strength. After a year in Egypt, Aziru was allowed to return home. He promptly defected to the Hittites. Amurru would remain Hittite territory into the 19th Dynasty:[17]

. . . troops of Hatti under Lupakku have captured cities of Amqu . . . Moreover we have heard the following. Zitana has come and there are 90,000 infantrymen that have come with him. We have, however, not confirmed the report, whether they are really there . . .

Aziru was not the only vassal to transfer his loyalty, and his tribute, to the Hittites. Mitanni (based in modern Syria and western Iraq), once Egypt's strongest Near Eastern ally and the birthplace of Tadukhepa, one of Akhenaten's most prominent wives, was left to face the new enemy alone.

Many pharaohs started their reigns with a brief military campaign designed to prove their ability to subdue Egypt's enemies. Some of these campaigns were genuine, some were minor spats deliberately engineered to allow the king to claim a great victory and some, we suspect, were simply 'borrowed' from earlier, more successful reigns. We have already seen Tutankhamun make reference to male and female slaves 'from the tribute of his Person's capturing' and have wondered if this standard phrase should be taken literally. Carved blocks bearing fragmented images from a dismantled east-bank Theban chapel named the 'Mansion of Nebkheperure Beloved of Amun Founder of Thebes' suggest that it should. Although there is no detailed text to explain the specifics of his campaign(s), we can 'read' the cartoon-like story of Tutankhamun's army adventures: we see the king storming a Syrian citadel, receiving booty which includes both prisoners and severed enemy hands threaded on spears, retiring home with a bound prisoner hanging from the royal boat, and offering the prisoners and other battle spoils to the gods of the Karnak temple. Separate scenes provide 'evidence' for a Nubian campaign.[18] The evidence from the Mansion is supported by scenes showing Asiatics and Nubians bearing tribute in the Theban tomb of the Viceroy Amenhotep-Huy (TT40), and scenes showing long lines of Asiatics and Libyans who appear both as prisoners and suing for peace in the Sakkara tomb of Generalissimo Horemheb. However, the fact that the early Ramesside kings would need to spend many years restoring Egypt's northern border indicates that, whatever they would like us to believe, Tutankhamun and Horemheb did not succeed in restoring Akhenaten's lost empire.

If his armies fought to maintain his empire, can we assume that Tutankhamun fought with them? The scenes from the Mansion imply that he was indeed present, and this impression is reinforced by his grave goods. The first artefact to be recovered from the Antechamber – the wooden chest known as the 'Painted Box' – had been plastered and painted over its entire outer surface with scenes of the king performing daring feats in his chariot (no. 21). On the lid he leads his men in an exciting and potentially dangerous desert hunt, and on the body he leads his men to victory against an army of Asiatics who have variously been identified as Syrians or Hittites. In both scenes Tutankhamun stands upright and alone in his chariot, his two prancing steeds controlled by the reins tied around his waist as he fires an arrow at his enemy. This is a standard royal pose seen on several New Kingdom exterior temple walls: in real life it would be almost impossible to control a chariot this way, and we would expect the king to be accompanied by a driver and probably a shield bearer too.

The standard nature of these scenes, and the lack of any supporting written details, makes us question their accuracy. All royal scenes are propaganda: they do not have to tell the truth as we recognise that concept today. We can understand this more easily if we consider the role of the king as priest. We are accustomed to seeing standard images of the king, and the king alone, making an offering to the gods on the walls of the state temples, but we do not fall into the trap of assuming that the king made every offering in every temple because we know that this would have been impossible. Although in theory the king was the only person who could communicate effectively with the gods, in practice he appointed deputies – priests – to make the offerings on his behalf. Generalissimo Horemheb was the head of Tutankhamun's army: he is also likely to have been his representative on the battlefield.

Other, less believable scenes of physical domination appear in Tutankhamun's tomb. One ceremonial shield shows the king grasping a lion by the tail to smite it; another shows him assuming the form of a crowned human-headed sphinx to trample human enemies (nos 379b and 379a). The gilded figures recovered from the Treasury show him balancing on a fragile boat to harpoon a hippopotamus (a traditional 'enemy' of Egypt's living Horus king, which is omitted from the scene lest it magically come alive in the tomb) and riding on the back of an animal which appears to be either a leopard or a panther (nos 275c, 275e, 289a, 289b). He hunts on the walls of the Mansion, too, where we see him in his chariot, chasing antelopes and lions. A dead wild bull has, we are told, been shot by the king. By physically vanquishing the forces of chaos, be they human enemies or wild animals, Tutankhamun fulfils his duty to preserve *maat* and in so doing pleases the gods. At the same time the harpooning of the hippopotamus equates Tutankhamun with the god Horus, who harpooned his uncle Seth in the form of a hippopotamus in their desperate fight for the crown.

To add support to this image of Tutankhamun man-of-action, his tomb has yielded a plethora of military and hunting equipment. The most conspicuous are six dismantled chariots of slightly differing design: three highly decorated and relatively light vehicles which were probably used for ceremonial appearances (nos 120, 121, 122) and a less ornate, more robust chariot, plus two light but undecorated vehicles which have been tentatively identified as hunting chariots (nos 161, 332, 333). These were accompanied by an impressive arsenal of weapons including sixteen bows, arrows, and an assortment of clubs, slings, throw-sticks, swords and daggers. To protect the king there were four ceremonial shields, four lighter and more practical shields, and a sleeveless cuirass made from leather scales sewn onto a linen lining (no. 587a).[19]

But, although Tutankhamun was buried with the weapons of a huntsman and soldier, it has been argued that he may not have been agile or even strong enough to wield this equipment. While Derry had believed him to be a well-nourished young man in reasonable health, the analysis published by the Supreme Council of Antiquities suggested that he had been a physically weak king suffering the effects of inbreeding and plagued by illness and disabilities, including malaria, scoliosis of the spine and a deformed left foot with signs of club foot (*talipes equinovarus*), two diseased metatarsals and a missing toe-bone.[20] If this diagnosis is correct, images of Tutankhamun performing skilful – and on several occasions foolhardy and clearly fictional – acts of bravery must be interpreted as routine propaganda depicting the king, whatever his actual appearance and character, as physically perfect and astonishingly brave. This seems reasonable, and it would certainly explain the 130 canes and walking sticks recovered from his tomb.

However, as so often happens in Egyptology, the diagnosis is not as clear-cut as we would hope. It is not unknown for 'club foot' in mummies to be the result of warping caused by the over-tight bandages. More importantly, an X-ray taken by Harrison's team in 1968 appears to show a healthy left foot with normal-shaped bones. As the abnormal metatarsals and missing bone are located close to an area of damage, this opens up the possibility that they are a post-1968 development.[21] Supporting the diagnosis of no deformity, Tutankhamun's shoes and sandals show none of the differences in construction that we might expect to find in footwear designed for someone with a club foot.

As the medics continue to argue over Tutankhamun's left foot, we must be very cautious in defining his many sticks as walking aids.[22] Throughout the Dynastic era the stick or staff was a symbol of elite male authority, and as such it was routinely carried by men who experienced no difficulty walking. Although primarily a status indicator, the stick could, if necessary, be used. Casual beatings were, for the less privileged, a hazard of daily life. Schoolboys were beaten by their teachers; servants were beaten by their overseers; the lower classes were beaten by their superiors; and tax collectors were armed with sticks that helped them to maximise their revenue. In the Middle Kingdom *Tale of the Eloquent Peasant* the unfortunate Khun-Anup, the hero of the story, is unfairly beaten both by the villain Djehutinakht and the official Rensi, and he accepts these assaults with resignation as the natural order of things. Although the Old Kingdom sage Ptahhotep tells us that 'wretched is he who injures a poor man', he also advises his elite male readers: 'Punish firmly, chastise soundly.'[23]

Finding himself in urgent need of resources to finance his restoration programme, Tutankhamun tasked Maya, Chief of the Treasury, with implementing a ruthless fundraising campaign. Visiting the major state temples from the southern border to the Mediterranean Sea, Maya ensured that the taxes that Akhenaten had diverted to the cult of the Aten were once again filling the temple coffers, and that the temples were in turn paying their dues to the crown:[24]

> *Regnal Year 8, third month of Peret, day 21 . . .*
> *On this day His Majesty [Tutankhamun] commissioned the hereditary prince and count, the fan-bearer at the right*

> *hand of the king, the king's scribe, the overseer of the treasury*
> *Maya, to tax the entire land and endow divine offerings for*
> *all the gods of Egypt . . .*

Restorations – the demolition of Akhenaten's short-lived Aten temples and the repair of the vandalised and neglected traditional temples – occurred throughout Egypt, although as Thoth of Hermopolis Magna, Ra of Heliopolis and Ptah of Memphis had managed to maintain low profiles throughout the Amarna Age, in many cases the only restoration needed was the re-carving of Amun's name where it occurred as part of the compound name Amenhotep.

Northern Egypt has yielded little evidence of restoration and rebuilding. An inscribed stone door frame recovered from the Giza plateau mentions both Tutankhamun and Ankhesenamun 'Beloved of Hauron', and may be the remains of a new chapel dedicated to the Canaanite god who was associated with the Great Sphinx.[25] This door frame was later usurped by the 19th Dynasty Ramesses II, who covered the original inscriptions in plaster and carved his own name. A stone lintel preserving a Horemheb restoration written on top of another king's name suggests that Tutankhamun's workmen were also active at Avaris in the eastern Delta.[26] As the door frame and lintel show, however, Tutankhamun was not the only late-18th Dynasty/early-19th Dynasty restorer active in the north. His successors Ay, Horemheb and the earlier Ramesside kings also undertook restorations, with Horemheb in particular habitually claiming credit for Tutankhamun's work.

To the south of the Aswan border, Nubia was under the firm control of the viceroy, Amenhotep-Huy, 'King's Son of Kush, Fan-bearer on the right hand of the King, Overseer of the gold-lands of Amun, Overseer of the cattle of Amun in this land of Kush, the brave of His Person in the cavalry, the King's Scribe'.[27] Reconstruction work was needed at Gebel Barkel and at Soleb, where Akhenaten had attacked his father's name, replacing the theologically unsound 'Nebmaatre Amenhotep' with the repetitious but more acceptable 'Nebmaatre Nebmaatre'. Kawa received a new temple, whose reliefs showed Tutankhamun worshipping Amun-Ra, Re-Horakhty, Atum, Min and Thoth, and the walled administrative centre of Faras benefited from a new temple and a new statue group featuring Tutankhamun sitting, godlike, between Amun and Mut.[28] It was here at Faras that Amenhotep-Huy's widow, Taemwadjsi, built a chapel in memory of her husband. The carved stone facings attached to the mudbrick chapel walls have survived to confirm that the chapel was associated with the cult of the divine Tutankhamun. Amenhotep-Huy appears adoring Tutankhamun's twin cartouches while his brother is described as 'Second Priest of Nebkheperure [Tutankhamun]' and his wife as the 'Chief of the Female Attendants of Nebkheperure'.

At Faras, it is clear, Tutankhamun has effortlessly achieved Akhenaten's dream: he is worshipped as a living god. This departure from orthodoxy can be matched by evidence from Kawa, where Tutankhamun was regarded as the living incarnation of Amun-Ra. In theory Egypt's living kings were semi-divine. They would only become fully divine after death. However, this subtle theological point was not always clear to their people. The colossal statues erected by Amenhotep III were not simply huge works of art. They were divine statues, deliberately placed outside the temple walls so that they might form an accessible focus for worship for those – the ordinary people – who were denied access to the temple gods. Each statue developed its own cult, its own priesthood and its own devotees. In theory these statues were representations of divine aspects of the living king rather than images of the living king himself, but it is doubtful that all those who left offerings and addressed petitions to the statues understood this fine distinction. Beyond Egypt's borders it seems that this complex theology could be relaxed. Amenhotep III and Tiy had been worshipped as living gods in Nubia; now Tutankhamun, too, is divine.

The most detailed evidence for Tutankhamun's restoration programme comes, as we might expect, from the Theban area. Here a vast swathe of land, stretching from the tombs and mortuary temples of the west bank of the Nile to the city and temples of the east bank, formed a sacred landscape dedicated to the god Amun (or his New Kingdom variant, Amun-Ra) and his divine family. Amun-Ra lived a hidden life within the Karnak temple complex but did, as the annual rituals demanded, make occasional visits to the homes of other gods. Concealed within the cabin of his sacred boat, carried high on the shoulders of his priests, he would process to the neighbouring Luxor temple or would cross the river to visit the gods of the royal mortuary temples. The times that the god emerged from his seclusion were national holidays: times of public feasting, drinking and celebration as the people of the Theban area came as close as they ever would to communicating with their god.

Akhenaten's vendetta against Amun had led him to attack not only the state temples and official art, but private tombs and non-royal statuary too, in a desperate attempt to erase all mention of the despised god from Thebes. Tutankhamun had little interest in restoring the desecrated private monuments – that could be left to the families concerned – but he was interested in grand gestures, and he was particularly keen to associate himself with his illustrious ancestor Amenhotep III.[29]

He therefore completed and decorated Amenhotep's entrance colonnade at the Luxor temple, and restored vandalised texts and reliefs within Amenhotep's east-bank mortuary temple at Kom el-Heitan. At Karnak statues of Amun-Ra, Mut and Amunet (a variant wife for Amun) were commissioned, the granary known as 'Amun rich in provisions' was restored, and temple texts and reliefs were repaired. The king's figure was inserted alongside that of Amenhotep III on the Third Pylon (a monumental gateway within the temple complex) and his name appeared on the Sixth and Eight Pylons. Meanwhile building work recommenced on the Tenth Pylon, a gateway which been started by Amenhotep III and abandoned by Akhenaten. Tutankhamun used blocks from Akhenaten's dismantled temples as fill within the gateway, while decapitated human-headed sphinxes originally designed for Akhenaten's solar temples were adapted to create an avenue of ram-headed sphinxes running between the Tenth Pylon and the temple of Mut. Between the paws of the sphinxes stood miniature figures of Tutankhamun himself, holding the crook and flail in his crossed arms.

Meanwhile, as the Aten temples were demolished their inscribed stone blocks were recycled into new buildings which might, as the centuries passed, themselves be recycled into even newer buildings, generating great archaeological confusion. The blocks of Tutankhamun's vanished Theban Mansion provide an excellent example of the complex life of a temple block. Cut originally for one of Akhenaten's Karnak sun temples, the blocks were reused first by Tutankhamun and then by Ay, who completed the Mansion as a memorial to his predecessor. Following Ay's death, Horemheb initially altered the inscriptions to suggest that he had restored the Mansion, then had a change of heart and dismantled it. This erasure of

Tutankhamun's building is a reflection of Horemheb's hardening attitude to the Amarna Age and all who were associated with it. Perhaps realising that history would not deal kindly with the 'heretic' kings, he had resolved to disassociate himself from his immediate past. Many of Tutankhamun's blocks were used as fill in the Second and Ninth Karnak Pylons. From there they made their way into the medieval buildings that sprang up around the Karnak temple complex. Finally, as the medieval houses have gradually been demolished, the blocks have entered the museum system.

The Karnak temple was not only to be restored; it was to be enhanced. A new relief on the exterior wall was decorated with gold foil that glittered in the sunlight. Here the inundation god Hapi and the harvest goddess Renenutet were flanked by two identical scenes showing Tutankhamun approaching Amun-Ra, Mut and their son, Khonsu. Sadly the relief is today badly damaged, the gold foil has been stolen and Tutankhamun's name has been overwritten by Horemheb. Within the temple many of the cult statues had been damaged, so Tutankhamun's sculptors picked up their chisels and set about repairing the shattered figures of Amun-Ra and his family that were crucial to the proper functioning of the cult. Art historians are easily able to identify their work as they made no attempt to replicate the original style; rather, they placed contemporary late-18th Dynasty body parts and features onto sculptures which, in some cases, were considerably older. It may be that when the statues were painted, as they all would have been, these discrepancies in style were less obvious.

With the majority of the temple statues damaged beyond repair, replacements had to be commissioned. Statues of the new king were needed, too. Tutankhamun was represented at life and colossal size, either as himself or as a god bearing his face, at both the Karnak and Luxor temples. Today he still sits, life-sized, within the Luxor temple with Ankhesenamun by his side. Technically the dyad represents the divine couple Amun-Ra and Mut, but the rounded faces are unmistakably those of the young king and his queen. This convention of applying the king's features to his god would continue throughout Tutankhamun's reign.

To gain a better look at Tutankhamun the man we need to turn to the 'Karnak cachette', a collection of over 2,000 outdated and unwanted temple artefacts, which were buried in a pit within the temple complex at the end of the Dynastic Age and re-excavated in 1903. Included with the almost 800 stone statues are two near-identical, slightly less than life-sized images of Tutankhamun, each striding forward on the left leg. Tutankhamun wears a *nemes* headcloth and an elaborately pleated kilt that stands proud of his body and sandals, and his body is masculine, muscular and perfectly proportioned with a broad chest and narrow hips. His hands, open with the palms downwards on his kilt, form the traditional gesture of humility assumed by a mortal in the presence of a god. This is not a 'boy-king': it is a thoughtful, mature ruler, a king at prayer.[30]

This mature Tutankhamun reappears in the form of the two life-sized wooden statues that stood guard over the blocked entrance to his Burial Chamber (nos 22 and 29). These show the king with a black, resin-painted skin and eyes and eyebrows highlighted in gold. Each wears a golden headdress: one a *nemes* headcloth and the other a *khat* headdress (a simplified version of the *nemes*). Each has golden jewellery, each stands with his left foot forward and each carries a staff in his left hand. Both golden kilts are inscribed with Tutankhamun's name and titles, and one (the figure with the *khat* headdress) states that he is the *ka*, or spirit, of the king and, perhaps, of his brother statue: 'the good god, of whom one be proud, the sovereign of whom one boasts, the royal *ka* of Horakhte, Osiris, the King Lord of the Lands, Nebk-heperure'.[31] Egyptologists, longing to find written documents within the tomb, once speculated that the kilts, which stand proud of their bodies, may have provided a hiding place for Tutankhamun's lost correspondence. Sadly, X-ray examination has confirmed that this is not the case.

We cannot expect Tutankhamun's statues to provide us with an accurate portrait. They will always present him as the ideal Egyptian king: a king virtually indistinguishable from all other kings. If we want to know what Tutankhamun actually looked like, we need to examine his body and the other clues packed in his tomb. An examination of his clothes is helpful here. The garments are in a poor state of preservation, but enough cloth has survived to allow the textile experts of the University of Leiden to take measurements and create modern reconstructions.[32]

The king's mummy, measured by Derry during the autopsy, was approximately 1.63 m in length. Allowing for shrinking during the desiccation process, this suggests that he stood 1.67 m tall: the same height as his two guardian statues. He would have been tall for an ancient Egyptian, but not freakishly so. Tutankhamun's upper body has suffered exten-sive damage, but measurements taken from the near-life-sized 'mannequin' indicate a chest circumference of 79.6 cm. His waist, estimated by combining measurements taken from his belts, sashes and the mannequin, measured a narrow 70–75 cm, with the variation in size reflecting the fact that the sashes and belts were designed to be worn over garments. In contrast, Tutankhamun's hips, measured from his loincloths, were a surprising 108 cm wide.[33] This wide-hipped, narrow-waisted physique is the shape that we see in representations of Akhenaten, leading us to speculate that Akhenaten's exaggerated Amarna art was an exaggeration of his own unusual body shape. The gilded statues recovered from the Treasury confirm another unusual physical trait: each, to a greater or lesser extent, shows the king as a fine-boned individual with obvious breasts. Breasts are not always an indication of femininity, of course. The fact that Akhenaten, too, seems to have breasts in many of his statues suggests that gynaecomastia ran in the family.

What about Tutankhamun's face? While the skin on his body was grey, brittle and cracked, his face, which had been protected from the funerary unguents by the funerary mask, was darker in tone, with a large lesion or scab on his left cheek. His lips were slightly parted, revealing the prominent front teeth that are observable in other 18th Dynasty royal mummies. To Carter, the newly revealed Tutankhamun appeared[34]

> . . . of a type exceedingly refined and cultured. The face has beautiful and well-formed features. The head shows strong structural resemblance to Akh-en-aten, suggesting the same affinity noticeable on the monuments. A resemblance in character which makes one inclined to seek [a] blood relationship.

It is a difficult and thankless – maybe even pointless – task to attempt to reconstruct the face of a long-dead king. Whatever the expertise and intentions of the scientist/artist, the result is always open to criticism by those who feel that it does not match their own expectations. Skin tone causes a particular problem: just how dark- or light-skinned would a late-18th Dynasty pharaoh be? Art is absolutely no help here, as the royal artists invariably painted their work in bright, traditional colours.

Several scientific reconstructions and many artistic portrayals of Tutankhamun have been attempted. The most realistic is likely to be one of the three faces commissioned as part of the 2005 virtual autopsy. The reconstructions were created by independent, specialist teams based in Egypt, France and the USA using CT scan data and the skull (or a plastic model of the skull in the case of the French and USA teams). However, two of the teams were told whose face they were re-creating and, as a press release issued by the Supreme Council of Antiquities tells us, 'made reference to ancient images of Tutankhamun'; the accuracy of their reconstructions therefore has to be questioned. The American team, who worked blind, gave Tutankhamun the appearance of a young North African man with a receding chin and prominent nose. Project leader Zahi Hawass has summarised the three faces for us:[35]

> *The three reconstructions (French, American and Egyptian) are all very similar in the unusual shape of the skull, the basic shape of the face, and the size, shape and setting of the eyes. The noses of all three are different, although the French and the American versions are more similar to each other than the Egyptian. Also, the chin is similar in the American and the French reconstructions; the Egyptian reconstruction has a stronger jaw and chin. In my opinion as a scholar, the Egyptian reconstruction looks the most Egyptian, and the French and American versions have more unique personalities.*

Other, more sensational facial and full-body reconstructions have followed, often incorporating the disputed weakness and left-leg deformity identified by the Supreme Council of

Antiquities examination. This frail modern version of Tutankhamun stands in stark contrast to the strong and powerful image that he himself wished to present to the world.

As Tutankhamun's reign progressed, the elite once again built family tombs reflecting the happy expectation of an eternal afterlife lived alongside Osiris in the Field of Reeds. Tomb art had more or less returned to 'normal': the distinctive Amarna figures had vanished, the traditional gods had been restored and the tomb owner was once again the focus of his own destiny. A number of prominent Amarna refugees built tombs in the Sakkara cemetery including, as we have already seen, the wet nurse Maia, the vizier Aper-el and the sculptor Tuthmosis. The most splendid tombs were those built by Tutankhamun's treasurer, Maya, and Generalissimo Horemheb. Here, in Horemheb's unused tomb, we can see Tutankhamun in action. A full-grown man, he stands at the palace balcony with Ankhesenamun by his side, rewarding the faithful Horemheb with a gift of golden collars.[36] Animals, as well as humans, might be buried at Sakkara. When the Apis bull, the avatar of Ptah of Memphis, died, Tutankhamun had him mummified and interred in the Sakkara Serapeum: the sacred bull cemetery. The bull's burial was looted in antiquity but four human-headed canopic jars, three faience pendants bearing Tutankhamun's prenomen and several wooden coffin fragments have survived.[37]

Four hundred miles upstream, Amenhotep-Huy's elaborately decorated Theban tomb allows us another glimpse of Tutankhamun as he goes about his civil duties.[38] The king sits beneath a ceremonial canopy, dressed in an elaborately pleated garment, wearing the Blue Crown and holding the crook and flail. He watches as an anonymous 'Overseer of the Treasury' (presumably the ubiquitous Maya) performs

Amenhotep-Huy's investiture as viceroy and in so doing reminds us that Nubia was an extremely valuable economic resource. In a separate scene Tutankhamun again sits in state to receive Nubian tribute from Amenhotep-Huy, who stands before him waving an ostrich fan.

After ten years on the throne, Tutankhamun died. Seen from the modern viewpoint, this seems a shockingly sudden tragedy; after he had survived birth and childhood and experienced (we assume) neither malnutrition nor a harsh working environment, we might reasonably have expected him to live for another twenty or thirty years. His contemporaries, more accustomed to the idea that death could strike at any moment, were perhaps less surprised than we are. A reign of ten years, in a land where elite adult males had a life expectancy of approximately forty years, was a long time. Tutankhamun had outlived many of his contemporaries and family members, and he died a man, not a boy. His death is nowhere announced and nowhere explained, but we would not expect it to be. However, the flowers included within his coffins – a wreath adorning the uraeus of the second coffin, a garland on the chest of the second coffin and a floral collar on the third coffin – were flowers which bloom from the middle of March to the end of April.[39] Assuming that these were picked for the funeral, and further assuming that the mummy spent the traditional seventy days in the embalming house, this floral evidence combines with the evidence provided by the dated wine jars to indicate that Tutankhamun died in either January or February of his tenth regnal year.

As in all the best detective stories, we need to examine the body to determine his cause of death. This is not, however, an easy matter. Tutankhamun's body was badly damaged prior to bandaging, whether in the undertaker's workshop or in an attack or accident it is difficult to tell. It was damaged again when the excavation team used what would today be considered brutal methods – a combination of heat, hot knives and force – to extract it from its innermost coffin and mask. To make matters worse, 3,000 years spent lying in unguent-soaked linen had charred the king's skin and destroyed his bandages. As Howard Carter explains:[40]

> . . . the farther we proceeded the more evident it became that the covering wrappings and mummy were both in a parlous state. They were completely carbonised by the action that had been set up by the fatty acids of the unguents with which they had been saturated.

The resin-hardened linen packing the chest cavity prevented Derry from conducting a full examination of the upper torso, and made it impossible for him to suggest a cause of death. This opened the floodgates of speculation. Soon it was rumoured – with no supporting evidence – that Tutankhamun had died of tuberculosis. More intriguingly, an excavation team member, Arthur Mace, had already speculated that Tutankhamun might have been murdered:[41]

> The rest is pure conjecture . . . We have reason to believe that he was little more than a boy when he died, and that it was his successor, Eye [Ay], who supported his candidature to the throne and acted as his advisor during his brief reign. It was Eye, moreover, who arranged his funeral ceremonies, and it may even be that he arranged his death, judging that the time was now ripe for him to assume the reins of government himself.

The 1968 Harrison X-rays revealed what Derry had been unable to see: extensive damage to the chest and sternum, with part of the ribcage missing. The 2005 team were able to add the pelvic bones and the heart to the list of missing body parts. Harrison was intrigued by a small piece of detached bone in the left side of the skull cavity:[42]

> *This could be part of the ethmoid bone [the bone separating the nasal cavity from the skull cavity], which had become dislodged from the top of the nose when an instrument was passed up the nose into the cranial cavity during the embalming process. On the other hand, the X-rays also suggest that this piece of bone is fused with the overlying skull and this could be consistent with a depressed fracture, which had healed. This could mean that Tutankhamun died from a brain haemorrhage caused by a blow to his skull from a blunt instrument.*

This bone fragment – actually there are two, on the right – has sparked a lot of debate. Though they were initially identified as evidence for a fatal bang on the head, it is now accepted that the fragments are parts of Tutankhamun's upper vertebra, detached during Derry's autopsy. They are not embedded in the resin but are free to move within the skull; they must therefore post-date the resin and post-date Tutankhamun's death.

Harrison felt that the base of Tutankhamun's skull was unusually thin. A clouded area in this region could perhaps indicate a haemorrhage caused by a blow with a blunt instrument. The idea that Tutankhamun might have been hit on the head gained huge popular acceptance, and still flourishes on the Internet today. However, re-examination of the Harrison radiographs has shown that the thin skull is an optical illusion caused by the angle of the skull when X-rayed, and the 2005 team has confirmed that there is no sign of a fatal blow.[43] While it has to be recognised that not all forms of murder leave traces that can be detected 3,000 years after death, there is absolutely no evidence to show that Tutankhamun was killed.

The 2005 investigation felt that as there were no signs of great trauma elsewhere on his body, the damage to Tutankhamun's chest must have occurred after his death. The investigative team focused their attention on Tutankhamun's left thigh, which had been broken at, or very close to, the time of death. This had already been noticed by Derry and Harrison but, as the king's fragile bones had been fractured many times post mortem, they had attached no importance to it. Now it was speculated that this injury may have caused his death: 'It is possible that this injury became infected and killed the king'.[44] Alternative interpretations of the evidence suggested that the shattered left leg might have triggered a fat embolism, or that Tutankhamun may simply have bled to death. Later, they suggested that he might have died from the effects of malaria on a constitutionally weakened body. This seems unlikely as, while malaria is life-threatening to the young, adults will usually have developed immunity to the disease.

There is, of course, no need to look for exotic or unusual causes of death. In 18th Dynasty Egypt diarrhoea or even a rotten tooth could kill. But his mangled body is a strong indication that the young Tutankhamun did not die from natural causes. The fact that his heart had apparently putrefied before it could be saved suggests either negligence in the undertaker's workshop or a delay in getting the body to the embalmers. This could indicate death on a foreign battlefield but, as we have already seen, there is no evidence that Tutankhamun actually set foot on a foreign battlefield. An accidental death, away from home, therefore seems more likely. Perhaps, as has recently been suggested, he was trampled by a hippopotamus, although we might have expected this to leave more damage on the rest of the body.[45]

There is another, far stronger possibility. Tutankhamun's golden ostrich-feather fan was recovered between the walls of the third and fourth shrines in his Burial Chamber, close to the king's body (no. 242). An inscription on its foil-covered handle tells us that the forty-two white and brown feathers which once adorned the top of the fan were taken from ostriches captured by the king while hunting in the desert to the east of Heliopolis (near modern Cairo). The embossed scene on the semi-circular top of the fan shows, on one face, Tutankhamun setting off in his chariot to hunt ostrich and, on the reverse, Tutankhamun triumphant, returning with his prey. Hunting ostriches was an ideal way for a king to demonstrate his control over the chaotic forces of nature. It was a young man's sport, spiced with speed and danger. It would have been extremely unlucky – possibly even danger-ous – to describe any king's actual death within his tomb. But we are left wondering whether the fan that was so deliberately placed so close to the king's body could have been provided as a cryptic clue to his untimely demise.

Tutankhamun had ruled Egypt for just ten years, many of which were spent under the guidance of his advisors and female relations. During this time he reversed the Amarna experiment and did much to restore the damage caused by Akhenaten's neglect. We can only guess what would have come next had he been allowed more time.

3

The Undertaker's Tale

Tutankhamun is Prepared for his Afterlife

Engraved on his stone sarcophagus, the goddesses Serket and Nephthys vow to protect the dead Tutankhamun (no. 240):[1]

Words spoken by Serket: My arms envelop he who is within so that I might protect the son of Ra, Tutankhamun. He shall not die a second time in the necropolis but shall exist as a great god in the presence of the gods of the Duat [Netherworld].

Words spoken by Nephthys: I have come [so that] I might serve behind my brother the Osiris, son of Ra, Tutankhamun . . . You shall exist as a living ba *[spirit or soul], assuming every form that you wish. Your* ba *shall not be separated from your corpse. You will follow Ra in the barque of millions and, together with him, you will set on the western horizon.*

Tutankhamun believed that his earthly life was but a fleeting moment in his eternal existence. Just as his coronation had made him one with all of Egypt's living kings, so his death would make him one with the divine deceased. As we have already noted, royal theology offered several exciting possibilities. A dead king might twinkle as an everlasting star, keeping permanent watch over the Two Lands. He might become one with the mummified Osiris, judging the deceased and ruling those who spent eternity toiling in the Field of Reeds. Or he might join the crew of the solar boat captained by the falcon-headed Ra, to fight the malevolent beings who threatened the sun during the dangerous hours of darkness. A degree of flexibility was allowed, so he might even take elements of each divine afterlife and combine them into his own specific destiny.

One thing was obvious, though. To achieve his potential, to become fully divine and live forever, Tutankhamun had to rely on the goodwill of his successor. Plan as he might, without the proper rituals – mummification, appropriate grave goods, a funeral and a functioning mortuary cult – he would not make this all-important transformation. In recognition of the vulnerability of the dead, it had been decreed that each new king should confirm his right to rule by burying his predecessor in appropriate style.

Uniquely, we can see this system in action. Painted on the north wall of Tutankhamun's Burial Chamber, Ay fulfils his duty of care towards his predecessor by performing the Opening of the Mouth and Eyes ceremony. The mummified Tutankhamun stands swathed in white linen, his crowned and bearded head exposed and his crossed arms clutching the crook and flail that symbolise his kingship. He has assumed the form of the king of the dead, Osiris. Facing him, a sprightly-looking Ay assumes the role of Osiris's son and heir, Horus. He wears the Blue Crown and a white kilt, and the leopard-skin cloak of a priest is draped over his shoulders. Wielding a ceremonial adze, Ay ritually unseals the mouth, nose and ears of his predecessor, granting him the potential to reanimate.

Ay's emergence as Tutankhamun's successor comes as a big surprise. Horemheb's biography, which we consulted when looking for details of an 18th Dynasty coronation, gives a clear account of his life as heir to the throne under the rule of an unnamed king who must surely be Tutankhamun:[2]

*So, this god distinguished his son in the sight of all the people
. . . the king's heart being content with his dealings, and
rejoicing at the choice of him. In order to guide the laws of
the Two Regions he appointed him as supreme chief of the
land and as Hereditary Prince of this entire land. He was
unique, without equal.*

As this is Horemheb telling his own tale we might suspect that
he is exaggerating his importance at Tutankhamun's court and
maybe even glossing over his less than orthodox route to the
throne by claiming a link with a king who is no longer alive
to contradict him. But his account is supported by inscriptions
created during Tutankhamun's reign. A stone doorway, part
of a now-vanished mudbrick building, tells us that Generalissimo Horemheb is the hereditary prince, and his elaborately
decorated Sakkara tomb makes it very clear that he is both
hereditary prince and deputy to the king.[3] This tomb would be
abandoned when King Horemheb became entitled to a royal
tomb in the Valley of the Kings.

Under normal circumstances Horemheb would have
remained heir to the throne until Tutankhamun fathered a
male child with a suitably high-ranking mother. This never
happened, and the fact that it is Ay who emerges as king
reminds us that the circumstances surrounding Tutankhamun's death were far from normal. It is tempting to speculate
that Horemheb was far away from Thebes, maybe in Northern
Syria, when the tragedy occurred. There is evidence to suggest
– without any concrete proof – that in Year 9/10 Tutankhamun's troops were battling, and failing, to retake the Syrian
city of Kadesh, which had fallen under the influence of the
Hittite king, Suppiluliuma.[4] We have few specific details of
this campaign, but carved scenes recovered from the Mansion

of Nebkheperure plus tribute scenes carved in the Karnak temple and on the walls of Horemheb's Sakkara tomb combine to suggest that the Egyptians faced a coalition of Syrian–Palestinian forces rather than Hittites. Horemheb played no part in Tutankhamun's funeral arrangements and this does seem odd: even if he was fighting in Syria, the lengthy embalming process would have allowed him sufficient time to return to Thebes. If we are generous, we can speculate that, with Egypt in urgent need of a king, Ay as deputy to the deputy stepped forward. More cynically, we can suggest that Ay saw an opportunity and seized it. Having served Amenhotep III, Akhenaten and Tutankhamun, he was already an old man and no one could have reasonably expected him to rule for more than one or two years. He was to exceed expectations in actually reigning for four. Ay did not appoint Horemheb as his successor.

For over a thousand years the elite way of death had underpinned the Egyptian economy. The urge to build the pyramids – gigantic stairways to heaven – had kick-started the civil service, with the need to supply the northern building sites with raw materials and many thousands of workers providing a steep learning curve. Now the Egyptian bureaucrats excelled in report writing, tax collecting and logistics. The pyramid age had ended but still, throughout the land, architects, masons, labourers, sailors, carpenters, accountants, artists, textile producers, metalworkers, potters and many more were involved on a daily basis, either directly or indirectly, in equipping the dead for eternity. With the tomb finally packed, the mummy installed and the door sealed, families and priests stepped forward to provide the regular offerings of food and drink that would sustain the dead for eternity. In many cases these offerings were financed by the income generated by generous endowments of land which had been bequeathed to the tomb by the tomb-owner. Meanwhile, tomb robbers were making their own contribution to the economy as they retrieved and recycled the grave goods so carefully and expensively chosen for the deceased. Not everyone, of course, had the privilege of mummification and a stone tomb. The vast majority of the population were buried as they always had been, in simple pit graves in the desert cemeteries. But those who aspired to a better class of death – those who wanted stone tombs and mummification – faced a serious drain on their family resources.[5]

As a vital part of the extensive funerary industry, mummification had become a ritual of huge importance. Even Akhenaten, whose religious beliefs had been far from traditional, sent his dead family to be wrapped like Osiris. It is therefore frustrating that we know very little about the actual process. Were the undertakers' mysteries too sacred to be shared with the uninitiated? Were they a trade secret? Or can we assume that while everyone knew what happened in the undertaker's workshop, no one felt the need to discuss it? Happily, not everyone was squeamish. A thousand years after Tutankhamun's death the Greek historian Herodotus delighted his readers with a lengthy account of his visit to Egypt: a curious land of pyramids, bold women and the most bizarre funeral rituals that anyone could imagine. He tells us that there were three methods of mummification – the cheap, the less cheap and the expensive. We can safely assume that the royal undertakers used 'the most perfect process' on Tutankhamun:[6]

> . . . as much as possible of the brain is extracted through the
> nostrils with an iron hook, and what the hook cannot reach
> is rinsed out with drugs; next the flank is laid open with a

flint knife and the whole contents of the abdomen removed; the cavity is then thoroughly cleansed and washed out, first with palm wine and again with an infusion of pounded spices. After that it is filled with pure bruised myrrh, cassia, and every other aromatic substance with the exception of frankincense, and sewn up again, after which the body is placed in natrum, covered entirely over, for seventy days — never longer. When this period, which must not be exceeded, is over, the body is washed and then wrapped from head to foot in linen cut into strips and smeared on the under side with gum, which is commonly used by the Egyptians instead of glue. In this condition the body is given back to the family, who have a wooden case made, shaped like the human figure, into which it is put.

Herodotus is not always accurate in his observations, and he omits the specifics that would help us to really understand the process. For example, he makes it clear that natron (a naturally occurring compound of sodium carbonate, sodium bicarbonate, sodium sulphate and sodium chloride which the Egyptians used as both a soap and a preservative) was used in the mummification process, but was the natron applied dry, or were the bodies soaked in a natron bath? Despite the lack of detail, his matter-of-fact description fits well with the evidence obtained from modern mummy autopsies, and from experiments conducted on animal and occasional human corpses. He does, however, underestimate an important aspect of the process that is highlighted in the few late-dating papyri that describe the rituals of mummification.[7] These make it clear that mummification was much more than an elaborate method of parcelling up the corpse for the grave. It was a religious rite, the all-important first step on the way to eternal life, and the embalmers were priests who wielded archaic tools, uttered spells and donned the jackal-head mask of the god Anubis as they transformed the dead into a latent god.

To understand why mummification was considered such an important rite, we need to consider what happened immediately after Tutankhamun's passing. The king had died, but he was not yet devoid of life. As his body commenced its physical disintegration it released a host of powerful royal entities that lingered, waiting for the rituals that would allow them to start their new lives. These entities, often interpreted as souls, spirits or life-essences, included a being known as the *ka*. If we return to the scene painted on the north wall of his Burial Chamber we can see Tutankhamun's *ka*, identical to the king himself but with the hieroglyphic sign of two raised arms on its head, supporting Tutankhamun as he is welcomed into the afterlife by Osiris.

Released from the body, the *ka* was a needy being with the same basic requirements as the living. It needed a home (the mummy within the tomb) and it needed a regular supply of food and drink. Ideally this sustenance would be provided in the form of regular offerings made by the descendants of the deceased or their representatives, but it could also be supplied by images and mentions of food and drink on the tomb walls, by models of food and food production included with the grave goods, and by actual food and drink buried with the mummy. The fine wines included amongst Tutankhamun's grave goods would have been a fitting accompaniment to the meats, legumes, pulses, spices, honey, cakes and fruits provided as an eternal banquet. Surprisingly, although beer was a staple of the Egyptian diet and was known to be a favourite of the gods, Tutankhamun's tomb did not include jars of beer. This did not matter: he had all the materials necessary to make his own. A model granary filled with grain (no. 277) would have allowed the dead king – or his *ka* – to bake an endless supply of bread that could be washed down with a tasty tomb brew.

Egypt's dead were separated from the living, but they remained very much a part of the living world. The cemeteries welcomed visitors, with most elite tombs including a decorated chapel where the living might look at colourful images, maybe enjoy a picnic, and ultimately leave a suitable offering for the deceased whose body lay hidden in the burial shaft. Tutankhamun's body, however, was to be housed in a tomb cut into the rock of a remote wadi. He did not expect visitors to make the long trek to the Valley of the Kings in order to present him with a loaf of bread or a jar of beer. Instead, following a precedent established at the start of the 18th Dynasty, he separated his offering chapel from his burial and built a conspicuous mortuary or memorial temple – his 'Mansion of Millions of Years' – on the desert edge. The two elements – the tomb and the mortuary temple – were physically separate yet they formed one unit, and the *ka*, which lived with the mummy, was able to pass magically between the two.

Tutankhamun's mortuary temple vanished many centuries ago, but we can make an educated guess at its location. It seems inconceivable that a self-proclaimed traditionalist would not have placed his own temple amongst the line of 18th Dynasty mortuary temples which already dominated the west bank of the Nile opposite the Karnak temple. We can further guess that he built it, at least in part, using blocks from Akhenaten's dismantled Theban Aten temples. The ruined west-bank temple of Ay and Horemheb hints at its position.[8] Situated close to the remains of the mortuary temple of Tuthmosis II and not far from the later-dating, more intact mortuary temple of the 20th Dynasty King Ramesses III, this temple has yielded the remains of several colossal statues, two of which show a king striding forward.[9] Art historians have suggested that these colossi strongly resemble Tutankhamun; they were, however, inscribed by Ay and overwritten by Horemheb. If they did start life as Tutankhamun, it is likely that Ay 'borrowed' them from his mortuary temple, which, given the size and weight of the colossi, was probably situated nearby. It may even be that the temple of Ay and Horemheb itself is Tutankhamun's repurposed mortuary temple. Although the temple has yielded several foundation deposits inscribed with Ay's cartouche, it is possible that these belong to a late building phase. If Ay did usurp Tutankhamun's mortuary temple, we can speculate that he transferred his predecessor's mortuary cult to the east-bank Mansion of Nebkheperure.

The *ka* was a vulnerable entity. While it remained in close contact with its corpse – not a disarticulated skeleton, but a recognisably human body – it would survive, allowing other aspects of the deceased's soul to flourish away from the tomb. But if the *ka* could not recognise its own host it would die, and the deceased would die again. This would mean a permanent erasure; there could be no return from the dreaded second death. It was therefore crucial that the *ka* should be able to recognise its corpse. While it was theoretically possible for the *ka* to survive in a statue or a two-dimensional image, these were very much last resorts. Ideally, the body would be preserved in a lifelike form, albeit a form simultaneously obscured and defined by bandages. Having come to know Tutankhamun as a living and breathing human in Chapters 1 and 2, the contrast when we start to consider the more graphic descriptions of his mummification process is quite stark. For many readers a visit to the undertaker's workshop may seem an indefensible invasion of his privacy: do we really need to know in full, gory detail what happened to Tutankhamun's body after his death? I would argue that we do, for two very different reasons. Firstly, because his mummification was the first, vital step on Tutankhamun's journey towards his eternal existence and, as such, should not be regarded as an insignificant, end-of-life routine. And secondly, because, if we are to use Tutankhamun's body as a source of evidence for his life, health and death, we need to understand the processes that it has undergone.

The Theban undertakers operated from tents pitched on the edge of the desert on the west bank. Theirs was a mysterious realm, part way between the Black Land – the fertile land: the controlled home to the living – and the Red Land – the desert: the chaotic home to wild animals and the dead. This isolation of the recently deceased emphasised their liminal status as neither living nor yet entirely dead. At a more practical level, banishing the undertakers to the edge of the community allowed the citizens to avoid the smells, flies and vermin generated during the long and very messy process. Nobody wanted to live next door to the embalming tent.

We might expect that in a hot land corpses would be hurried to the undertaker's workshop as soon as death was confirmed. But this diagnosis of death was not necessarily the simple matter it would be today: in countries with limited medical skills the onset of putrefaction is often the only way to be certain that a person has indeed died. This may explain why the Roman Period papyrus known as the *Rituals of Embalming* stipulates that the body should remain at home for four days, allowing the family time to mourn, to organise the embalming and, presumably, to make absolutely certain that death has occurred. Herodotus adds that there were other, more sinister reasons why a corpse might be less than fresh:[10]

When the wife of a distinguished man dies, or any woman who happens to be beautiful or well known, her body is not given to the embalmers immediately, but only after the lapse of three or four days. This is a precautionary measure to prevent the embalmers from violating the corpse, a thing which is said actually to have happened in the case of a woman who had just died. The culprit was given away by one of his fellow workmen.

The newly dead Tutankhamun was clearly not hurried anywhere. The fact that his heart was missing and his brain had vanished, leaving his ethmoid bone intact – the 1969 Harrison X-rays show the bone still in place; it has since sustained some damage – is a strong indication that decomposition was well advanced by the time he reached the embalmer's workshop. His brain, we can assume, had simply decayed and trickled down his nose. This would have been considered convenient rather than a problem: although Egypt's doctors understood just how serious a brain injury might be, the undertakers regarded it as a useless organ and simply threw it away.

The resin-soaked linen which the undertakers used to pack and shape Tutankhamun's chest is still in place: now rock-solid, it cannot be removed. So we can be confident that, unlike the king's wandering penis, his heart was lost prior to mummification. As the heart was believed to be the organ of reasoning, this was a serious matter that might cause problems in the afterlife. As a precautionary measure, Tutankhamun would be provided with a replacement heart: a large black resin scarab mounted in gold would be suspended by a long, beaten gold wire from his neck (no. 256q). Inscribed on the scarab, spell 29b from the *Book of the Dead* offered protection against the loss of the heart: 'The souls on earth will do as they desire, and the soul of the deceased will go forth at his desire'.

What caused this delay in sending Tutankhamun to the undertaker's tent? We have already speculated that he experienced a fatal accident while hunting in the northern desert. Could he then have been transported south either for medical attention – his young companions being in denial over his death – or for mummification? A fatal accident involving any king is likely to cause panic and confusion, but this would have been a very poor decision as, even with the help of the wind, the boat journey from Heliopolis to Thebes would have taken many days. It would have been preferable to mummify Tutankhamun in Memphis, then transport his mummy south for burial, as would happen when the 19th Dynasty kings Seti I and Ramesses II died while residing in the north.

Herodotus has already provided us with a good overview of events in the undertaker's workshop. Examination of Tutankhamun's unwrapped body allows us to add more specific detail to his account, breaking the process down into six specific stages: initial preparation, removal of the brain, emptying of the body cavity, desiccation, washing and dressing, and wrapping. Looking at the process overall, it is clear that, although there are signs of haste and somewhat shoddy workmanship in the provisioning and packing of Tutankhamun's tomb, his body was appropriately and respectfully mummified.

On arrival in the undertaker's workshop Tutankhamun was stripped, shaved and washed. As he lay supine on a sloping table, the undertakers turned their attention to his head. The removal of the brain could easily be accomplished by poking a long-handled spoon up the left nostril (breaking the ethmoid bone in the process) and whisking until the liquidised matter started to trickle down the nose. But in Tutankhamun's case this was unnecessary. His empty skull was flushed out with natron solution and then – either before desiccation or immediately after – part-filled with resin. As his 1968 head X-ray shows two distinct resin layers at right angles to each other, this must have been a two-phase operation, with one layer being introduced via the nose while the body lay flat on its back, and the other introduced through the base of the skull either when the body lay on its front with the head tipped back or, more unlikely, the upper body hung upside down

It was important that the organs most prone to decay – the stomach, the intestines, the lungs and the liver – be removed as soon as possible. The kidneys might be removed too – accidentally, we assume – or left in place. To achieve this, a transverse slit almost 9 cm long was cut in Tutankhamun's left flank, parallel to a line running from the navel to the hip bone. The embalmer would then insert a hand, locate the required organs and extract them, cutting through the diaphragm in order to access the lungs. Nine centimetres is longer than the normal embalming incision, yet seems absurdly small when compared to the modern Y-shaped autopsy cut, which runs across the body from the tip of each shoulder to join at roughly the level of the nipples and continue down to the pubis. Diodorus Siculus, another Classical visitor with a fascination for Egyptian funerary rituals, tells us why the undertakers may have been wary of inflicting too much obvious damage on a body:[11]

> *Now the men who treat the bodies are skilled artisans who have received this professional knowledge as a family tradition; and these lay before the relatives of the deceased a price-list of every item connected with the burial, and ask*

them in what manner they wish the body to be treated. When an agreement has been reached on every detail and they have taken the body, they turn it over to men who have been assigned to the service and have become inured to it. The first is the scribe, as he is called, who, when the body has been laid on the ground, circumscribes on the left flank the extent of the incision; then the one called the slitter cuts the flesh, as the law commands, with an Ethiopian stone and at once takes to flight on the run, while those present set out after him, pelting him with stones, heaping curses on him, and trying, as it were, to turn the profanation on his head; for in their eyes everyone is an object of general hatred who applies violence to the body of a man of the same tribe or wounds him or, in general, does him any harm.

The men called embalmers, however, are considered worthy of every honour and consideration, associating with the priests and even coming and going in the temples without hindrance, as being undefiled. When they have gathered to treat the body after it has been slit open, one of them thrusts his hand through the opening in the corpse into the trunk and extracts everything but the kidneys and heart, and another one cleanses each of the viscera, washing them in palm wine and spices.

The embalming wound would normally be covered and magically healed by an embalming plaque; an oval gold plate discovered in the bandages on the left side of his body may be Tutankhamun's misplaced embalming plaque.

The recent scans have revealed that Tutankhamun's diaphragm is present and intact, indicating that while the undertakers used the traditional route – the embalming slit – to draw the intestines, liver and stomach from his lower abdomen, they took advantage of the gaping hole in his chest to extract his lungs. At the same time they conducted some restoration work, rearranging his mangled upper body to give the king a more natural chest shape beneath the bandages. While some of Tutankhamun's ribs are broken and some are missing, others show the smooth edges indicative of post-mortem cutting of the fresh bone with a narrow blade.[12]

As Tutankhamun would need his internal organs in the afterlife, they too had to be washed and preserved in natron. The embalmed viscera would eventually be stored in a set of beautifully decorated human-shaped golden coffinettes dedicated to the four protective Sons of Horus: the human-headed god Imseti, guardian of the liver; the baboon-headed god Hapy (lungs); the jackal-headed god Duamutef (stomach); and the falcon-headed god Qebehsenuef (intestines) (no. 266g). As the contents of the coffinettes have never been subject to medical examination we cannot be certain exactly what lies within. In particular, given the relatively large size of the human liver, we cannot be certain that the organs were preserved intact, and it is interesting to note that during his experimental human mummy project, Dr Bob Briar was forced to section the liver in order to squeeze it into its canopic jar.[13]

His canopic coffinettes depict Tutankhamun as Osiris, wearing the *nemes* headdress and holding the crook and flail. They are very similar to his middle coffin: so similar, in fact, that when an image of a coffinette was used to advertise the 2019–20 *Tutankhamun: Treasures of the Golden Pharaoh* exhibition in London, many visitors were bemused to find that what they had assumed to be a full-sized coffin was only actually 39 cm tall. Howard Carter noted that at least one of the coffinette lids was neither a perfect match nor a good fit for its base, and suggested that they may have been the work of different craftsmen working independently to a given design. More recently it has been recognised that the coffinettes were not actually created for Tutankhamun, as the cartouches included in the inscriptions on their linings shows clear signs of alteration.[14]

The coffinettes, fastened by linen ribbons tied at the neck and ankles, were wrapped in linen and placed in separate cylindrical compartments carved into the base of a semi-translucent calcite canopic chest whose four corners were protected by the carved images of the funerary goddesses Isis (southwest), Nephthys (northwest), Serket (northeast) and Neith (southeast) (no. 266b). The same four goddesses stood at the corners of the sarcophagus to protect Tutankhamun's body. At some point – either in the embalming house or as part of the funerary ritual – the coffinettes were liberally coated in the same unguents that would be used to cover the life-sized coffins and mummy. The canopic compartments were then plugged by four delicately carved human-headed lids wearing the *nemes* headcloth with a vulture head and uraeus on the brow. Although undoubtedly kings, these calcite heads do not bear a great resemblance to Tutankhamun's other images, raising the possibility that they, too, were designed for someone else. Finally, the sloping lid of the canopic chest was lowered and tied in place with linen cords.

Within the tomb this chest would be housed in the Treasury, where, standing on a wooden sled, it would be covered by a linen shroud and surrounded by an engraved golden shrine (no. 266a), which was itself surrounded by a gilded canopy mounted on a wooden sled and protected by the four freestanding funerary goddesses (no. 226). Carter, who was not a man given to excessive demonstrations of emotion, was greatly taken by the beauty of the canopic assemblage:[15]

Facing the doorway, on the farther side, stood the most beautiful monument that I have ever seen – so lovely that it made one gasp with wonder and admiration. The central portion of it consisted of a large shrine-shaped chest, completely overlaid with gold, and surmounted by a cornice of sacred cobras. Surrounding this, free-standing, were statues of the four tutelary goddesses of the dead – gracious figures with outstretched protective arms, so natural and lifelike in their pose, so pitiful and compassionate the expressions upon their faces, that one felt it almost sacrilege to look at them. One guarded the shrine on each of its four sides, but whereas the figures at front and back kept their gaze firmly fixed upon their charge, an additional note of touching realism was imparted by the other two, for their heads were turned sideways, looking over their shoulders towards the entrance, as though to watch against surprise. There is a simple grandeur about this monument that made an irresistible appeal to the imagination, and I am not ashamed to confess that it brought a lump to my throat.

The elongated proportions, slightly tilted heads and pleated clothing of the canopic goddesses all indicate that the shrine is a recycled Amarna artefact. As goddesses would have had no part to play in Akhenaten's austere afterlife, we can speculate that all four started life as queens – Nefertiti, perhaps? – with their defining crowns being a late addition to make them a better fit with Tutankhamun's official religious beliefs.[16]

Back in the undertaker's workshop, the hollow king was re-washed and his finger- and toenails tied in place. His torso was packed with small bags of natron salt and sawdust, and his entire body was covered in natron salt. Beneath the heaped salt, Tutankhamun's eyes were part-open and his eyelashes were still in place. Forty days later his desiccated body, now lighter in weight and darker in colour, was retrieved from the salt, washed and oiled. Tutankhamun's nose and eyes were plugged with linen-impregnated resin, and his lips were sealed, still slightly open, with resin. His abdomen and chest were packed with resin-impregnated linen to restore and retain his shape, and a beaded 'bib' was glued across his chest to disguise and perhaps magically heal his wound. Derry could not remove the bib – it was too firmly stuck – and he remained unaware of the traumatic injury beneath. This bib was missing, presumed stolen with resulting damage to the body, when Harrison examined Tutankhamun in 1968.

Finally, Tutankhamun was ready for the wrapping that would protect and preserve his body and confirm his new divine identity. In the absence of any ancient Egyptian guide to wrapping a mummy, we are forced to rely on the Roman Period *Rituals of Embalming* plus the document known as the *Apis Embalming Ritual*, which, as the name suggests, details the mummification of the sacred Apis bull, the avatar of the god Ptah of Memphis.[17] Bulls are obviously very different in size and shape to people, but the underlying theory of the wrapping ritual remains the same. This was not simply a tidying-up operation: it was an intricate, time-consuming and vastly expensive ritual requiring huge quantities of linen sheets, pads and bandages, all of which had to be hand-woven.

Supervised by a specialist priest, the 'master of secrets', operating in a dedicated wrapping room, the junior undertakers prepared the pads and bandages, then anointed and wrapped the corpse in a prescribed order, working from head to foot. Sixteen layers of bandages were wound around Tutankhamun's body, with the finest linen being reserved for the innermost and outermost layers, while over 150 charms and amulets were distributed within the wrappings. The fingers, toes and limbs were wrapped individually, and Tutankhamun's arms were crossed horizontally across his chest, close to his waist, with his left arm over his right. This is a variant on the usual placement – other 18th Dynasty kings had their crossed arms angled upwards – but we must be wary of interpreting it as either a mistake or a deliberate message. It is all too easy for modern observers to identify 'rules' that might not have actually existed, and to then use these rules to accuse the ancients of making 'mistakes'. If we take a close look we can identify several 'mistakes' in Tutankhamun's mummification: the placement of his arms, the size and location of his embalming slit, and the two layers of resin in his head are all unusual. Similarly, we can spot 'errors' within his tomb: the placement of his canopic coffinettes and magical bricks, for example, are not what we would have expected them to be. But, as Tutankhamun's was the first funeral to be conducted in the Valley of the Kings in almost thirty years, can we reasonably expect everything to be done exactly as before? And can we assume that things were always done perfectly in the past? If an explanation for Tutankhamun's arms is needed, we can speculate that the atypical placement was in some way connected to the damaged chest.

Within his bandages Tutankhamun was dressed in a golden kilt or apron that extended from his waist to his knees. Golden sandals were placed on his feet. His jewellery included finger and toe stalls, bracelets (seven on the right arm and six on the left), rings on his fingers and an array of collars and pectorals on his chest, placed at different levels. Two daggers, one of gold (no. 256dd) and one of enormously valuable meteoritic iron (no. 256k), were attached to girdles tied around his waist.

A close-fitting beaded skullcap covered his shaved head, its four gold and faience cobras displaying an early version of the name of the Aten (no. 2564t). It seems odd that the conspicuously orthodox Tutankhamun would be buried with such an intimate reference to his rejected god, and various theories have been proposed to explain it, ranging from a deathbed conversion to a simple misunderstanding in the mortuary. Other headdresses were to be incorporated in the bandages. A curious conical 'headdress' of wadded linen 'wrapped in the manner of modern surgical bandages' reminded Carter of a crown – a link to the crowned god Osiris, perhaps? – although he also speculated that this may have been 'merely a pad intended to fill up the space that otherwise would have been left empty in the hollow of the headdress of the mask' (no. 256:4u).[18] This was topped by the remains of what appeared to be a linen *khat* headdress, held in place by a gold band (no. 256:4pbis). Above this came an inlaid golden diadem with hanging ribbons whose detachable uraeus and vulture head were found separated within the bandages wrapping the thighs (no. 256:4o).

With the wrapping complete, a pair of hands holding the crook and flail was sewn onto the bandages (no. 256b(1)). A human-headed *ba*-bird hovered below the hands (no. 256b(2)), topping a network of inscribed funerary bands – two longitudinal bands and four transverse bands – which had been made for someone else, and were not a good fit for Tutankhamun's mummy (no. 256b(3)). Their original cartouches had been erased, with just one, naming Smenkhkare, left in place. Finally, a helmet-like golden funerary mask was placed over the king's head and shoulders, and a triple string of disc beads was attached to the front of the mask (no. 256a). These beads are usually removed when the mask is on public display.

Tutankhamun's funerary mask links its wearer with the gods, who were known to have golden skin.[19] More specifically, it links him with the god of the dead, Osiris, who was routinely depicted with a bandaged body and exposed hands and face. The mask wears a *nemes* headdress inlaid with stripes of blue glass, with the vulture and cobra on the brow ready to defend their king. The eyebrows, eyelids and eye cosmetics are made of lapis lazuli; the eyes are made of quartz and obsidian and show (wrongly) red discolouration in both the inner and outer corners; the ears, as we have already seen, have covered functional piercings capable of wearing earrings. The narrow, plaited beard is a separate piece made of gold inlaid with now-discoloured faience. In August 2014, it hit the headlines when, while being removed from its case for cleaning, the beard fell off the mask. Initially inexpertly glued back with fast-drying and highly visible epoxy glue, the beard has since been restored and reattached with beeswax (the 'glue' used by the ancient craftsmen), and the damage can no longer be seen.

The mask is inscribed on the shoulders and the back, with the text on the back coming from the *Book of the Dead*, Spell 151. This is a spell spoken by the jackal-headed god Anubis that will not only allow the mask to become the face of the deceased, but also allow it to help the deceased as he faces challenges in the afterlife:[20]

> . . . *Your right eye is the Night-Barque, your left eye is the*
>   *Day-Barque,*
> *Your eyebrows are the Ennead, your brow is Anubis,*
> *The back of your head is Horus, your hair is Ptah-Sokar.*
> *You are in front of the Osiris, so he may see because of you.*

There has been a lot of speculation as to whether or not this mask was made for Tutankhamun. Citing the pierced ears, and suggesting that Tutankhamun's cartouches show signs of alteration, the British Egyptologist Nicholas Reeves has argued that the mask was originally created for a woman.[21] But many remain unconvinced and, while we cannot accept the mask as a portrait, its facial features do appear to match other formal images of the king.

Seventy days after entering the undertaker's workshop, Tutankhamun had assumed his new, bandaged form and was ready to make his final journey across the desert. There was one further important task to be done. The undertakers gathered the materials used in his mummification. These could not be thrown away: they too needed to be buried. They were to resurface when, on 21 December 1907, an excavation team funded by American lawyer and amateur Egyptologist Theodore M. Davis discovered a stone-lined pit or unfinished tomb shaft (KV54) housing up to a dozen extra-large storage vessels. No photographs or plans were taken of the jars *in situ* and, as Davis made no formal record of his discovery, we cannot be certain how many there originally were. The vessels were taken to Davis's house, where they were opened to entertain a distinguished visitor. Here the Egyptologist and museum curator Herbert Winlock takes up the tale:[22]

> *Sometime early in January 1908, I spent two or three days with Edward Ayrton, to see his work for Mr Davis in the Valley of the Kings. When I got to the house the front 'lawn' had about a dozen gigantic white pots lying on it . . . At that time Ayrton had finished a dig up in the Valley of the Kings just east of the tomb of Ramesses XI. He had quite a job on his hands to find something to amuse Sir Eldon Gorst, the British diplomatic agent who was to be Mr. Davis's self-invited guest soon . . . as he had opened one of the great pots*

and found a charming little yellow mask in it, everybody thought they were going to find many more objects in the other jars . . . That evening I walked back over the hills to the Davis house in the Valley, and I have still got a picture in the back of my head of what things looked like. What in the morning had been fairly neat rows of pots were tumbled in every direction, with little bundles of natron and broken pottery all over the ground . . .

Davis, who had high expectations of the jars, was deeply disappointed to find them filled with what seemed to be a random jumble of bric-a-brac: broken seal impressions bearing Tutankhamun's name, linen-wrapped bundles of natron salt and sawdust, linen sheets and bandages, three head-covers, floral collars, large quantities of broken pottery, animal bones (duck, goose, cow and sheep or goat). The finds were considered insignificant, and were donated to the Metropolitan Museum of Art in New York. It was not until 1941, almost two decades after the discovery of Tutankhamun's tomb, that Winlock recognised the importance of the jars and their contents.[23] KV54 had housed Tutankhamun's embalming cache, and the jars were packed with the remnants of his embalming materials plus the remains of the funeral feast held not for the living, but for the statues and images of the deceased. The floral garlands were the flowers which had adorned the king's coffins and statues during the various stages of his funeral, the three linen headscarves had perhaps been worn by the embalmers as they worked on his body, and a curious collection of about twenty burnt sticks may have been used by the embalmers to check the rate of desiccation beneath the heaped natron salt. Winlock believed that the embalming material, being simultaneously important and impure, had been deliberately buried away from the main tomb.[24] Others believe that the vessels were initially stored in the passageway of Tutankhamun's tomb. When it was decided to fill the passageway with stone chips, the embalming cache was, for some unknown reason, moved to a new, secure location just over 100 m away.[25]

As no king wanted to run the risk of dying without a tomb to house his body and a mortuary temple to house his cult, funerary building programmes were given top priority. Tutankhamun was no exception. As a child-king he might have anticipated replicating the thirty-plus years' reign of his grandfather Amenhotep III, but, as the untimely deaths of Smenkhkare and at least four of Akhenaten's daughters showed, death was no respecter of either youth or royalty. Abandoned building works in the Royal Wadi indicate that he started to build an Amarna tomb immediately after his accession, but this project came to an abrupt end when the court left Amarna. As a self-proclaimed devotee of Amun-Ra, Tutankhamun now wished to be buried alongside his illustrious Amun-worshipping ancestors in the reinstated Theban royal necropolis. Given his constant desire to associate himself with his grandfather Amenhotep III, it is likely that he selected a site in the Western Valley. Here, Amenhotep's extensive tomb (WV22) incorporated passageways, multiple chambers and subsidiary burial suites for close family members.

There are two Western Valley possibilities for Tutankhamun's tomb. The first, the unfinished WV25, consists of a flight of steps and a descending passageway. We could reasonably expect Tutankhamun's tomb to have been far more advanced than this. The return of the skilled tomb-building workforce from Amarna may have caused a slow start, but the multi-titled Maya, 'Overseer of Works in the Place of Eternity' and 'Overseer of Works in the West', had been directing building work for at least six years, and probably more, by the time Tutankhamun died. The fact that Ramesses I could be buried in a comparatively small but appropriately regal tomb after less than two years on the throne demonstrates that these six years would have provided ample time to create a viable royal tomb. It therefore seems logical to identify WV25 as the abandoned tomb of Amenhotep IV, built before he changed his god and his name and fled to Amarna. In contrast, the neighbouring WV23 is an 18th Dynasty royal tomb equipped with two descending stairways, two corridors, a stairwell and three chambers.

WV23 was not, however, made ready for Tutankhamun's burial. Instead, he was to be interred in KV62, a modest private tomb, one of three late-18th Dynasty non-royal rock-cut tombs cut into the floor of the main Valley.[26] Originally one simple room accessed by sixteen descending steps and a narrow, sloping passageway (measuring in length 8.08 × width 1.68 × height 2 m), the new tomb had been extended with the addition of three extra rooms.[27] Carter's team provided these rooms with modern names. The 'Antechamber' was the original chamber, a rectangular room (7.85 × 3.55 × 2.68 m) cut 7.1 m below the Valley floor and orientated north–south. This allowed access via a sealed doorway to the storage room known as the 'Annexe' (4.35 × 2.6 × 2.55 m; orientated north–south). The floor of the Annexe was almost a metre below the floor of the Antechamber. The 'Burial Chamber' (6.37 × 4.02 × 3.63 m; orientated east–west) was separated from the Antechamber by a plastered dry-stone partition wall with a hidden doorway and it, too, was built at a lower level than the Antechamber. Opening off the Burial Chamber, but not hidden behind blocking, the 'Treasury' was a storage chamber (4.75 × 3.8 × 2.33 m; orientated north–south).

Although its primary purpose was to serve as a home for the mummy, its *ka* and the grave goods, the tomb was far more than a storage depot. It was a place of powerful ritual activity. But KV62 was far smaller than Amenhotep III's extensive tomb, and space was severely limited. This was a problem. There would be little room to perform the rituals that played an important part in a royal funeral, and the grave goods that had been accumulating for a decade would have to be squeezed in with little regard to presentation. A more immediate difficulty was posed by the tomb doorways, which were too narrow to allow the larger grave goods to pass. Some, including the chariots and the beds, could be dismantled, but the sarcophagus carved from a single block of granite could not, and the four gilded shrines which were to be erected around the sarcophagus were too large to pass even when dismantled. The workmen were forced to cut away the bottom six steps leading to the passageway and the lintel and jambs of the door opening onto the antechamber, restoring them in stone, wood and plaster once the tomb was filled. The archaeologists would have to reverse this operation when they extracted the shrine panels from the tomb.

Why was Tutankhamun not buried in his own tomb? This is nowhere explained, but as Ay was responsible for Tutankhamun's funeral we should look to him for an answer. It may be that there was a structural problem in the Western Valley tomb which forced Ay to bury Tutankhamun in a substitute tomb that was already in use either as a necropolis workshop or, more likely, housing the burial of a minor royal. But it is possible to reconstruct a more elaborate scenario. We know that Ay came to the throne as an elderly man. He had already built a private tomb at Amarna, and a second private tomb in the floor of the Valley of the Kings. Nobody's fool, he must have realised that he would not have enough time to build himself a third, more splendid tomb. His decision would have been an easy one. Tutankhamun would be buried in the tomb that Ay had been preparing for his own private burial, while King Ay would take over the unfinished tomb in the Western Valley. Just four years after Tutankhamun's death, Ay himself was indeed buried in the splendid, still-unfinished tomb close by the tomb of his former employer, Amenhotep III. Ay's burial was ransacked in antiquity, and his mummy and grave goods have never been found.

While Tutankhamun slowly desiccated beneath his heap of salt, plans were under way to fill his tomb with his belongings. This must have been a logistical nightmare. Chests, boxes and baskets had to be built, packed, labelled, then transported to the Valley. While some came from the nearby Malkata palace or from Tutankhamun's mortuary temple, others came by boat from as far away as Memphis. All had to be crammed into the too-small tomb. We have no way of knowing how typical his grave goods are, but, although it is tempting to imagine longer-lived kings lying in warehouse-like tombs surrounded by hundreds of thousands of artefacts, we have no reason to assume that Tutankhamun was not provided with everything necessary for his afterlife. As his Burial Chamber was too small to hold anything other than the actual burial, the Treasury – the room closest to the body – was filled with the more ritual- and funerary-focused grave goods, while the Annexe became a storage room for food, drink and oils, with some furniture added. The Antechamber, which held a high percentage of everyday and practical items, posed a problem as a pathway had to be left for the mummy to access the Burial Chamber and the canopic box to access the Treasury. While some items could be stacked against the walls, other grave goods would have had to be put into temporary storage outside the tomb. Meanwhile the funeral-specific grave goods – the coffins, canopic box, funerary figures and *shabtis* – had to be gathered for the funeral procession, and food, drink and ritual implements had to be organised for the funeral and the feast that followed.

The brief description of royal afterlife expectations that started this chapter makes the underlying theology seem simple and clear-cut. In reality we find a degree of confusion and conflicting religious beliefs reflected in Tutankhamun's grave goods and tomb art. Each object prepared for his burial had its own valid purpose, but if we consider the assemblage as one large collection we see a jumble of mixed expectations and traditions. This does not mean that Tutankhamun himself would have been confused or dissatisfied. Those of us who approach Christmas with Advent calendars and letters to Santa, or who celebrate Easter with hot cross buns and chocolate bunnies, can understand the happy mingling of different traditions. We should not expect Tutankhamun's tomb to tell a simple tale of death and the afterlife: Egyptian theology was never that simple. This becomes obvious when we take a second look at the painted walls of his Burial Chamber and see scenes of both an Osiris-based and a Re-based afterlife, and obvious again when we consider the *shabti* figures included with his grave goods.

Shabtis, or servant figures, were an important part of the elite burial equipment throughout the New Kingdom. Their very specific duty – to deputise for the tomb owner – is outlined in Spell 6 of the funerary text known as the *Book of the Dead*:[28]

> O shabti, *if counted upon . . . to do any work that has to be done in the underworld . . . you shall substitute for me*

in cultivating the fields, irrigating the riverbanks, or trans-
porting by boat the sand of the east to the west. 'Here I am,'
you shall say.

Animated by magic, the *shabtis* will pick up their miniature tools – Tutankhamun's *shabtis* were equipped with tiny baskets, picks, hoes and yokes – and perform any menial agricultural task that Osiris might allocate to their master. Tutankhamun was buried with 413 *shabtis* made from various materials, of varying design and artistic quality. He had a labourer for every day of the year plus thirty-six overseers (one for each ten-day week) and twelve supervisors (one for each month of the year). This would be evidence of sensible planning if it were not for one very important fact. Kings did not expect to perform menial agricultural labour in the afterlife: they therefore had no need for deputy workers. Royal *shabtis* would always be redundant. Tutankhamun was not the only king confused over this fairly basic theological point: many kings were buried with *shabtis* that they did not need, and, as we have already seen, they have even been found at Amarna, where Akhenaten certainly did not expect to experience an Osirian afterlife. The 19th Dynasty Ramesses III was perhaps the most confused king: a scene in his Medinet Habu mortuary temple actually shows him performing menial agricultural work for Osiris.

We can attend Tutankhamun's funeral vicariously via a series of scenes painted on his tomb walls. Eighteenth-Dynasty royal tombs were traditionally decorated with texts and scenes taken from a collection of religious writings known as the *Books of the Underworld* or the *Guides to the Afterlife*. In Tutankhamun's tomb, however, only the Burial Chamber was plastered and painted, and it seems that this was a rush job. Mould on the walls and on the grave goods, and humidity damage suffered by a number of artefacts, tell us that the plaster was not fully dry when the tomb was sealed. It seems that Ay's tomb switch was a last-minute decision. From our viewpoint this late painting is a good thing, as we can be certain that his wall scenes (unlike many of his grave goods) were specifically designed for Tutankhamun. They reflect, if not his own afterlife expectations, then at least the expectations that Ay had for him.

On the east wall we can see the mummified king. He lies in a coffin resting on a bier protected by a garlanded shrine. The shrine stands on a boat that is itself standing on a wooden sled. The canopic box, which would also have processed across the desert, is absent from the scene, as are the mourning women whom we see attending 18th Dynasty private funerals. There is no sign of the widowed Ankhesenamun and we have no means of knowing how she has reacted to Tutankhamun's untimely death. Twelve of Egypt's highest-ranking dignitaries, dressed in white linen, have been recruited to pull the ropes that drag the sled over the desert sands to the tomb. Amongst them, distinguished by their shaven heads and clearly labelled, are the viziers Pentu and Usermont. All the men chant mournfully as they pull: 'Nebkheperure come in peace, O god, protector of the land.' The image makes the journey across the desert look effortless; archaeology shows that it was a bumpy ride that damaged Tutankhamun's bandaged feet as they rubbed against the sides of his coffin.

The north wall takes up the tale with three scenes intended to be read from right to left. The first, which we visited at the start of this chapter, shows an abbreviated version of the funerary rites. Tutankhamun's mummy has been propped upright and Ay, dressed in the leopard skin of a priest, is wielding the serpent-headed knife to conduct the Opening of the Mouth and Eyes ritual. Indirect confirmation that Tutankhamun's mummy would be raised from the horizontal to the vertical during the ceremony is provided by two holes roughly punched into his funerary mask, which would allow his flail to be tied in place and prevent it from flopping forward when the mummy stood up.[29] Funerary scenes depicted in non-royal tombs indicate that this ceremony was performed at the tomb entrance. We don't know how long the ritual would have taken – the painted image allows no sense of time – but the presence of the three animal-form beds and four gilded shrines within the tomb has led to the suggestion that it may have continued for up to three days and four nights.[30] Next we see Tutankhamun – now a man rather than a mummy – being welcomed into the afterlife by the goddess Nut. Finally, we see the king and his *ka* embracing the god Osiris. The damaged south wall preserves the remains of a scene showing Tutankhamun being greeted by the funerary deities Hathor, Anubis and Isis.

The west wall tells a tale belonging to a very different theology. In a scene from the funerary text known as the *Book of the Hidden Chamber Which is in the Underworld* (more popularly known today as the *Amduat*) we are shown the first hour of night: the hour known as 'Smiter of the Heads of the Enemies of Ra'. It is sunset – neither day nor night – and the solar boat is being welcomed into the underworld by the twelve singing baboons who represent the twelve hours of night. This is the boat that Tutankhamun will help to crew. The sun god Ra has grown old and tired, but on Tutankhamun's wall his boat offers him the hope of rebirth by featuring the youthful beetle god Khepri, a manifestation of himself. Had the Burial Chamber been larger, it is possible that we would have been able to follow Ra's crew on their nocturnal adventures through the next eleven hours. We would have seen them fight the evil serpent Apophis, watched a knife-wielding, cat-headed being decapitate the enemies of Osiris, observed Ra visit Egypt's most secret and ancient gods, witnessed the last judgement of the damned and finally rejoiced as the divine crew drag the sun boat through the body of the coiled snake Mehen allowing Ra to be reborn.

At some point during the funeral the priests offered a last meal to the funerary statues and, maybe, the mummy. This started with the presentation of food on tables and wine in jars and ended with living visitors consuming the food and perhaps smashing the vessels. The remaining food and any smashed pottery were gathered together and stored in large jars, which were left in the passageway along with other, random artefacts, including a number of small red offering cups.

Tutankhamun's mummy and canopic box and the ritual artefacts used in the funeral ceremony were carried down sixteen steps, along the narrow passageway, through the packed Antechamber and into the Burial Chamber. Here his heavy coffin bases were ready and waiting, stacked inside the stone sarcophagus. Tutankhamun was garlanded and placed in his innermost coffin, and the priests muttered spells as they poured at least two buckets of resin-based unguents over their king, carefully avoiding the face and feet. The three coffin lids were closed and sealed in turn, and the broken sarcophagus lid was, with some difficulty, lowered and 'mended' with plaster and paint. This part of the operation must have taken longer than expected as the toes of the outermost coffin had to be planed down to allow the lid to lie flat, leaving telltale curls of wood in the sarcophagus base.

The canopic box was placed within its pre-assembled shrine. Then, with the Treasury complete, work could start on erecting the four concentric, floorless gilded shrines around the sarcophagus (from outer to inner, nos 207, 237, 238, 239). With great difficulty – they were too large to pass into the Burial Chamber without widening the entrance – they were brought in largest first, stacked against the wall, then assembled from smallest (innermost) to largest (outermost). The lack of space in the Burial Chamber caused problems for both the ancient carpenters and the modern archaeologists, who, as Carter tells us, 'bumped our heads, nipped our fingers, we had to squeeze in and out like weasels and work in all kinds of embarrassing positions' as they attempted to dismantle the shrines.[31] Despite helpful instructions scratched or painted onto the shrine components, the shrines were not properly assembled. There were dents and gaping cracks, carpenter's debris was left on the floor and, most surprising of all, the shrines were misaligned so that their doors faced east, not west towards the setting sun.

With the shrines in place, their double doors bolted and sealed, the masons were able to build up the doorway separating the Burial Chamber from the Antechamber. The new south wall was painted, and the artists exited the Burial Chamber by crawling through a small hole. The priests sealed four 'magic bricks' into the walls of the Burial Chamber, then they, too, left. Working from the Antechamber, the masons blocked the hole into the Burial Chamber and plastered it so that – it was hoped – the king's body would remain hidden forever, although the very obvious placement of the two Guardian Statues was something of a giveaway to future robbers. The remaining grave goods were then packed into the Antechamber with a few being abandoned in the passageway. The last living person to leave the tomb swept the ground behind him, so that no footprint would disturb the harmony of the sacred place. Finally, the priests blocked and sealed the tomb door and filled the descending stairway with rubble.

Alone in the dark, Tutankhamun waited for nightfall and the start of his next big adventure. Meanwhile, his bandages slowly started to smoulder. The resins and unguents, so lavishly applied by the undertakers and priests, were charring his skin and reducing his wrappings to soot.

4

The Queen's Tale

Tutankhamun's Sister-Wife, Ankhesenpaaten

A widowed Egyptian queen writes to the king of the Hittites:[1]

*My husband has died. A son I have not. But to thee, they say,
the sons are many. If thou wouldst give me one son of thine, he
would become my husband. Never shall I pick out a servant of
mine and make him my husband! . . . I am afraid!*

Ankhesenpaaten is a familiar Amarna figure. She makes her
first appearance as a baby in a family scene engraved on a
small private stela recovered from an unknown Amarna villa.[2]
Immortalised in limestone and once-bright pigments, a young
family is relaxing beneath the sun's rays. The father, seated on
a cushioned stool, holds his first-born and most important
daughter. He tickles her, and leans forward to kiss her. Facing
him, his wife holds their second daughter, who, eager to join
the fun, has to be restrained on her mother's knee. Almost
unnoticed, a third, tiny daughter has clambered onto her
mother's shoulder and is reaching forward to grab a tempting
ornament dangling from her elaborate headdress. Behind the
father, eight pottery vessels hold enough beer to quench the
fiercest of thirsts. At first glance this could be any ancient
Egyptian family enjoying a picnic. A closer look confirms that
this is a far from normal scene. The parents are wearing the
diagnostic crowns that identify them as Akhenaten and his
consort, Nefertiti. The sun that shines above them is the Aten,

Above. The 'Painted Box', recovered from Tutankhamun's tomb, was decorated with scenes of the king performing daring feats in his chariot and packed with a seemingly random assortment of grave goods.

Below. Akhenaten, Nefertiti and their three eldest daughters are blessed by the rays of the Aten. There are no royal sons in this scene; does this mean that they did not exist?

Above. The young pharaoh Tutankhamun wears the traditional king's Blue Crown. This head comes from a broken statue which originally depicted Tutankhamun standing before a seated god.

Right. Tutankhamun presents himself as a traditional 18th Dynasty pharaoh.

Below. A range of different sized crooks and flails, symbols of Egyptian kingship and a link to the king of the dead Osiris, recovered from Tutankhamun's tomb.

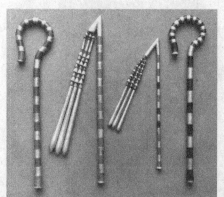

The Theban god Amun and his consort Mut have been given the faces of King Tutankhamun and his consort Ankhesenamun.

Left. The damaged face of the coffin recovered from tomb KV55. The coffin, originally intended for an elite woman, has been modified to accommodate a royal burial. Could this be the last resting place of the ephemeral King Smenkhkare?

Below. The east wall of Tutankhamun's burial chamber allows us to observe his funeral. The king lies in a coffin resting on a bier and protected by a shrine. Twelve of Egypt's highest dignitaries will drag the coffin across the desert on a wooden sled.

THE GREATEST REVELATION OF ARCHAEOLOGY, PART OF THE MAGNIFICENT GOLD SHRINE, SEEN THROUGH THE BROKEN DOORWAY, BETWEEN SENTINEL STATUES.

Above. Tutankhamun's tightly-packed burial chamber is revealed to the world. The two near-identical 'guardian statues' represent the king and his *ka*, or spirit.

Right. The 'Little Golden Shrine' is covered with gold foil decorated with images of Queen Ankhesenamun supporting her husband. Carter originally identified these as simple domestic scenes; Egyptologists now believe that they have a deeper meaning.

Left. Tutankhamun's golden canopic shrine is protected by the goddesses Isis, Nephthys, Serket and Neith, who are depicted in the Amarna art style. This suggests that it was either created early in his reign, or 'borrowed' and adapted from an elite Amarna burial.

Below. Tutankhamun's preserved organs were placed in four miniature coffins, which were stored in separate compartments in a semi-translucent canopic chest guarded by the same protective goddesses. The compartments were plugged by delicately carved human-headed lids.

Left. The goddess Nephthys guards Tutankhamun's granite sarcophagus. She and her sister goddesses are late additions to the sarcophagus: originally these figures had arms but no wings, leading to speculation that they may have represented one or more of the royal women.

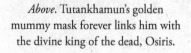

Above. Tutankhamun's golden mummy mask forever links him with the divine king of the dead, Osiris.

Right. The mummified Tutankhamun was protected by three similar but not identical nested anthropoid coffins, the innermost coffin being made of gold. Experts have speculated whether the three coffins were originally a set.

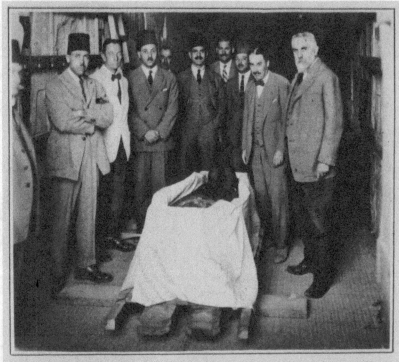

THE EXAMINATION OF TUTANKHAMEN'S MUMMY, FOUND TO BE THAT OF A YOUTH OF EIGHTEEN: THE ARCHÆOLOGISTS AND EGYPTIAN GOVERNMENT OFFICIALS PRESENT ON THE OCCASION.

Above. The king's autopsy is reported in the *Illustrated London News.* For the first time, Egyptologists have proof that Tutankhamun was not an elderly king.

Left. The child-king Tutankhamun, taking the form of the sun god Ra, emerges from a lotus blossom in a recreation of a myth describing the beginning of the world.

the god who dominates every aspect of their life. The baby captivated by her mother's crown is Ankhesenpaaten: she will change both her name and her god, will become queen to her brother, and will outlive her entire family.

Ankhesenpaaten is naked. Her lack of clothes allows us to see that the artists, unaccustomed to depicting children, have given her the awkward shape of a miniature Nefertiti: she has a pear-shaped body, heavy thighs, an indented waist and spindly arms and calves, and, although she is climbing and her arms seem reasonably fluid, her legs are locked stiffly together. Her shaven head has an unnaturally elongated shape. Her sisters are slightly larger but have an identical body shape and the same exaggerated head. As Meritaten is looking backwards, towards her mother, we can see that she also has a thick side-lock plait. These egg-shaped heads, with or without a side-lock, appear repeatedly at Amarna both in two-dimensional art and in sculpture, allowing us to identify otherwise unlabelled princesses. Initially Egyptologists speculated that the head shape might be evidence for the deliberate manipulation of the soft bones of the skull at birth, but, although artificial cranial modification (head binding) was practised worldwide in antiquity, no mummies with a characteristically distorted skull have been discovered. The fact that Ankhesenamun's head appears completely normal when, fifteen years later, she appears beside Tutankhamun at Thebes confirms that this is not the case and also allows us to discount the suggestion that all six of Nefertiti's daughters suffered from hydrocephalus. It seems far more likely that the elongated heads are a deliberate exaggeration of a family tendency towards long skulls that is made obvious by Harrison's 1968 X-ray of Tutankhamun's head. The *Great Hymn to the Aten* confirms that Akhenaten was interested in the idea of the egg as a source of life, and it seems that he has linked this to his own young daughters:[3]

> *You make the seed grow in women and create people from fluid. You give life to the son in his mother's womb and calm him to stop his tears. You are the nurse within the womb, who gives breath to animate all that he makes when it comes down from the womb. On the day he is born you open his mouth to supply his needs. When the chick is in the egg, speaking within his shell, you give him breath within it to live. When you have made his time for him to break himself out from the shell, he comes out of the egg to proclaim his birth, and goes about on his two legs when he comes out of it.*

Amarna had an insatiable demand for royal art. Akhenaten, Nefertiti and their daughters appeared on the boundary stelae that encircled the city, on tomb and temple walls, in private and public chapels, and in significant locations throughout the city. There were statues of stone, metal and wood, frescos, small carved and brightly painted stelae, and large carved and brightly painted walls. Dictators routinely erect large statues to celebrate themselves, but this plethora of royal images reflects more than a simple desire to dominate the cityscape. As the old gods are relegated, Akhenaten is reassigning the roles formerly held by the traditional solar deities. Atum, the god who emerged from the waters of chaos at the beginning of time, has become the Aten. His twin children, Shu, the god of the atmosphere, and Tefnut, the goddess of moisture, have become Akhenaten and Nefertiti. Akhenaten's daughters now represent the divine children born to Shu and Tefnut, and their descendants.

As time goes by we see an increasingly older Ankhesenpaaten attending royal engagements with her sisters. She stands on the palace balcony and helps her father to throw gold to his favourites, and she attends the international gathering in Year 12. An isolated inscribed sandstone block of unknown provenance shows her in the care of 'the nurse of the King's Daughter Ankhesenpaaten, Tia'. Tia offers bread to the young princess and both stand close to a super-sized, truncated royal male who must be Akhenaten. It is clear that Ankhesenpaaten is a very important person: she is one of the select group of females who are allowed to encircle the king. But as the third daughter she is never as important as Meritaten, the first-born, who is accorded the honour of sitting on their father's knee, and she is never as important as Meketaten, the second-born, who is effectively Meritaten's deputy. Just as Akhenaten's status was elevated by the death of his elder brother, Tuthmosis, so Ankhesenpaaten's status must have been boosted by Meketaten's early death.

Towards the end of Akhenaten's reign two young princesses suddenly join in the outer ranks of the royal family. Their titles, which are both complicated and damaged, make it clear that they are the daughters of an unnamed king or kings.[4] Their names, Meritaten Tasherit (Meritaten-the-Younger) and Ankhesenpaaten Tasherit (Ankhesenpaaten-the-Younger), allow speculation that they were named after their mothers. Despite the fact that father–daughter marriages are extremely rare in Dynastic Egypt, it was initially assumed that both Meritaten and Ankhesenpaaten had married their father and borne his children, a theory that still flourishes on the Internet today. In fact, there are several possible parents for either or both girls, including Meritaten and Smenkhkare, Kiya and Akhenaten (have we found Kiya's unnamed daughter?), any unrecorded harem queen and Akhenaten, and, as an outside possibility, Meketaten and an unknown husband. Ankhesenpaaten and

Tutankhaten make an unlikely set of parents as Tutankhaten would have been too young to father two children while living at Amarna. The fact that Meritaten and Ankhesenpaaten later married Smenkhkare and Tutankhaten serves as proof, if proof were needed, that neither had previously married, as widowed Egyptian queens did not remarry.

While royal father–daughter marriages were rare, royal brother–sister marriages were not. These marriages were perceived as beneficial. They allowed the king to marry a woman trained for her role; they ensured that the queen had no conflicting loyalty to her birth family or country; they restricted the number of claimants to the throne by limiting the number of royal grandchildren; they provided appropriate husbands for princesses who might otherwise find it difficult to marry. They even linked the royal family to the gods, who were also inclined to marry their sisters, although the divine marriages were at least in part due to a shortage of eligible partners. No one would have objected to Tutankhaten marrying his full or half-sister Ankhesenpaaten as no one would have been aware that their marriage might have unfortunate consequences.

All Egyptians, from commoners to gods, were expected to marry, irrespective of sexual preference. A man without a wife was seen as incomplete, and schoolboys were advised to marry early and father as many children as possible:[5]

Take a wife when you are young, that she may make a son
for you. She should bear for you while you are still youthful;
it is proper to make people. Happy is the man whose people
are many; he is acclaimed on account of his offspring.

For most people marriage and the family unit offered the only reliable guard against sickness, misfortune and poverty in old age. Tutankhaten, of course, had no need to worry about age-related poverty, but he was still expected to approach marriage in a businesslike way, and he did need to father children.

Ankhesenpaaten was to become Tutankhamun's consort, or 'Great Wife'. She would be an essential component of her husband's rule, with the king and queen forming a partnership – a male/female balance – that would serve the gods, guide Egypt and confound chaos. Her most obvious duties would be to support the king and provide him with a nuclear family, which would ideally include a male heir and a couple of spares, plus a few daughters who could add their feminine support to their father's rule and, of course, marry their brothers. However, the consort was far more than a baby-machine and Ankhesenpaaten's responsibilities would be varied and complex. Frustratingly, the spotlight that constantly shines on the king blinds us to the queen and makes her work difficult to see. Occasional mentions in the *Amarna Letters* show that a consort might play a part in diplomacy, while a couple of explicit titles – 'God's Wife' and 'God's Hand' – hint at female rituals designed to arouse male gods. A few consorts are even known to have ruled Egypt, temporarily, on behalf of an absent husband or an infant son. Their 'reigns', entirely hidden within the reigns of the husband or son, are invisible unless the king chooses to thank the queen for her loyalty.

One wife would not be enough. The king, unlike his people and his gods, had a duty to marry many times, acquiring simultaneous wives of different status carrying different duties and expectations. Some of his marriages would be – we assume – made to Egyptian women, purely for pleasure. These queens would be less important than the consort but there was always the possibility that one might, at a time of dynastic crisis, be plucked from relative obscurity to become the next King's Mother. More important were Tutankhamun's diplomatic marriages: both the high-level marriages that would persuade his allies that they were indeed his brother kings, and the lower-level marriages that would bind his less important vassals to Egypt by effectively holding their daughters hostage in his harem. These marriages were regarded as personal bonds between individual kings; if either monarch died, the bond broke and a new marriage was needed. So, when Tadukhepa, daughter of Tushratta of Mitanni, moved into the Egyptian harem as the bride of Akhenaten, she found herself living alongside her aunt Gilukhepa, daughter of Shutturna II of Mitanni, who had moved into the Egyptian harem as the bride of Akhenaten's father, Amenhotep III. All the matches contracted by Akhenaten would need to be re-established and so, despite the fact that he was not yet a teenager, the first years of Tutankhamun's reign would have been spent marrying a series of foreign brides. At the same time he would have been acquiring foreign women – servants as well as wives – as gifts. We have already seen Abdi-Astarti of Qiltu's casual mention of a gift of '10 women'; he was far from the only correspondent to send anonymous women to Egypt.

We can see that Tutankhamun assumed responsibility for a significant number of women: not just his wives and their children, but their servants, too. Gilukhepa may not have been unusual in arriving in Egypt with a retinue of 317 attendants, many of whom would have been women. In addition, there would be the pharaoh's aunts, sisters and cousins, and the women inherited from Akhenaten, Smenkhkare and Amenhotep III. It would have been impossible to house all these women at court. Instead they were sent to independent harem complexes: self-contained and self-supporting female communities that derived their income from endowments of land, rents paid by tenant farmers and a flourishing textile business.

It is ironic that while the relatively humble houses and tombs of the Amarna workmen's village have survived more or less intact, the extensive harem complexes and their associated cemeteries have vanished almost without trace.

Although we have multiple inscriptions and images to testify to the fact that Ankhesenpaaten became Tutankhamun's Great Wife, we have no record of their marriage. Tutankhamun's tomb has yielded a painted chest occasionally described as the 'marriage contract' casket, but there is nothing to support the implied assumption that it once held important legal documents (no. 40). The chest, cut from an alabaster block and bearing the incised cartouches of the 'Great God, Lord of the Two Lands, Son of Ra, Lord of Diadems' Tutankhamun and the 'Great Royal Wife' Ankhesenamun, held a mass of decayed horsehair and some balls of what might have been human hair, prompting Carter to suggest that it might have been 'a kind of extra canopic coffin for the king's hair'. If we return to the Hermopolis block which first introduced us to Tutankhaten, we can see a second hieroglyphic inscription referring to the 'King's Daughter of his body . . . one greatly favoured by the Lord of the Two Lands'. Their proximity – originally the two inscriptions faced each other across the now-broken block – suggests that the texts are linked. It may even be that they are the 'captions' identifying two missing figures that once stood together on the temple wall. Most of the King's Daughter's name is missing, but a lone reed hieroglyph suggests that it ended in the word 'Aten'. Four of Akhenaten's six daughters bore names ending with the name of his god, but Egyptian names were not always written with the hieroglyphs ordered in the way that they were pronounced, and in only one case was the Aten element regularly written at the end of the name.[6] We can therefore be confident that the text refers to Ankhesenpaaten. With less confidence we can suggest that Tutankhaten and Ankhesenpaaten stand together in this official context because they are already husband and wife and Ankhesenpaaten has become the heiress apparent to Nefertiti and Meritaten. This would explain the use of the epithet 'greatly favoured by the Lord of the Two Lands', which is unique to her.

Following Tutankhamun's coronation Ankhesenamun became an active consort like her mother and her grandmother before her. She appears on a number of Tutankhamun's monuments, is mentioned in inscriptions, and appears as the face of Mut in the Luxor temple. However, she only has her husband's ten-year reign in which to make her mark on the archaeological landscape, and that is not long enough. The best place for us to seek evidence for Ankhesenamun in action is in her husband's tomb. Not on the walls – she does not appear in any of the painted scenes – but on some of his decorated grave goods. The 'Little Golden Shrine', a beautiful and intensely magical artefact and one of Tutankhamun's most enigmatic grave goods, is a good place to start (no. 108). The shrine – a double-doored wooden box with a sloping roof, covered in thick gold foil and mounted on a sledge – is a replica of *Per-Wer*, the shrine of the vulture goddess Nekhbet of el-Kab, tutelary deity of Upper Egypt. Like many of the boxes in Tutankhamun's tomb, the shrine was targeted by robbers and so, when rediscovered, it held a random collection of rejected artefacts: an ebony pedestal for a stolen statuette, parts of a corselet and collar, and a beaded necklace bearing an amulet of Weret Hekau, the Great Enchantress. Weret Hekau suckles Tutankhamun to prepare him for his coronation; she embraces him with her left arm and guides his mouth to her breast with her right hand. The miniature Tutankhamun, 'King of Upper and Lower Egypt, Nebkepherure, beloved of Weret Hekau, the mistress of heaven', stands on a pedestal beside the giant snake, wearing a crown, kilt, sandals and jewellery.

The shrine has retained its gold foil exterior, and it is here that we can see Tutankhamun and Ankhesenamun interacting in a series of engraved panels described by Carter as[7]

> . . . depicting, in delightfully naïve fashion, a number of episodes in the daily life of king and queen. In all of these scenes the dominant note is that of friendly relationship between the husband and the wife, the unselfconscious friendliness that marks the Tell el Amarna school . . .

Carter, a talented artist himself, has clearly absorbed the propaganda of the Amarna idyll and it has persuaded him to forget that formal Egyptian art carries significance far beyond its decorative value. He has equated the fluid, Amarna-style movement with informality and has decided that the vignettes are, although charming, essentially insignificant. He has not paused to wonder why the artists would go to the trouble and expense of depicting a married couple going about their humdrum daily lives on an artefact important enough to be included in a king's tomb. A century on, we have a far better understanding of both the complexities of Egyptian art and the role of the queen consort. When we examine the shrine we see a queen offering her feminine support to a king who is seated, not because he is weak but because he is too powerful to stand. Assuming the role of Weret Hekau, the queen pours liquid into the king's cup; as Maat, the divine personification of the concept of *maat*, she squats to receive the water that the king pours into her hands. The link to Weret Hekau, who is mentioned several times in the uninformative lists of names and titles inscribed on the shrine exterior, suggests that

Ankhesenamun is preparing her husband for his coronation and his participation in the New Year ceremonies that will follow. This is confirmed by the lower scene on the back of the shrine that shows Ankhesenamun offering the enthroned Tutankhamun two notched palm ribs, the hieroglyphic symbol for 'years', together with the symbols for jubilee festivals, eternity and the 'tadpole', which signifies 100,000. Above, in a separate scene, we see Ankhesenamun anointing her husband, presumably as part of his coronation ritual.

Ankhesenamun is equally prominent on the centre panel of the back of the king's 'Golden Throne' (no. 91). Standing just over a metre tall, this is a wooden chair with a solid, slightly sloping back panel, arms, openwork side panels and four legs carved as lion legs. Originally the legs were connected by a carving representing the unification of the Two Lands, but this was stolen by tomb robbers. The throne is covered in gold and silver foil and inlaid with colourful stones, glass and faience. The two side panels display winged uraei wearing the double crown of Upper and Lower Egypt; on these panels, Tutankhamun's name is given as 'Tutankhaten'. Like the Little Golden Shrine, the throne has its artistic roots in the Amarna period, though a serious attempt has been made to adapt the discredited Atenist theology to the new orthodoxy. Once again, it is interesting to read Howard Carter's interpretation of the scene on the back panel:[8]

> *The scene is one of the halls of the palace, a room decorated with flower-garlanded pillars, frieze of uraei (royal cobras), and dado of conventional 'recessed' panelling. Through a hole in the roof the sun shoots down his life-giving protective rays. The king himself sits in an unconventional attitude upon a cushioned throne, his arm thrown carelessly across*

> *its back. Before him stands the girlish figure of the queen,*
> *putting, apparently, the last touches to his toilet: in one hand*
> *she holds a small jar of scent or ointment, and with the other*
> *she gently anoints his shoulder or adds a touch of perfume*
> *to his collar. A simple homely little composition, but how*
> *instinct with life and feeling it is, and with what a sense of*
> *movement!*

Carter's use of the term 'girlish' is perhaps intended as a compliment, though it is an awkward one and not one that many women would appreciate today. Ankhesenamun is a grown woman, a queen consort with important political and ritual duties. Carter's words are probably influenced by a sentimental view of upper-class women as passive, emotional and caring; a view which he has transposed to ancient Egypt. This has the unfortunate effect of diminishing Ankhesenamun's importance. This is not a cosy domestic incident – an intimate moment between two young lovers: it is, once again, an anointing ritual, and Ankhesenamun is the priest.

The royal couple are shown within a floral pavilion or bower. Ankhesenamun stands before her husband, wearing an elaborately pleated robe with sleeves, a Nubian-style bobbed wig and a complicated crown incorporating cow horns, a sun disc and two tall feathers, which suggests a link with the falcon sun god Horus, Hathor, the daughter and Eye of Ra, and, most relevant here, with Amun of Thebes. Tutankhamun, dressed in pleated kilt, collar, tall crown and colourful jewellery, sits in an elaborate chair with his feet on a footstool. Above the royal couple the Amarna-style sun disc once again shines, its long rays ending in small, human-style hands. As Ankhesenamun extends her right hand towards Tutankhamun, she assumes the role of Weret Hekau.[9]

All is not what it seems, however. If we look closely we can see that the scene has been altered. The tall headdresses interrupt the sun's rays and so must be late additions to the image, as normally the height of the headdress would be adjusted to fit the space available. The names of the royal couple, which are given in their later, Amun-based form, show clear signs of alteration from their earlier -aten and -paaten versions. It seems that the throne was made at a time when the Aten was Egypt's dominant god, then adapted to suit Tutankhamun's changed circumstances. It has been suggested that it was originally made for an entirely different king but, if this is the case, who were the original couple? Experts have variously argued for Akhenaten and Nefertiti, Akhenaten and Kiya, and Smenkhkare and Meritaten. Given that the cartouches have undergone only minimal alteration, it seems most likely that the throne was made soon after Tutankhaten's accession, and that the queen was always intended to be Ankhesenpaaten/amun.

If the Little Golden Shrine and the Golden Throne confirm Ankhesenamun's role in supporting Tutankhamun's living kingship, his sarcophagus hints that she also, at the start of his reign, had a role to play in supporting him in death (no. 240). It only takes a quick glance to see that his sarcophagus and its lid are not a matching set. The lid is carved from red granite that has been painted in a not entirely successful attempt to match the colour of the quartzite base. It is generally assumed that the original lid was dropped, but it is equally likely that the original base suffered a catastrophic accident, forcing the masons to improvise and maybe 'borrow' a base from an older tomb. When, with the funeral rapidly approaching, a second incident resulted in a crack running across the centre of the lid, there was not time to find a substitute, so the damage was 'mended' with plaster and paint.

The sloping sarcophagus lid is carved with a winged sun disc and three vertical lines of funerary text that reference the funerary deities Anubis, Thoth and, unusually, the falcon god Behdety. The base, which also carries funerary texts, is protected by four goddesses carved in raised relief, one standing at each corner, looking towards Tutankhamun's head. Isis, Nephthys, Serket and Neith extend their winged arms to encircle the sarcophagus and in so doing eternally embrace and protect the dead Tutankhamun. However, the four goddesses originally had human arms rather than feathered wings. Initially carved as women, or as one woman four times, they were re-carved as goddesses to reflect Tutankhamun's changed afterlife expectations. At the same time, the funerary texts underwent substantial changes. The fact that the base is unfinished, with some areas merely blocked out and others completed in paint, suggests that this remodelling occurred shortly before Tutankhamun's funeral; this in turn supports the idea that Tutankhamun was not a weak and sickly king (a king with an imminent need for a sarcophagus) when he died. Here we can draw a parallel with Akhenaten's smashed granite sarcophagus, fragments of which have been recovered from the Amarna royal tomb. These show that Akhenaten was protected in death not by four goddesses – that would have been unacceptable, given his religious beliefs – but by four versions of Nefertiti, one standing at each corner of his sarcophagus. As we have already noted, it is possible that Tutankhamun's sarcophagus base was taken from an earlier burial. But if it was indeed purpose-made for him, we can deduce that it originally displayed four images of Ankhesenpaaten. Like her mother before her, it seems that Ankhesenpaaten has the power to protect the dead king.[10]

Before we leave Tutankhamun's tomb there is evidence for one other aspect of Ankhesenamun's life that we must consider. The Treasury housed the most sacred and intimate of Tutankhamun's grave goods, including his canopic shrine. Here, casually resting on a jumbled heap of boxes, model boats and other artefacts, the excavation team found a plain wooden box whose displaced lid had originally been tied and sealed in place (no. 317). Inside the box were two tiny anthropoid coffins lying side by side and head to foot, one measuring 49.5 cm and the other 57.7 cm in length (nos 317a,b). The coffins had been tied shut with linen ribbons around the neck, waist and ankles, and sealed with the cemetery seal. Both coffins were made of wood, both had been painted with resin, and both bore standard funerary inscriptions that named the deceased as 'Osiris'. They were slightly too large for their box, and, mirroring what had happened to Tutankhamun's own coffin, it had been necessary to trim down the toes of the larger coffin to force the lid shut.

Each coffin held an inner coffin covered in gold foil, and each inner coffin held a tiny bandaged mummy. The first mummy wore a golden funerary mask too large for its head. It was unwrapped by Carter, who had not expected to find human remains, then passed to Derry, who identified it as the well-preserved body of a premature girl, measuring 25.75 cm from the top of her head to her heels.[11] There was no sign of an abdominal incision and so no way of knowing how the baby had been mummified. She had been wrapped with her arms fully extended and her hands resting on the front of her thighs. She had neither eyelashes nor eyebrows, but there was fine baby hair on her head. Her skin was grey, brittle and almost transparent; a portion of her umbilical cord was still attached. Derry estimated that she had died at five months' gestation.

The second tiny body was equally well wrapped, but lacked a mask. By a curious quirk of fate, this was already in Cairo

Museum. Davis had, in his botched 1907 excavation of Tutankhamun's embalming cache, discovered a miniature golden mask in one of the storage jars. This had been claimed by the Antiquities Service and sent to Cairo. When the remaining jars were donated to the Metropolitan Museum of Art, Davis also donated an entirely unrelated miniature mummy mask retrieved, perhaps, during his 1906 excavation of KV51, a tomb which yielded the mummified remains of three monkeys, three ducks, one ibis and one baboon. This unexplained substitution confused everyone, and the painted plaster mask was published as a part of Tutankhamun's embalming cache.[12] As Davis kept no record of the opening and emptying of the storage jars we do not know whether the original mask was found with the embalming materials or with the remains of the funerary feast, or whether everything was jumbled together. This means that we cannot work out how the miniature mask came to be included. Was it discarded in the embalmer's workshop, perhaps because it was too small to fit on the wrapped head? This would suggest that at least one of the babies was mummified at the same time as Tutankhamun. Or was it dropped within the tomb, and swept up with the remains of the funerary feast? If the latter is the case, it suggests that the babies, like the statues, the figurines and, of course, the royal mummy, played a part in Tutankhamun's funeral.

Derry unwrapped the second mummy himself, revealing a baby girl, measuring 36.1 cm from the top of her head to her heels. Although her body and skull cavity had been emptied and packed with resin-soaked linen, she was less well preserved than the other mummy. Her extended arms lay beside the thighs. She had eyebrows and eyelashes and her eyes were open. She had little head hair, but Derry felt that this may have come away with the bandages. There was no umbilical cord but, after examining her navel, Derry suggested that this had been cut away. He believed that this baby had been stillborn at approximately seven months' gestation. Harrison, who re-examined the baby several years later, estimated eight or nine months' gestation. He diagnosed that she had suffered from Sprengal's shoulder – a deformity of the clavicle – in conjunction with spina bifida and lumbar scoliosis.[13] More controversially, it has been suggested that the girls may have been twins, their difference in size being attributed to Twin-Twin Transfusion Syndrome.[14] This suggestion has not been widely accepted. The babies and their coffins were sent to Cairo, where they were separated – the coffins entered the Museum while the bodies were sent to the Medical School, where they lay forgotten for many years. In 1977, one of the mummies was rediscovered and a tissue sample taken which revealed blood group O/M. This is consistent with Tutankhamun being the father.

We do not know why two baby girls would be included amongst the grave goods in a royal tomb in the Valley of the Kings. Nor, as Tutankhamun's is the only substantially intact 18th Dynasty royal tomb to be discovered, do we know if this was standard practice. Is it a coincidence that both babies were female, or were they deliberately included in his burial so that they might add their feminine protection to that offered by Ankhesenamun? It does seem highly likely that these are Tutankhamun's own stillborn daughters, born to Ankhesenamun. Carter certainly believed that they were Ankhesenamun's babies and, apparently oblivious to the fact that children have two parents, asked:[15]

Was it the result of an abnormality on the part of the little Queen Ankh-es-en-Amen [sic], or was it the result of polit-

> *ical intrigue ending in crime? These are questions, I fear,*
> *which will never be answered, but it may be inferred that*
> *had one of these babies lived there might never have been*
> *a Rameses.*

Egypt had no role for a childless, widowed consort. We should therefore not be too surprised that Ankhesenamun disappears as Ay takes her husband's throne, bringing an end to a line of kings stretching back almost 200 years to the reign of Tuthmosis I. We can imagine her retiring from public life and retreating to the harem palace, where she might spend the next thirty or forty years in luxurious obscurity. Burial in one of the lost harem cemeteries would follow. This was the fate of the vast majority of Egypt's queens.

A quick Internet search, however, will turn up the popular theory that the widowed Ankhesenamun remained at court to marry her husband's successor, Ay. Theirs would have been a curious match: Ay was considerably older than Ankhesenamun and there is strong circumstantial evidence to suggest that he was both Queen Tiy's brother and Queen Nefertiti's father, and therefore both grandfather and great-uncle to Ankhesenamun. We have no precedent for a widowed queen remarrying and no precedent for a grandfather–granddaughter marriage either within the royal family or elsewhere. Nor is there any record of Ankhesenamun playing any part in Ay's reign. The only evidence for their marriage is provided by a blue glass or faience ring decorated with the side-by-side cartouches of Ankhesenamun and Ay. This ring was acquired in 1931 by a 'Mr Blanchard of Cairo' (presumably the American antiquities dealer Ralph Huntington Blanchard), from an unspecified site in the Nile Delta. The Egyptologist Percy Newberry accepted the ring as a genuine antiquity and based his reconstruction of events following Tutankhamun's death on it. For him, this was proof beyond reasonable doubt that the commoner-born Ay had consolidated his claim to the throne by marrying the only surviving Amarna princess. Newberry, however, was writing in 1932, when the 'heiress theory' of Egyptian kingship was flourishing. This theory, developed from a superficial (mis-)understanding of African matriarchies, stipulated that the right to the Egyptian throne passed through the female line. As Newberry himself explains:[16]

> *A man generally became king by virtue of his marriage to the Hereditary Princess, she being the eldest surviving female of the reigning house. She might be the king's widow, or his eldest surviving daughter, or a more distant relative. The Hereditary Princess did not herself reign . . . she was only the channel through which the kingship was transmitted to her husband.*

The ring has since disappeared. However, a ring displaying the same cartouches was purchased by the Berlin Museum in the 1970s. Newberry's theory was accepted without question, possibly because it provided an acceptable explanation for the consanguineous royal marriages that many Egyptologists found shocking. It only takes a quick glance at Tutankhamun's family tree to see that the heiress theory has no basis in fact. While Tutankhaten and Ankhesenpaaten are likely to have been siblings or half-siblings, neither Amenhotep III nor Akhenaten chose a sister as consort. Indeed, Amenhotep III made his wife's relatively humble parentage very clear by informing the world that she was 'The Great Royal Wife . . . The name of her father is Yuya and the name of her mother is Thuya.'[17] Ay's actual consort can be seen on the walls of his

Western Valley tomb, where Tiye, whom we first met as wet nurse to Nefertiti, bears the title of Great Royal Wife. Could the ring have been a forgery or a mistake, with the artist, who may have been unable to read, simply copying the wrong names? Or, as seems most likely, does it reflect an amicable relationship between Ay and Ankhesenamun, who may, perhaps, have continued to perform her priestly role throughout her grandfather's reign?

Ay ruled Egypt for no more than four years before he was succeeded by Generalissimo Horemheb. We do not see Ankhesenamun again.

The *Deeds of Suppiluliuma* is a biographical account of the reign of Tutankhamun's contemporary, the Hittite king Suppiluliuma I. It was written after his death by his son Mursili II, and stored in the royal archives of the Hittite capital, Boghaskoy (now in modern Turkey). It has survived on a fragmented series of clay tablets, written in the same cuneiform 'wedge' script used for the *Amarna Letters*. Embedded within Suppiluliuma's history is the curious tale which started this chapter:[18]

> . . . *when the people of Egypt heard of the attack on Amka they were afraid. And since, in addition, their lord Nibkhururiya had died, therefore the queen of Egypt, who was Dahamunzu (?), sent a messenger to my father and wrote to him thus: 'My husband has died. A son I have not. But to thee, they say, the sons are many. If thou wouldst give me one son of thine, he would become my husband. Never shall I pick out a servant of mine and make him my husband! . . . I am afraid!' When my father heard this, he called forth*

the Great Ones for council (saying): 'Such a thing has never
happened to me in my whole life!' So it happened that my
father sent forth to Egypt Hattusaziti, the chamberlain,
(with this order): 'Go and bring thou the true word back to
me! Maybe they deceive me! Maybe (in fact) they do have
a son of their lord! Bring thou the true word back to me.'

At first sight, this is a simple story. A widowed queen of
Egypt has written to Suppiluliuma, asking him to send one of
his sons as her bridegroom. Frustratingly, however, the name
of the letter writer, 'Dahamunzu', is simply a phonetic version
of the Egyptian queen's title *'ta hemet nesu'* or 'King's Wife'.
Because we know that Suppiluliuma was one of Akhenaten's
correspondents, we know that we are looking for a queen who
was widowed towards the end of the Amarna Age. This leaves
us with three or four candidates: Nefertiti, Meritaten, the
enigmatic Neferneferuaten (who is probably Meritaten) and
Ankhesenamun. Experts have argued long and hard for each of
these. But, as we have seen, Akhenaten had made the succession clear. After his death the throne would pass to Smenkhkare and then either to Smenkhkare's son or to Tutankhamun.
Unless we are facing the unexpected and unevidenced double
tragedy of Ankhesenamun and Tutankhamun dying together,
only Tutankhamun's widow was likely to be in the position of
seeking a new king. The fact that the dead king's name, Nib-
khururiya, sounds like a distorted version of Tutankhamun's
prenomen, Nebkheperure, adds weight to our assumption that
the letter writer is Ankhesenamun.

Suppiluliuma was confused by this request. Everyone
knew that Egypt's kings were averse to the idea of one of their
princesses marrying a foreigner. This is made very clear in the
Amarna Letters when the king of Babylon – whose anonymous

daughter has married Akhenaten – pleads for a princess bride or, if that is really not possible, for a woman who can be passed off as a princess:[19]

> . . . you, my brother, when I wrote [to you] about mar-
> rying your daughter, in accordance with your practice of
> not gi[ving](a daughter), [wrote to me], saying, 'from time
> immemorial no daughter of the king of Egy[pt] is given to
> anyone.' Why not? You are a king; you do as you please.
> Were you to give (a daughter), who would say anything? . . .
> grown daughters, beautiful women, must be available. Send
> me a beautiful woman as if she were [you]r daughter. Who
> is going to say 'she is no daughter of the king'? But holding
> to your decision, you have not sent me anyone.

If the idea of an Egyptian princess serving as a hostage at a foreign court was abhorrent, even worse would be the idea of inviting a foreigner to take control of Egypt. The king of Egypt was, after all, tasked with the duty of defending the Two Lands against chaotic foreigners, and the walls of the great state temples were decorated with scenes showing pharaohs smiting Nubians, Libyans and Asiatics (who would include the Hittites). The timing of the letter adds to the confusion. We have speculated that Horemheb was unable to attend Tutankhamun's funeral because he was campaigning against Hittite allies in northern Syria, yet here is an Egyptian queen begging a favour of a Hittite king who, if not exactly an enemy, cannot have been considered a friend.

Suppiluliuma sent his chamberlain, Hattusaziti, to make enquiries in Egypt. Weeks later, in the spring, Hattusaziti returned to Hatti. He had questioned the queen, and she in turn had sent a message via her own envoy, Hani:[20]

Why didst thou say 'they deceive me' in that way? Had I a son, would I have written about my own and my country's shame to a foreign land? Thou didst not believe me and hast even spoken thus to me! He who was my husband has died. A son I have not! Never shall I take a servant of mine and make him my husband! I have written to no other county, only to thee have I written! They say thy sons are many: so give me one son of thine! To me he will be husband, but in Egypt he will be king.

These repeated journeys must have taken far longer than the seventy days that we would expect Tutankhamun to spend in the undertaker's workshop. Could the funeral have been put on hold, presumably with Ay's agreement, to wait for Suppiluliuma's response? Eventually, it came. Optimism, or perhaps greed, had overcome prudence and Suppiluliuma had despatched a son, Zannanza. Unfortunately, Zannanza died en route to Memphis. Whether or not this was a natural death is unclear; but it certainly caused a rift in the already lukewarm relationship between Egypt and the Hittites. There is no mention of this correspondence, or of the death of Zannanza, in the Egyptian records.

This highly unsatisfactory ending leaves us with a whole host of unanswerable questions. Did Ankhesenamun really have the power to control Egypt's destiny in this way? Would she have been so desperate that she would enter negotiations for a foreign husband? Would she have been able to persuade her courtiers, including the ambitious Ay and Horemheb, that her new husband (be he Egyptian or foreign-born) should become king? Given her own impeccable royal pedigree, would she not have considered ruling herself? Female rule was never ideal but it was certainly possible, and

The Queen's Tale

Ankhesenamun would have known that both the 12th Dynasty Sobeknofru and the earlier 18th Dynasty Hatshepsut had reigned as female kings. We have to conclude by considering the possibility that the letter was a trap: either an irresistible offer devised to cause friction between two powerful states, or a trap designed to cause friction within the Hittite court. The author of the trap, be they Egyptian or Hittite, remains unknown.

5

The Thief's Tale

Tutankhamun and the Tomb Robbers

A thief confesses to robbing the tomb of Ramesses VI (KV9):[1]

The foreigner Nesamun took us up and showed [us] the tomb of King Nebmaatre-meryamun [Ramesses VI] . . . And I spent four days breaking into it, we being [present] all five. We opened up the tomb and we entered it . . . We found a basket (??) lying on sixty . . . chests (?). We opened it. We found a cauldron (?) of bronze; three wash bowls bronze; a wash bowl . . . We weighed the copper of the objects and of the vases and found it to be 500 deben, 100 deben falling to the share [of each man?]. We opened two chests full of clothes . . .

Egypt's elite decorated their tomb chapels – the public rooms in their tombs – with carved scenes painted in bright colours. These scenes were intended to be seen. Visitors would light a torch, open the tomb door and step into a cool, dimly lit land of order and prosperity. Today the wooden tomb doors have been replaced by metal grilles and the faded walls are lit by harsh electric light, but we can still observe the tomb owners as they go about their daily tasks, and we can relax with them as they enjoy a sumptuous banquet washed down with a bottomless jar of beer. There are scenes of boating, board games and family life. Musicians play their instruments, children play their games and attractive young women dance. In the background servants perform their daily tasks with admirable efficiency: everyone knows his or her place and is happy with his or her lot. We have to look very hard to catch a glimpse of anyone who does not appear to be having a good time. The Dynastic Egyptians, it seems, have mastered the art of living the perfect life.

But this, of course, is an illusion. The tomb paintings are not snapshots of lives lived, but wishes for the perfect life to come as seen from the perspective of the elite tomb owner. Beyond the tomb door an unhappy combination of poverty, sickness, misfortune, crime and simple bad luck ensured that life in the land of the living was far removed from this idyll. With Egypt's great wealth controlled by the educated elite – an estimated 10 per cent of the population, almost all male – and with very little opportunity for social mobility, the vast majority of the people were destined to repeat the lives lived by their parents and grandparents before them. A lifetime of hard physical work and, for many women, multiple pregnancies would be 'rewarded' by burial in a simple pit grave in a desert cemetery. We can only speculate on the afterlife that these anonymous unmummified Egyptians expected to achieve.

While cleverness and hard work did not necessarily bring material rewards, the Egyptian way of death offered ample opportunities for the unscrupulous to acquire wealth. Morally, robbing the dead was indefensible: it was, after all, an attack on the eternal life of the deceased that might cause the dead to curse the living. We will consider the veracity of Tutankhamun's curse myth in Chapter 8. Physically it could be extremely dangerous: burrowing beneath the surface of a desert cemetery or tunnelling through a passageway packed with stone chips was fraught with risk. The discovery of a squashed dynastic robber, caught in the act by a rock fall in the Riqqeh cemetery and represented only by a pair of skeletal arms reaching out towards his mummified victim plus a heap of bones on the floor, emphasises just how hazardous the life of a tomb robber could be. As the excavator observed, 'It appeared as if he had been suddenly crushed while in a standing, or at least a crouching position when the fall occurred.'[2] Those who were caught faced a painful end: the 'questioning' of suspects might include the twisting of limbs, cutting, or beating with a stick, while those found guilty were mutilated, sent to work in the mines or quarries (effectively a death sentence), or in extreme cases impaled on a wooden stake as a warning to others. Nevertheless, the rewards were potentially huge, and many were prepared to run those risks.

Post-dynastic robberies, state-sanctioned clearances and modern archaeological excavations have completely emptied the royal tombs, sweeping away the evidence for earlier, more modest crimes. But a survey of cemeteries throughout dynastic Egypt makes one thing clear. All too often those who robbed the dead were those tasked with their care. Specialist knowledge and unquestioned access to the cemeteries provided many opportunities. Undertakers could take short cuts with the rituals and processes and, as no one could see beneath the tightly wrapped bandages, could steal linen, unguents and amulets with impunity. Gravediggers preparing for a new burial might stumble across an old tomb and loot it. State employees excavating a royal tomb might cut into an earlier burial and steal the grave goods. Priests resealing a family vault might help themselves before bolting the door. Necropolis guards and officials might accept a bribe to look the other way, or might even rob the tombs themselves.

Reading through this litany of petty crime, and adding in the professional gangs who methodically targeted the cemeteries, we might reasonably ask why the ancients made this possible. Why, for 3,000 years, did the elite Egyptians persist in taking their treasures to the grave when they knew that these same treasures would prove an irresistible temptation to thieves? Why did they continue with the expensive and time-consuming ritual of mummification when they knew that bodies would survive in a desiccated but still recognisable form complete with skin and hair if buried, unwrapped and uncoffined, in the hot, sterile desert sands? A combination of religious pressure (the identification of the mummification ritual as a means of accessing the afterlife) and social pressure (being seen to do the right thing), plus, perhaps, a reasonable fear of being trapped in a sand-filled grave for eternity, allowed the funerary industry to flourish. The elite continued to place a misguided reliance on physical barriers, on guards and on threats that they believed would be effective regardless of the fact that the illiterate thieves could not read them:[3]

> *(With regard to) any person*
> *who shall do anything evil to this (tomb)*
> *(or) enter therein (with the intention of doing evil?)*
> *The crocodile shall be against them in the water,*
> *the snake shall be against them on land,*
> *the hippo shall be against them in the water,*
> *and the scorpion shall be against them on land.*

Robberies have obscured the evidence for what we might call 'official' thefts: the recycling of grave goods created for others. As Tutankhamun's is the only royal burial to survive substantially intact we cannot know how often this happened in the Valley of the Kings, but we do not have to look too closely at his grave goods to see that he at least was buried with a mixture of his own property and artefacts made for others. Some of the latter are obviously funerary gifts: we know, for example, that six of Tutankhamun's larger and better-made *shabtis* were dedicated by the courtiers Maya (no. 318b; see also no. 331a) and Nakhtmin (nos 318a,c and 330i–k).

Some of Tutankhamun's grave goods – those conspicuously inscribed with the names of deceased royal family members, including Tuthmosis III, Amenhotep III, Tiy, Akhenaten, Nefertiti, Meritaten and Neferneferuaten – were classified by Carter as 'heirlooms', although we can never be certain whether these are genuinely items of sentimental value, or simply old artefacts retrieved from the Amarna royal tombs via the KV55 workshop and reused by Tutankhamun (or Ay). The most intriguing of these heirlooms was a miniature wooden anthropoid coffin found in the Treasury (no. 320). This had been coated in resin, bound at the neck and ankles with linen ribbons, and sealed with the necropolis seal. It proved to be the outermost of a series of four coffins holding a gold pendant in the form of a squatting king wearing the Blue Crown that has been identified on stylistic grounds as either Amenhotep III or Tutankhamun, and a plait of hair folded in a linen cloth labelled with the name and titles of Queen Tiy. This hair is considered a key piece of evidence in the search for Tiy's mummy.

Groups of grave goods showing differences in style and execution – the mismatched collection of *shabtis*, for example – may reflect the work of different craftsmen working simultaneously on the same project, rather than grave goods acquired from different sources. But other artefacts, including Tutankhamun's mummy bands, at least one of the gilded shrines surrounding his sarcophagus, his canopic chest and his miniature canopic coffins were clearly made for others before being adapted to become part of Tutankhamun's own equipment. Their reuse is made obvious by their style (late Amarna

Period), by their lack of similarity to other key artefacts in the tomb and, most importantly, by their inscriptions, which show signs of alteration. Some experts would add the middle one of Tutankhamun's three nested coffins (no. 254) to this list on the grounds that, although the three fit perfectly together, it is not a stylistic match to the other two. Of course, it should also be considered that the other two are the 'borrowed' items (nos 253 and 255). Other experts, as we have already seen, believe that Tutankhamun's funerary mask was created for Neferneferure.

A lock of hair may indeed be an 'heirloom' or a sentimental link with the past: the Victorians who influenced Carter's childhood certainly thought so, as they routinely wore mourning jewellery incorporating the hair of the beloved deceased. Mummy bands and canopic coffins are an altogether different matter. These are not optional or insignificant items: they are the essential, intimate components of a royal burial. Most experts now accept that Tutankhamun's 'borrowed' grave goods were made for Neferneferuaten, leaving us to wonder why this enigmatic individual did not need them. It may be that these were unwanted spares, retrieved from the Amarna royal workshop. But it seems more likely that they came from Neferneferuaten's own Amarna burial via the temporary workshop in KV55. This prompts us to ask why Tutankhamun did not have his own funerary equipment. We might reasonably have expected such essential items as canopic chests to have been prepared early in his reign and stored, in his mortuary temple perhaps, until needed. Given the last-minute switching of his tomb, it is tempting to link the substituted grave goods to Ay, the elderly successor who feared that he lacked the time to commission his own tomb and grave goods. If KV55 was filled with artefacts retrieved from the Amarna Royal Wadi, it would have been a simple matter to make a strategic swap, allowing Ay to be buried with the grave goods originally intended for Tutankhamun, while Tutankhamun was given the grave goods prepared for, and maybe used by, various members of his family.

Surrounded by his new and repurposed grave goods, the dead Tutankhamun was significantly more wealthy and considerably more vulnerable than the vast majority of Egypt's living. The entrance to his tomb had been blocked, plastered, sealed and buried, but his property was far from secure and there were many – including those who had built his tomb, those who had packed it with grave goods and those who had assisted in the performance of the funerary rituals – who knew exactly what lay underground. This danger had been recognised by the architect Ineni, who boasted of building a Valley tomb for Tutankhamun's ancestor Tuthmosis I, 'none seeing, none hearing'.[4] Ineni is, of course, exaggerating: the Valley was never a well-kept secret. But his claim contains more than a grain of truth. While each of the highly conspicuous pyramids of the Old and Middle Kingdoms had been built by approximately 20,000–30,000 temporary labourers summoned under a system of national service to work in three-month shifts for up to twenty years, the rock-cut tombs of the Valley were built using a much smaller, specialist workforce: the 'Servants in the Place of Truth'.

The Servants lived and died apart from the general Theban population, in the purpose-built, state-owned workmen's village known today as Deir el-Medina. This was far from total isolation – the workmen had access to other west-bank settlements and could cross the river to the city whenever they wished – but their remote village was a constant reminder of their own unique role. The location of Deir el-Medina in the dry desert half a mile from the destructive damp of the cultivated land has allowed its archaeology to survive to an astonishing degree. The houses, with their lower walls substantially intact, still stand behind the remains of a stout mudbrick wall. Peering over this wall we can see rows of near-identical terraced houses whose interiors have been customised by their owners so that no two are the same. Beyond the village wall there are tombs cut into the hillside, chapels, the desert and a large dry hole known today as the 'Great Pit'. We do not, however, see the one thing that we might expect to see: a well. The Great Pit had failed to hit the water table and, as the Nile flowed two miles to the south of the village, every drop of water had to be supplied by the state. Every day an endless chain of donkeys carried the heavy water jars to and from the village.

The unusually literate villagers took full advantage of the fact that they had access to an endless supply of writing materials: ink in various colours plus the limestone flakes (ostraca) that littered the desert floor. When the Valley of the Kings lost its place as the royal necropolis at the end of the New Kingdom, forcing Deir el-Medina to close and its residents to relocate, they abandoned a remarkable archive of written material and informal art that allows us to gain an insight into the rhythm of their working lives:[5]

> *The scribe Neferhotep greets his lord in life, prosperity and health . . . I am working in the tombs of the royal children which my lord ordered to be constructed. I am working very well and very efficiently, with good work and with efficient work. May my lord not be concerned about it! Indeed I am working very excellently. I do not tire at all.*
>
> *Addressed by the scribe Nebnetjeru to the scribe Ramose . . . Please be attentive and fetch me some(?) ink because [my] superior has told [me] the good (ink) has deteriorated.*

Every ten days the workmen would leave the village and walk to the Valley. They would spend the next eight days labouring in the tombs by day – working two four-hour shifts each day with a break at noon for lunch – and sleeping in temporary huts at night, before returning home for the two-day weekend. Meanwhile those left behind – the wives, the young, the old and the sick – lived an atypical existence where the women rather than the men ran village life.

Archaeological evidence identified by Howard Carter indicates that not long after Tutankhamun's funeral a gang of robbers evaded, or maybe bribed, the necropolis guards and made a hole in the upper-left corner of the blocked tomb doorway. Once inside, they lit their torches, hurried down the passageway and forced their way through the second door to access the Antechamber. Boxes and chests were emptied onto the floor. Small and light items – ointments, jewellery, metals and textiles – were snatched; large and unwieldy artefacts, and artefacts covered in gold leaf rather than made of solid gold, were rejected. One robber wrapped eight gold rings and two scarabs in a scarf, then dropped it in a box for Carter to find and weave into an intricate tale on the object record card (no. 44b):

> *Doubtful what the original contents had been. The present contents were obviously a miscellaneous collection gathered hastily together after the robbery was discovered and thrown carelessly into the box. Indeed this box gives us the best clue yet as to the details of the tomb robber. On the top were two objects which must obviously have been seized from the person of one of the thieves –*
>
> > *(1) 4 pieces of gold plate open granulated work. These were bent & folded over together for convenience in handling.*

(2) *a long shawl, in the centre of which had been
twisted up a collection of eight gold rings & 2 scarabs.*

*No thief would throw these objects away in however
great a hurry he was, and he must have been apprehended
with the objects on him. The objects [below] must have come
originally from a number of boxes. Thus just a position here
has no meaning . . . This cloth was used by one of the thieves
to wrap his loot up . . . just exactly in the way a modern
Arab wraps up valuables in his head shawl, he placed the
objects in the centre of the cloth, held up the ends to form
a kind of hanging bag, closed the bag by twisting the cloth
several times, and then with the closed bag made a simple
loop knot.*

The loot was presumably rushed across the river and sold in
Thebes.

The robbers returned again and again until, inevitably, the
necropolis officials noticed the open tomb. Violated tombs
were routinely tidied and resealed. If the thefts could not be
prevented, they could at least be hidden, allowing the officials
to pretend that all was well in the necropolis. After all, no one
wanted an official enquiry from the vizier's office. Tutankhamun's tomb was therefore tidied in a rather haphazard fashion,
with items crammed into random boxes and chests so that just
one of the boxes in the Antechamber now housed contents
that agreed with its original label. With the tomb restored to a
semblance of its previous condition, the internal doorway was
re-blocked and resealed, and, as an extra precaution, the passageway was filled to its roof with limestone chips. Several small
objects, including items dropped by the robbers and items
swept into the tomb with the stone chips, were accidentally
incorporated in the fill. Finally, the outer doorway was resealed.

The next set of thieves entered by the old robbers' hole and, faced with a blocked passageway, employed their engineering skills (and possibly their state-owned tools) to tunnel through the stone chips. They were able to access all the tomb chambers but, ignoring the ritual items that were concentrated around the burial, focused on the everyday items in the Antechamber and Annexe. Again, boxes were opened, pottery was smashed and gold was ripped from wood. Now, however, the robbers were constrained in their choice of loot by the size of their tunnel. History repeated itself as the necropolis officials once again noticed the violation. The tomb was restored, the tunnel filled with dark stone chips and the outer doorway again made whole and sealed with the necropolis seal. This pattern would have continued had the weather not intervened.

While the Valley of the Kings is normally hot and dry, it occasionally experiences severe thunderstorms. When this happens the ground cannot absorb the rainwater that pours down the mountainside, forming large streams carrying a mass of stone, sand and rubble. As the streams collide and mix, the central Valley – the location of Tutankhamun's tomb and KV55, both of which were cut directly into the bedrock – becomes a lake. When the water eventually recedes it leaves a hard deposit of mud, chalk, shale and limestone. The ancient architects, aware of the dangers of flooding, attempted to protect their dead kings by digging a large drainage channel and by erecting diversionary walls near individual tombs. Despite these precautions, all the lower-lying tombs have suffered the effects of repeated floods. When a fierce storm struck within four years of Tutankhamun's burial, the Valley filled with water and his tomb was lost beneath a sea of mud and debris. Soon after, the tomb already forgotten, the workmen engaged in building Horemheb's tomb (KV57) constructed their huts directly over its entrance. Finally, almost 200 years later, the workmen cutting a tomb for the 20th Dynasty Ramesses VI (KV9) also built their huts and dumped their rubbish over the lost tomb entrance.[6]

Fate had ensured that, after an initial spate of robberies, Tutankhamun would lie safe within his vanished tomb for 3,000 years. Other kings were not so lucky. Security in the Valley was to a large extent dependent upon the goodwill of the workmen who built and decorated the tombs. It was a matter of the utmost importance that these workmen were paid promptly and in full. During the 18th Dynasty this had not been a problem. But as royal authority started to wane towards the end of the 19th Dynasty, it was not always possible to meet this obligation. A document known today as the *Turin Strike Papyrus* describes discontent amongst the workers during the 20th Dynasty reign of Ramesses III, and includes a casual mention of thefts from the tombs of Ramesses II (KV7) and his sons (KV5): 'Now Userhat and Patwere have stripped stones from above the tomb of Osiris King Usermaatre Setepenre [Ramesses II] . . . and Kenena son of Ruta did it in the same manner above the tomb of the royal children of King Usermaatre Setepenre . . .'[7]

As Egypt's economy collapsed, crimes against the dead increased. The west-bank residents had the knowledge and skills needed to attack the elite and royal tombs. The gangs were well organised and well informed, and they often had the tacit backing of the officials responsible for protecting the cemeteries. In Year 16 of Ramesses IX we find the court meeting to consider the confession of Amenpanufer, a stonemason and robber who has raided the tomb of the 17th Dynasty King Sobekemsaf II. It is worth reading his confession in full as it not only provides details of the well-planned robbery, but also indicates the extent to which bribery and corruption had become a fact of life:[8]

We went to rob the tombs as is our usual habit, and we found the pyramid tomb of King Sobekemsaf, this tomb being unlike the pyramids and tombs of the nobles which we usually rob. We took our copper tools and forced a way into the pyramid of this king through its innermost part. We located the underground chambers and, taking lighted candles in our hands, went down . . . [We] found the god lying at the back of his burial place. And we found the burial place of Queen Nubkhaas, his consort, beside him, it being protected and guarded by plaster and covered with rubble . . . We opened their sarcophagi and their coffins, and found the noble mummy of the king equipped with a sword. There were a large number of amulets and jewels of gold on his neck, and he wore a headpiece of gold. The noble mummy of the king was completely covered in gold and his coffins were decorated with gold and with silver inside and out, and inlaid with various precious stones. We collected the gold that we found on the mummy of the god including the amulets and jewels which were on his neck . . . We set fire to their coffins . . . [an easy way to release the gold leaf and precious inlays].

After some days the district-officers of Thebes heard that we had been robbing in the West, and they arrested me and imprisoned me in the office of the mayor of Thebes. I took the 20 deben of gold that represented my share and I gave them to Khaemope, the district-scribe of the landing quay of Thebes. He released me and I rejoined my colleagues and they compensated me with a share again. And so I got into the habit of robbing the tombs . . .

Two and a half centuries after Tutankhamun's death, the king of Egypt could no longer be considered the all-powerful ruler of a united land. The civil service had grown bloated and corrupt, and personal and local loyalties were vying with – and often trumping – loyalty to the crown. As state income plummeted, the warehouses, which functioned as banks, were running low. Thebes was suffering from food shortages and the west-bank settlements were vulnerable to raids by Libyan nomads who swooped down from the western desert. The Valley of the Kings was a lawless zone and, on the desert edge, the mortuary temples had been vandalised and stripped of their valuables. Ramesses XI, the last monarch of the New Kingdom, abandoned Thebes and fled north, never to return. His death, in 1069 BCE, saw Egypt split in two. The former provincial governor Smendes became the first king of the 21st Dynasty, ruling northern Egypt from the new Delta city of Tanis. Simultaneously Generalissimo and High Priest of Amun Herihor, his successor, Pinudjem I, and his descendants ruled middle and southern Egypt from Thebes.

Egyptologists have designated the next four centuries the 'Third Intermediate Period'. This is in every way a misleading term, suggesting as it does that Egypt had, for the third time, plunged into a temporary dark age of chaos and confusion. It is true that this was a time of decentralisation and population movement, with large numbers of Libyans and Nubians settling in Egypt. But archaeological and, to a lesser extent, written evidence demonstrates that the Third Intermediate Period was for many a time of relative peace and prosperity. Increasingly, it is becoming obvious that the modern distinctions made between the controlled 'Kingdoms' and the lawless 'Intermediate Periods' are by no means as clear-cut as was once believed.

With the king absent, the Priests of Amun assumed responsibility for the maintenance of the royal necropolis in the Valley of the Kings. They found the tombs in a disgraceful condition: they had been opened and their contents stolen, and their mummies had been cut open and occasionally burned in a ruthless hunt for jewellery and amulets. To restore the burials to their former glory would be time-consuming, hugely expensive and ultimately pointless, as the rob–restore–rob cycle would simply start all over again. A new strategy was needed. If the promise of hidden treasure was attracting robbers to the tombs, perhaps the well-publicised removal of that treasure would allow the kings to rest in peace. Any treasure recovered during this operation would make a valuable addition to the Theban coffers, which were sadly depleted after many years of near-civil war.

The necropolis officials set to work. The royal tombs were opened and emptied, and their contents transferred to temporary workshops throughout the Theban necropolis. Here the mummies were unwrapped, rebandaged, labelled and placed in wooden coffins whose gold leaf had been stripped away. In a gesture of respect, several of the rewrapped royal mummies were provided with (cheap) floral garlands. The coffins were stored in chambers throughout the necropolis. Gradually these collections of mummies were amalgamated until there were just two: one royal cache sealed in the Valley tomb of Amenhotep II (KV35); and a second royal cache sealed in the family tomb cut by the 21st Dynasty high priest Pinodjem II, high in the Deir el-Bahri cliff (DB320).

Our consideration of Tutankhamun's life, death and immediate after-death experiences ends with his mummy lying surrounded by grave goods while his spirit flourishes in his chosen afterlife. His name has been omitted from the official list of kings but he has left enough statues and writings to ensure that he will not be forever forgotten. He will rest in peace for almost 3,000 years, before he re-emerges to become Egypt's most famous pharaoh.

PART TWO

LUXOR 1922 CE

6

The Lawyer's Tale

Looking For Lost Kings

The lawyer and Egyptologist Theodore M. Davis abandons his quest to find an intact royal tomb:[1]

I fear that the Valley of the Tombs is now exhausted.

The Valley of the Kings has never been a 'lost' archaeological site. Its name – the Biban el-Moluk, or 'Gates of the Kings' – betrayed its original purpose, and several of the tombs were obvious, open and empty. However, no one knew who had built the tombs or when, and estimates of their number varied. Diodorus Siculus hazarded a guess at forty-seven:[2]

There are also in this city [Thebes], they say, remarkable tombs of the early kings . . . Now the priests said that in their records they find forty-seven tombs of kings; but down to the time of Ptolemy son of Lagus [Ptolemy I], they say, only fifteen remained, most of which had been destroyed at the time we visited . . .

In 1743, the cleric and traveller Richard Pococke published his *Observations on Egypt*, an engaging introduction to a land vaguely familiar to his British readers through the Bible and a handful of Classical writers. Arriving in Luxor, he looked in vain for the hundred gates mentioned by Achilles in Homer's *Iliad*: 'Thebes of Egypt, where treasures in greatest store are laid up in men's houses,—Thebes which is a city of an hundred gates wherefrom sally forth through each two hundred warriors with horses and cars'.[3] Pococke visited Karnak, 'a very poor village, in which the people have mostly built their cottages among the ruins to the south of the temple', then, crossing the Nile, borrowed a horse from the local sheikh and rode to the Valley:[4]

> *By this passage we came to the Biban-el-Maluke, or Bab-il-Meluke, that is, the gate or court of the Kings, being the sepulchres of the Kings of Thebes . . . The vale where these grottos are, may be about one hundred yards wide . . . There are signs of about eighteen of them . . . However, it is to be remarked that Diodorus says seventeen of them only remained till the time of the Ptolemies; and I found the entrances to about that number, most of which he says were destroyed in his time, and now there are only nine that can be entered into. The hills on each side are high steep rocks, and the whole place is covered with rough stones that seem to have rolled from them; the grottos are cut into the rock in a most beautiful manner in long rooms or galleries under the mountains . . . The galleries are mostly about ten feet wide and high; four or five of these galleries, one within another, from thirty to fifty feet long, and from ten to fifteen feet high, generally lead to a spacious room, in which is seen the tomb of the King . . .*

The simplified map that accompanied his account showed a T-shaped valley with very obvious open doors cut into the rock face at ground level.

When, in 1768, the British explorer James Bruce visited Luxor he, too, tried to find the hundred gates and failed. His account of a visit to the 'magnificent, stupendous sepulchres of Thebes' is an exaggerated action-packed adventure, but he was able to visit seven tombs, and his observations are largely sound:[5]

> *In one panel were several musical instruments strowed upon the ground, chiefly of the hautboy kind, with a mouth-piece of reed. There were also some simple pipes or flutes. With them were several jars apparently of potter-ware, which, having their mouths covered with parchment or skin, and being braced on their sides like a drum, were probably the instrument called the tabor, or tabret, beat upon by the hands, coupled in earliest ages with the harp, and preserved still in Abyssinia, though its companion, the last-mentioned instrument, is no longer known there.*
>
> *In three following panels were painted, in fresco, three harps, which merited the utmost attention, whether we consider the elegance of these instruments in their form, and the detail of their parts as they are here clearly expressed, or confine ourselves to the reflection that necessarily follows, to how great perfection music must have arrived, before an artist could have produced so complete an instrument as either of these.*
>
> *As the first harp seemed to be the most perfect, and least spoiled, I immediately attached myself to this, and desired my clerk to take upon him the charge of the second. In this way, by sketching exactly, and loosely, I hoped to have made myself master of all the paintings in that cave, perhaps to have extended my researches to others, though, in the sequel, I found myself miserably deceived.*

Fear of the 'banditti that live in the caverns of the mountains' caused Bruce to flee. Back home, the publication of a highly imaginative sketch of the musical scene sparked great public interest. Henceforth, the tomb would be known as the 'Tomb of the Harpists'. Today we know it as the tomb of the 20th Dynasty pharaoh Ramesses III (KV11).

Egypt had experienced almost 300 years of Ottoman (Turkish) rule when, in 1798, Napoleon Bonaparte launched the invasion which he hoped would block the British from accessing India via the Red Sea. The French campaign started well, and by 21 July the Battle of the Pyramids had been won. This was, however, a short-lived triumph. On 1 August, Horatio Nelson led the British navy to victory against the French fleet and, with their ships destroyed, the French troops found themselves stranded in Egypt. Napoleon himself escaped in 1799. The French held Cairo for three years, gradually extending their control as far south as Aswan. Then, on 18 March 1801, the British landed and took Alexandria. When the Turkish army arrived to support the British, the French were forced to retreat and Cairo fell. Egypt was once again under Ottoman rule.

Included on Napoleon's civilian staff was the *Commission des Sciences et Arts d'Égypte*, a group of scholars tasked with recording the natural, modern and ancient history of Egypt. Their multi-volumed publication *Description de l'Égypte*, a book so large that it was supplied with its own storage cabinet, recorded just eleven tombs in the main Valley plus one, the tomb of Amenhotep III, in the Western Valley. The *Description* sparked a Europe-wide fashion for 'Nile-style' that was reflected in the clothing, jewellery and architecture of the Napoleonic age. But the academic community remained unimpressed. Ancient Egypt was regarded as a cultural dead end: its history lost, its customs crude – animal worship in particular was seen as primitive – and its art decorative but ultimately stagnant. Museums did little to discourage this view by presenting their limited Egyptian collections as curiosities rather than artefacts worthy of study.[6]

The first European to make a systematic attempt to find the lost Valley tombs was the Italian-born, British passport-bearing ex-circus strongman and hydraulics expert Giovanni Battista Belzoni. His interest in the Valley was sparked by a visit to the Tomb of the Harpists. Wandering into the remote Western Valley, he immediately found Ay's tomb and added a new inscription over its entrance: 'discovered by Belzoni 1816'. The next year he returned to the Western Valley and discovered the unfinished WV25, the tomb started by Amen-hotep IV. Relocating to the main Valley, his engineer's eye allowed him to find empty tombs with relative ease but, to his great disappointment, there was no sign of an intact royal burial. His greatest discovery came on 16 October 1817, when he discovered a tomb that he first identified as the 'Tomb of Apis' (because it yielded a mummified bull), then as the 'Tomb of Psammethis', but which we now know to be the tomb of Seti I (KV17). This, one of the longest, deepest and most beautifully decorated tombs in the Valley, formed the basis of a hugely successful exhibition held, appropriately enough, in the newly built Egyptian Hall in London. Visitors were enthralled by Belzoni's drawings, Seti's blue-glazed *shabtis* and – the highlight of the exhibition – the king's translucent alabaster sarcophagus.[7] The king's mummy, of course, had not been found. Undeterred, Belzoni supplied a random mummy which, ever the showman, he unrolled before a public audience.

As Belzoni toiled in the Valley, linguists and antiquarians were engaged in a frenzied race to translate the ancient Egyp-tian language and, simultaneously, decode the hieroglyphic script. The 1799 discovery of the 'Rosetta Stone' had made this a real possibility.[8] The Stone bore an inscription written in three different scripts and two different languages: a readable ancient Greek text, an unreadable ancient Egyptian text written in a script resembling modern Arabic (ancient demotic), and a second unreadable ancient Egyptian text written in hieroglyphs: it therefore offered the possibility of using the Greek text as a key to interpreting the other two. When, in 1822, the French linguist Jean-François Champollion won the race, it was finally possible to read the texts that decorated Egypt's tomb and temple walls. These revealed a knowledgeable, sophisticated and very ancient culture. Almost overnight, Egyptology was elevated from a quirky hobby to a respectable academic discipline, and those who had believed that the origins of Western civilization lay solely in the Classical world were forced to think again. The museums that had once been so dismissive of ancient Egyptian artefacts were now scrabbling to acquire more. Meanwhile tourism was booming and Luxor was filled with Western visitors eager to spend their money on souvenirs. Everyone wanted genuine antiquities (or what they fondly imagined to be genuine antiquities) and the locals were happy to oblige. Finally, the sterile desert was yielding a valuable crop.

In 1858, the National Antiquities Service was established to protect Egypt's increasingly valuable heritage. When, in the 1870s, the antiquities market was flooded with Third Intermediate Period funerary artefacts, the Service – having bought two funerary papyri for the new Cairo Museum – sprang into action. The chief suspects were the el-Rassul brothers, a well-known family of antiquities dealers and tomb robbers who had inexplicably grown wealthy. Their house – which, like many in the west-bank village of Gurna, was attached to an ancient tomb – was searched, but nothing was found. Attempts to bribe the brothers to reveal their secret failed, and so Ahmed el-Rassul and his brother Hussein were arrested and sent to the provincial capital to be interrogated. They were 'questioned'

– Hussein was left with a permanent limp – then, after two months, sent home. Eventually a third brother, Mohammed el-Rassul, agreed to a deal. In return for immunity from prosecution, a £500 reward and a position working for the Antiquities Service, he told the story of a remarkable find.

Roughly ten years earlier his younger brother Ahmed had been searching the Deir el-Bahri cliff for a lost goat – a pretext, almost certainly, for searching for lost tombs – when he stumbled across a depression that indicated a possible tomb shaft. After what must have been a considerable amount of effort the shaft was emptied of its fill, the blocked entrance at its base was breached and the el-Rassuls were able to enter the tomb of the Pinodjem family (DB320). The tomb still housed both the original Pinodjem burials and the cache of restored royal mummies kept there at the end of the New Kingdom. As the royal mummies had already been stripped of their valuables, the brothers started to rob the Pinodjem family.

On 6 July 1881, Mohammed el-Rassul led a museum curator, Émile Brugsch, and his colleague Ahmed Kamal to the deep, dark and well-hidden tomb shaft. A rope was secured around a palm log and Brugsch cautiously descended the shaft. Clutching a lighted candle, he crouched to pass through a tiny doorway, entering a low corridor lined with several large coffins and many small-scale funerary items, including boxes of statuettes, bronze and stone vessels and canopic jars. The corridor curved and ran, via a short flight of steps, to a chamber stacked with coffins housing some of Egypt's greatest New Kingdom kings and queens. Further along the corridor a second chamber held the sorry remnants of the Pinodjem family burials.[9]

While the tomb was known only to the el-Rassul brothers it was relatively safe. Now that the secret was out, rumours of a great treasure of diamonds and rubies were spreading across the west bank, making both the mummies and the archaeologists vulnerable. While the Antiquities Service regarded the people of Gurna as thieves happy to plunder Egypt's heritage, the people of Gurna equally regarded the Antiquities Service as thieves happy to deny poor people access to the vast fortune so fortuitously hidden on their doorstep. Fear of the locals may explain why Brugsch decided to empty the tomb immediately, without making detailed plans, cataloguing the finds or taking photographs. Three hundred men were hired to empty the tomb and transport the coffins: those who worked in the tomb were required to work naked, to prevent them stealing small objects. The coffins were wrapped in matting, sewn in canvas sheets and hauled up the shaft to lie in the hot sun. Less than a week after their discovery they were on a steamer bound for Cairo. The more obvious grave goods went with them; smaller-scale artefacts and fragments were abandoned in the tomb. Installed in Cairo Museum, the mummies reacted badly to their new, more humid conditions, and started to rot.

Back in the Valley of the Kings, French Egyptologist Victor Loret was now looking for the lost royal tombs. On 8 March 1898, he discovered the tomb of Amenhotep II (KV35).[10] The tomb was long and dangerous, with steep corridors and stairways, low ceilings and an open shaft designed to catch both robbers and rainwater. It had been robbed, but it was not empty. Loret found Amenhotep II himself lying in a wooden coffin inside his stone sarcophagus in his burial chamber. The king had been 'restored' and helpfully labelled by the Third Intermediate Period priests. He was not alone. There were random human remains scattered throughout the tomb and, to the excavator's great joy, a room housing nine coffined and labelled New Kingdom royal mummies. The coffined mummies were transferred to Cairo, and so too, after various attempted robberies, was Amenhotep II.

A sealed side chamber opening off the main pillared hall yielded a further three unlabelled, unwrapped and unconfined mummies arranged in a row on the floor. All three had been badly damaged, apparently by tomb robbers:[11]

The first seemed to be that of a woman. A thick veil covered her forehead and left eye. Her broken arm had been replaced at her side, her nails in the air. Ragged and torn cloth hardly covered her body. Abundant black curled hair spread over the limestone floor on either side of her head. The face was admirably conserved and had a noble and majestic gravity.

The second mummy, in the middle, was that of a child of about fifteen years. It was naked with the hands joined on the abdomen. First of all the head appeared totally bald, but on closer examination one saw that the head had been shaved except in an area on the right temple from which grew a magnificent tress of black hair . . . The face of the young prince was laughing and mischievous, it did not at all evoke the idea of death.

Lastly the corpse nearest the wall seemed to be that of a man. His head was shaved but a wig lay on the ground not far from him. The face of this person displayed something horrible and something droll at the same time. The mouth, which was running obliquely from one side nearly to the middle of the cheek, bit a pad of linen whose two ends hung from a corner of the lips. The half closed eyes had a strange expression, he could have died choking on a gag but he looked like a young playful cat with a piece of cloth . . .

Loret had been misled by the shaven, wigless head of the third, female body. As it was assumed that all three were insignificant members of Amenhotep's family he resealed them in the side chamber that he believed was their original tomb.

There is no evidence to confirm that any of these three mummies is royal, and absolutely nothing to date them to the late 18th Dynasty. It is unlikely that the Third Intermediate Period priests who left them lying naked on the floor thought that they were important people and, as we are relying on the priests' labels to identify the cached New Kingdom royals, we should give some weight to this opinion. But there is nothing that Egyptologists like more than to match anonymous mummies to lost royalty and so the first mummy, known today as the Elder Lady (KV35EY) has over the years been identified as, amongst others, the female pharaoh Hatshepsut, Akhenaten's consort, Nefertiti, and his mother, Queen Tiy. This mummy still has, as Loret had noted, abundant hair. Anatomist Grafton Elliot Smith, who later autopsied the body, described her as[12]

> . . . a small, middle-aged woman with long, brown, wavy, lustrous hair, parted in the centre and falling down both sides of the head on to the shoulders. Its ends are converted into numerous apparently natural curls. Her teeth are well-worn but otherwise healthy. The sternum is completely ankylosed. She has no grey hair.

In 1976, skull X-rays and measurements indicated the Elder Lady had the same distinctive skull shape as Thuya, mother of Queen Tiy. Soon after, a sample taken from the heirloom hair discovered in Tutankhamun's Treasury (no. 320) was found to be a scientific match to a hair sample taken from the Elder Lady.[13] Although with an estimated age at death of forty years she is perhaps younger than we might have expected of Akhenaten's mother, the Elder Lady was immediately accepted as Queen Tiy. Doubts then started to surface over the accuracy of the analytical technique used to compare the hair samples, which some experts feared might have been too general to produce any meaningful result.[14] The identification was further weakened when tissue testing showed that the Elder Lady is blood group O/N. This, while not impossible, is not what we would expect from a child of Thuya and Yuya, Tiy's parents, who are both blood group A2/N.[15] At the same time there came a growing realisation that a label on a box cannot prove the ownership or origin of anything within that box. The identity of the Elder Lady was no longer considered proven beyond all reasonable doubt.[16] In 2010, scientists working for the Egyptian Antiquities Service under the leadership of Dr Zahi Hawass used genetic analysis to identify KV35EL as the grandmother of Tutankhamun and the daughter of Yuya and Thuya: an identification which has been happily accepted by the media, and more cautiously received by Egyptologists.[17] If this is indeed Tiy, we can reconstruct her after-death earthly journey as burial at Amarna followed by restoration in KV55, then reburial (with her husband in WV22?) and finally transfer to KV35 during the Third Intermediate Period.

The mystery of the empty tombs had been solved and the missing royal mummies had been recovered. But not every king was accounted for. If we list the 18th Dynasty kings, their tombs and their bodies as identified in 1908, we can see that some possessed a tomb (which we assume he/she had used), some had a mummy recovered from a cache, and a few had both:

Ahmose: tomb?, mummy DB320

Amenhotep I: KV39?, mummy DB320

Tuthmosis I: KV20/KV38, mummy DB320?

Tuthmosis II: tomb?, mummy DB320

Tuthmosis III: KV34, mummy DB320

Hatshepsut: KV20, mummy part DB320?

Amenhotep II: KV35, mummy KV35

Tuthmosis IV: KV43, mummy KV35

Amenhotep III: WV22, mummy KV35?

Akhenaten: Amarna Royal Tomb, mummy?

Smenkhkare: Amarna Royal Tomb?, mummy?

Tutankhamun: tomb?, mummy?

Ay: WV23, mummy?

Horemheb: KV57, mummy?

Just two 18th Dynasty kings lacked both a tomb and a body. Smenkhkare was, however, a shadowy figure and it was not at all clear that he had enjoyed independent rule. It could reasonably be assumed that he had lived, died and been buried at Amarna. Tutankhamun was a different matter. He would surely have planned to be buried alongside his ancestors in the Valley of the Kings. So where was he? There were many Egyptologists eager to hunt for the missing king but the Antiquities Service, intent on avoiding the chaos of rival excavations, decreed that only one would be granted the concession to work in the Valley. In 1902, this prize was awarded to Theodore Monroe Davis, the wealthy American lawyer whom we first met as he excavated Tutankhamun's embalming cache (KV54).

Davis was driven by the twin urges to collect Italian Renaissance art and discover an intact Egyptian royal tomb. As he lacked the skills necessary to conduct his own fieldwork, he started his Egyptological career by sponsoring Antiquities

Service excavations, working in close association with three successive Inspectors: Howard Carter (1902–4), James Quibell (1904–5) and Arthur Weigall (1905). This system worked well, allowing the underfunded Antiquities Service to explore the Valley at someone else's expense. Davis's team discovered many tombs and pits, and had a spectacular success in 1905 when they found the virtually intact tomb of Yuya and Thuya (KV46). However, as the Inspector's official duties increased, the overworked Weigall encouraged Davis to employ a free-lance Egyptologist to lead his team.[18] This Davis did, working successively with Edward Ayrton (1905–7), Harold Jones (1908–11) and Harry Burton (1912–14). An unfortunate effect of this move away from direct supervision by the Antiquities Service was that Davis's fieldwork, which had always been hasty, now became irresponsibly poor and ill-documented.

On 6 January 1907, Ayrton's men were excavating not far from the recently discovered tomb of Yuya and Thuya.[19] They cut through a layer of solidified chippings and flood debris to uncover the rough flight of steps leading to the blocked doorway of the workshop-tomb KV55.[20] Seal impressions confirmed that the workshop had been closed during Tutankhamun's reign, then reopened and resealed some time before the late-18th Dynasty flood covered the Valley floor. Inside the doorway the short descending passage was blocked by a gilded wooden panel: one of the four sides of Queen Tiy's funerary shrine. As the fragile panel could not be moved without conservation treatment, the excavation team built a plank bridge which allowed them to cross into the single-tomb chamber. A rare excavation photograph confirms that this chamber was a mess, its floor covered in rubble fallen from the ceiling and littered with a random assortment of grave goods: the remaining shrine panels, a cosmetic box, alabaster jars, a decayed

funerary pall, faience objects, beads, vessels inscribed for
Amenhotep III and funerary bricks bearing Akhenaten's titles
with his cartouche erased.

A niche in the south wall – probably an abandoned doorway – held four stout canopic jars topped by delicate human-
headed lids. On the basis of their Nubian-style bobbed wigs
and fine facial features there is general agreement that the lids
represent either Kiya or Meritaten: as we would have expected
Queen Meritaten to wear a crown, Kiya seems the more likely
option. The lids do not sit well on their heavy bases, and
may not be the original stoppers.[21] Close examination confirms that these bases have a complicated history. Originally
giving their owner's name, the inscriptions were then erased,
leaving the cartouches of Akhenaten and the Aten intact.
Finally, the cartouches were chiselled away.[22] When opened,
the jars yielded a 'hard, compact, black, pitch-like mass surrounding a well-defined centrally-situated zone of different
material, which was of a brown colour and friable nature'.[23]

An anthropoid coffin decorated with inlaid feather-like
'rishi' patterning lay on the floor, its golden face ripped away
and its lid sufficiently dislodged to allow a glimpse of the
mummy that still rested within. Davis had already concluded
that this must be the burial of Queen Tiy. Davis's companion,
Emma Andrews, entered the tomb soon after its opening and
was able to observe the coffin *in situ*:[24]

> *1907, Jan 19. At the Valley . . . I went down to the burial*
> *chamber and it is now almost easy of access; and saw the*
> *poor Queen as she lies now just a bit outside her magnificent*
> *coffin, with the vulture crown on her head. All the wood-*
> *work of the shrine, doors &c. is heavily overlaid with gold*
> *foil and I seemed to be walking on gold . . .*

Davis believed that the coffin had originally rested on a wooden bier that had rotted and collapsed, precipitating the coffin to the ground and shifting its lid to expose its contents. The 'vulture crown' would therefore be a dislodged pectoral that had once decorated the mummy's chest. However, as there is no recorded trace of any bier, it is probable that the coffin always rested on the floor. There is evidence of water dripping into the tomb – the mummy was found to be damp – and evidence to suggest that a falling rock split the coffin lid. It seems likely that an intruder – either a robber or a necropolis official tasked with closing the workshop – stole the coffin's golden face and the mummy's golden mask.

Davis tells us that the mummy was 'covered with pure gold sheets'.[25] These were probably the detached coffin lining rather than a separate mummy cover. Now housed in Cairo Museum, they are inscribed but impossible to read. The six gold bracelets found on the mummy's arms were sent to Cairo, too; unfortunately these were stolen on the day that they were unpacked. This was not the only theft. It was a widely known 'secret' that KV55 had been robbed immediately after its discovery. Howard Carter was able to help Davis trace some of the stolen artefacts but, as their provenance was now compromised, they could not be included in the 'catalogue of the objects discovered' in KV55. Artefacts retained by Davis, or given away by him, were also excluded from the catalogue, as were a few items that were seen at the tomb opening but which have not been seen since.

The rotten coffin disintegrated as it was removed from the tomb. By 1915, museum conservators had rebuilt the lid but the base had vanished, only to reappear in the State Museum of Egyptian Art in Munich.[26] Reconstructed and reunited, the coffin tells a complicated story. It is obvious, from the quality of the inlays, that it was made for an important person. The arms of the coffin are crossed over the chest – an arrangement seen on both male and female coffins – but the exposed hands are empty and can offer no clue to the coffin's owner(s). The damaged texts suggest that it had two manufacturing stages and at least two owners. The first owner, who would have been named on the strips of inlaid hieroglyphs running down the lid and around the base, was a woman described as the '[wife and greatly beloved of] the King of Upper and Lower Egypt, living on *maat*, Lord of the Two Lands [Neferkheperure Waenre: Akhenaten], the perfect child of the living Aten, who shall live continuously for ever . . .'[27] As the head of the coffin wears a Nubian-style wig, it is likely that this woman was Kiya. The inscriptions were then altered from feminine to masculine and the epithets 'perfect little child of the Aten', 'great in his lifetime' and 'perfect ruler' were added. At the same time the coffin was fitted with the uraeus and curled beard (the type worn by gods) that made it appropriate for its second owner: an unidentified royal male.

The autopsy was conducted quickly, and the mummy was soon reduced to a skeleton with a shattered front tooth and a broken skull. The excavator, Theodore Davis, describes the autopsy:[28]

> *Presently, we cleared the mummy from the coffin, and found that it was a smallish person, with a delicate head and hands. The mouth was partly open, showing a perfect set of upper and lower teeth. The body was enclosed in mummy-cloth of fine texture, but all of the cloth covering the body was of a very dark colour. Naturally it ought to be a much brighter colour. Rather suspecting injury from the evident dampness, I gently touched one of the front teeth (3,000 years old) and*

*alas! it fell into dust, thereby showing that the mummy could
not be preserved. We then cleared the entire mummy . . .*

The absence of photographs means that we are reliant on eyewitness accounts and, as so often happens with such accounts,
these show considerable variability. Davis, for example, reports
that the hands were clasped while Ayrton tells us that the left
arm was bent with the hand resting on the breast and the
right arm was extended along the thigh. Weigall saw mummy
bands, but no one else did:[29]

*. . . when we removed the lid of the coffin we found a band
or ribbon of thin gold which had evidently passed round the
body. When we had gathered up the bones and fragments
and dust we found another similar band which had evidently passed down the back of the mummy. These bands,
as I remember them, were about two inches wide and were
inscribed with the titles of Akhenaten, but the cartouche was
in each case cut out, so that there was simply an oval hole in
the band, wherever it occurred.*

He tells us that the bands were sent to Cairo, where he saw
them in the museum workshop, but they were omitted from
the official catalogue, and '. . . I am now not sure whether
they are still somewhere in the Cairo Museum, or whether
they have disappeared.'

Davis enlisted the services of two doctors: the local Dr
Pollock and an unnamed American obstetrician who was win-
tering in Luxor. He tells us that both pronounced the remains
female on the basis of the wide pelvis, but Weigall disagrees: 'I
saw Dr Pollock in Luxor the other day, who denies that he ever
thought that it was a woman, and says he and the other doctor
could not be sure.'[30] When the bones arrived in Cairo, Smith

immediately saw that 'Queen Tiy' was male, and all anatomists who have since examined the bones have agreed with him.

What else can we say about this mummy? Derry and Harrison agreed that he stood approximately 170 cm tall, the same height as Tutankhamun. He also shared Tutankhamun's distinctive 'broad and flat-topped (platycephalic)' skull shape. Harrison's team later confirmed that KV55 and Tutankhamun shared the same relatively rare blood group (A2/MN) and both showed signs of a non-debilitating hereditary condition – epitrochlear foramen – that caused a hole through the humerus.[31] Combined, these points of similarity are enough to suggest that Tutankhamun and KV55 are closely related. They are either brothers or father and son. As Tutankhamun was himself less than twenty years old when he died he could not have outlived a near-adult son, and if he left a living son we would know about it. We can therefore rule out this option.

We are left with two strong possibilities. If the bones are those of a younger man, they are likely to be Tutankhamun's brother or half-brother (or, less likely, father) Smenkhkare. If the bones are those of an older man, they are likely to be Tutankhamun's father (or, less likely, grandfather), Akhenaten. As we know that Akhenaten ruled for at least seventeen years, and we can see his first-born daughter in Theban temple scenes dating from the start of his reign, we can safely assume that he was at a minimum thirty years old when he died, and probably several years older. The age of KV55 is crucial to our investigation.

Smith initially estimated an age at death of twenty-five years:[32]

The question has been put to me by archaeologists: 'Is it possible that these bones can be those of a man of twenty-

*eight or thirty years of age?' . . . No anatomist would be
justified in denying that this individual may have been
twenty-eight, but it is highly improbable that he could have
attained thirty years if he had been normal.*

Then, persuaded by the evidence from the coffin, including
the mysterious mummy bands, that the bones must be Akhenaten, he revised his diagnosis:[33]

*I do not suppose that any unprejudiced scholar who studies
the archaeological evidence alone would harbour any doubt
of the identity of this mummy, if it were not for the fact
that it is difficult from the anatomical evidence to assign an
age to this skeleton sufficiently great to satisfy the demands
of most historians, who want at least 30 years into which
to crowd the events of Khouniatonou's [Akhenaten's] event-
ful reign . . . If, with such clear archaeological evidence to
indicate that these are the remains of Khouniatonou, the historian can produce irrefutable facts showing that the heretic
king must have been 27, or even 30, years of age, I would
be prepared to admit that the weight of the anatomical
evidence in opposition to the admission of that fact is too
slight to be considered absolutely prohibitive.*

Derry examined the bones and teeth in 1931 and disagreed,
believing that they indicated a male in his early twenties.[34]
Harrison's team agreed with Derry: mummy KV55 had died
at less than twenty-five years of age and, indeed, 'if certain
variable anatomical criteria . . . are to be utilized, it is possible to be more definite that the age at death occurred in the
20th year'.[35] Several anatomists have since agreed with this
diagnosis. Harris and his team, however, having examined
the head and teeth, suggested an age at death of thirty to

thirty-five.[36] The more recent Egyptian examination produced a split opinion, with one expert arguing that the bones are those of a younger man, and another arguing that they belong to a man at least forty-five to fifty and possibly as old as sixty.[37] The fact that the team was unable to reach agreement on this matter is troubling, and an age at death of sixty causes big problems. If Akhenaten was sixty when he died in regnal Year 17 he would been older than his own mother (identified by the same team as KV35EL), who died, apparently in her forties, after the court moved to Amarna. The age stated in the official report is thirty-five to forty-five years but no evidence has been published to support this statement.[38] On this basis, the bones have been officially identified as Akhenaten, and it is as Akhenaten that they are now displayed to the public. There are many, however, including the present author, who would disagree and, accepting the younger age, regard the bones as the remains of Tutankhamun's brother Smenkhkare.

There is just one further point for us to consider. Could Smenkhkare have been Tutankhamun's father rather than his brother? The archaeological evidence suggests that this is possible as we have no idea when either Smenkhkare or his wife Meritaten were born. The age of the KV55 bones is again crucial here. If this is Smenkhkare, and if he did die in his twentieth year, it seems unlikely that he would have been succeeded by an eight-year-old son.

Davis's report, *The Tomb of Queen Tiyi*, was published in 1910. It was widely regarded as inadequate:[39]

> *The history of excavation Egypt presents, side by side with much splendid work, an almost continuous series of disasters. The greatest disaster of all is when the results have remained completely unpublished. But it is also a disaster when the*

*publication is incomplete or inaccurate. This is unfortu-
nately what has happened with Theodore M. Davis's volume
entitled* The Tomb of Queen Tiyi, *London, 1910.*

Davis went on to make more important finds, including
KV57, the tomb of Horemheb. But he was a disappointed
man; he had always hoped that he would find Tutankhamun.
In fact, he had come very close. As the photographer Harry
Burton observed:[40]

*If Mr Theodore Davis, of Boston, for whom I was exca-
vating in 1914, had not stopped his last 'dig' too soon I am
convinced he would have discovered the present tomb of
King Tutankhamen. We came within six feet of it. Just then
Mr Davis feared that further digging would undermine the
adjacent roadway and ordered me to cease work.*

Davis had destroyed much of the evidence preserved in
KV55 and had not realised the significance of the fact that his
two unrobbed tombs – KV46 and KV55 – lay close together
in the Valley floor. He had also failed to recognise three vital
clues that strongly suggested that Tutankhamun lay not too far
away. We have already discussed one of these: the embalming
cache found in KV54. To this must be added the 1905–6 discovery 'under a rock' of a faience cup bearing Tutankhamun's
name, which had, presumably, been dropped by tomb robbers,
and his discovery in 1909 of a small, undecorated chamber
(KV58), which yielded an uninscribed *shabti* and the gold
foil from a chariot harness inscribed with the cartouches of
Tutankhamun, Ankesenpaaten and Ay. Davis published KV58
as Tutankhamun's rather disappointing tomb.[41] How could
Tutankhamun have ended up in such a mean pit? Had he, too,
been 'restored' in antiquity?[42]

Such are the few facts that we know about Touatânkha-manou's life and reign. If he had children by his queen Ank-hounamanou or by another wife, they have left no trace of their existence on the monuments; when he died, Aiya [Ay] replaced him on the throne, and buried him. I suppose that his tomb was in the Western Valley, somewhere between or near Amenothes III [Amenhotep III] and Aiya [Ay]: when the reaction against Atonou [the Aten] and his followers was complete, his mummy and its furniture was taken to a hiding place . . . and there Davis found what remained of it after so many transfers and plunders. But this also is mere hypothesis, the truth of which we have no means of proving or disproving as yet.

In 1914, Davis retired from Egyptology believing that the Valley had yielded all its secrets. Not everyone agreed with him.

7

The Archaeologist's Tale

Discovering Tutankhamun

The British archaeologist Howard Carter remains convinced that the Valley of the Kings has not yielded all its secrets:[1]

Sir Gaston Maspero, Director of the Antiquities department, who signed our concession, agrees with Mr Davis that the site was exhausted, and told us frankly that he did not consider that it would repay further investigation. We remembered, however, that nearly a hundred years earlier Belzoni had made a similar claim, and refused to be convinced. We had made a thorough investigation of the site, and were quite sure that there were areas, covered by the dumps of previous excavators, which had never been properly examined

Today Carter is widely credited with the discovery of Tutankhamun's tomb. In 1922, events were seen very differently. Tutankhamun belonged to Carter's patron, the Earl of Carnarvon, as the headlines – 'Great Find at Thebes. Lord Carnarvon's Long Quest' – made quite clear.[2] If anyone thought about Carter it was as a favoured employee or, as *The Times* worded it, the 'trusty helper'. Carter was the means by which Carnarvon achieved his archaeological dreams; he was the Ayrton to Carnarvon's Davis. So, when in December 1922 the head of the Antiquities Service, Pierre Lacau, wrote to congratulate the team on their magnificent discovery, it was naturally to Lord Carnarvon that he wrote. An edited version of his letter was reproduced in *The Times* on 14 December:

> *All my colleagues are greatly impressed, not only by the extraordinary results obtained, but also by the method by which your work has been carried out. They wish unanimously to associate themselves with their President [Lacau himself] in the expression to you of all their congratulations and thanks. You have attached your name to one of the greatest discoveries made not only in Egypt, but in all the domains of archaeology.*
>
> *As regards your collaborator, Mr Howard Carter, who has conducted the work during so many years, it is for him the finest crowning of a career and the most astonishing reward that any archaeologist could have. Such a reward is truly merited, for he has afforded a fine example of method and patience, the rarest virtue in an excavator. May he often be emulated.*

George Edward Stanhope Molyneux Herbert, 5th Earl of Carnarvon, was – as his title makes obvious – a British aristocrat. His ancestral seat, the 300-room Highclere Castle, is known to many today as the setting for the ITV historical drama *Downton Abbey*. Visitors in search of the authentic Downton experience may still enjoy a visit to the castle's *Egyptian Exhibition*, 'celebrating the 5th Earl of Carnarvon's discovery of the tomb of Tutankhamun'. Even by the standards of the Edwardian aristocracy, Carnarvon was extremely wealthy. His money came not only from his various inheritances, but also from his prudent marriage to the nineteen-year-old Almina Wombwell. Ostensibly the natural daughter of the banker Alfred de Rothschild, she received a marriage settlement from him that included a £500,000 dowry (approximately

£70,000,000 purchasing power in 2021), plus an annual income of £12,000 and the repayment of Carnarvon's out-standing gaming and personal debts.[3] Following her husband's death, Almina financed the team until Tutankhamun's tomb was empty; a generous act for a woman with no interest in ancient Egypt.

Carnarvon had ample funds to finance his hobbies: collecting art and rare books, sailing, racehorses and fast cars. In 1901, his love of speed having nearly killed him, he turned to Egyptology. Carnarvon's sister Winifred Burghclere tells us that her brother '. . . was a splendid driver, well served by his gift – a gift which also served him in shooting and golf – of judging distances accurately, whilst processing that unruffled calm in difficulties which often, if not invariably, is the best insurance against disaster'.[4] Nevertheless, driving at speed along a straight and apparently empty road in Germany, this splendid driver failed to anticipate two bullock carts hidden in a dip in the road. Unable to stop, he wrenched the car sideways and crashed into a heap of stones. As its tyres burst the car overturned and landed on Carnarvon, squashing him into the mud. He was left with substantial injuries – his sister lists concussion, burns, a broken wrist, temporary blindness and injuries to the jaw and mouth – which made him prone to headaches and chest infections. His doctors, worried about the British damp, recommended that he winter in Egypt.

Like Theodore Davis before him, Carnarvon quickly developed a fascination with ancient Egypt and the hunt for lost treasure. He did not want to buy antiquities; he wanted the thrill of finding them himself. But, while he had the funds to finance a dig, he too lacked the skills necessary to conduct a proper, scientific excavation. If he wished to excavate the most promising archaeological sites – the Valley of the Kings being the most promising of all – Carnarvon needed to find a professional archaeologist to lead his team. In 1909, Gaston Maspero introduced him to Howard Carter, with the suggestion that the two might work profitably together.

Carnarvon could not have found a better field director. Carter was a talented artist with an impressive archaeological CV. He had trained with Percy Newberry in the rock-cut tombs of Beni Hasan and el-Bersha, with Flinders Petrie at Amarna, and with Édouard Naville at Deir el-Bahri. He had then spent five years as Chief Inspector of Antiquities for Southern Egypt and a year as Chief Inspector of Antiquities for Northern Egypt. The Antiquities Service was familiar with his work, and Arthur Weigall, the current Antiquities Inspector for Southern Egypt, recognised his expertise and integrity. As a team, Carnarvon and Carter could be trusted to investigate Egypt's more promising sites, and they embarked on a series of archaeologically interesting if unspectacular excavations. However, the one site that they both desperately wanted to excavate remained frustratingly out of reach. It was not until 1914 that Theodore Davis relinquished his concession to excavate in the Valley of the Kings. In 1915, it was agreed that 'the work of excavation shall be carried out at the expense, risk and peril of the Earl of Carnarvon by Mr Howard Carter; the latter should be constantly present during excavation'.[5] However, with the world at war a full fieldwork season was impossible, and it was not until late 1917 that Carnarvon and Carter finally started their search for Tutankhamun.

Carter, mindful of the location of Davis's recent discoveries of KV46 and KV55, decided to focus his attention on the Valley floor. He had determined on a bold strategy that he himself recognised as a 'rather desperate undertaking'; the floor would be systematically stripped down to the bedrock in the area between the tombs of Ramesses II, Merenptah and Ramesses VI.[6] The Valley floor would be mapped, and approximately 200,000 tons of rubble and old excavation debris would be moved, allowing the archaeologists to confirm that nothing had been cut into the Valley floor.[7] A light-railway system would be employed to move the rubble: this would later prove useful in transporting Tutankhamun's grave goods across the desert to the river.

During his first season Carter cleared some of the rubble and ancient huts beneath the entrance to the tomb of Ramesses VI (KV9). Again, echoing Davis, he came very close to finding Tutankhamun but stopped just short of the hidden entrance when his work started to disrupt the flow of tourists visiting Ramesses's tomb. Oblivious to the near miss, he continued work elsewhere. This was not the exciting archaeological adventure that Carnarvon had anticipated. It was dull, dirty, repetitive and unrewarding labour. Maybe Davis had been right: Tutankhamun had indeed been buried in the Chariot Tomb, and the team should find another site to excavate? There were rumours that Carnarvon was becoming tired of the financial drain, although, given the extent of his wealth, this seems unlikely. Local labour was cheap and a few weeks' work would have cost no more than a few hundred pounds. It seems more likely that he was becoming bored with Egyptology, and was ready to move on. Whatever the reason, Carnarvon and Carter agreed that the 1922–3 excavation season would be their last attempt to find the lost king:[8]

> *Six full seasons we had excavated there, and season after season had drawn a blank; we had worked for months at a stretch and found nothing, and only an excavator knows how desperately depressing that can be; we had almost made*

up our minds that we were beaten, and were preparing to leave The Valley and try our luck elsewhere; and then – hardly had we set hoe to ground in our last despairing effort than we made a discovery that far exceeded our wildest dreams. Surely, never before in the whole history of excavation has a full digging season been compressed within the space of five days.

On 1 November 1922, the team returned to the area beneath the tomb of Ramesses IV. Here, having removed the remains of the 20th Dynasty workmen's huts, they cut through 91 cm of what Carter described as 'soil' or 'heavy rubbish', but what contemporary photographs show to have been flood debris.[9] Three days later, while Carter was at his house and Carnarvon was in England, the workmen uncovered what proved to be the first of a flight of sixteen stone steps. These led down to a blocked doorway covered in gypsum plaster and stamped with oval seals including the seal of the necropolis; a jackal (the god of mummification Anubis) crouching above nine bound captives. Summoned by the workmen, Carter rushed to the site. He made a small hole and, employing his newfangled electric torch, was able to peer into a passage packed with stone chips. His pocket diary entry for 5 November 1922 is a laconic 'Discovered tomb under tomb of Ramesses VI. Investigated same & found seals intact.' His same-day entry in the official excavation journal tells a far more thrilling tale:

Towards sunset we had cleared to the level of the 12th step, which was sufficient to expose a large part of the upper portion of a plastered and sealed doorway. Here before us was sufficient evidence to show that it really was an entrance to a tomb, and by the seals, to all outward appearances that it was intact . . . The seal-impressions suggested that it belonged to somebody of high standing but at that time I had not found any indications as to whom . . . Though I was satisfied that I was on the verge of perhaps a magnificent find, probably one of the missing tombs that I had been seeking for many years, I was much puzzled by the smallness of the opening in comparison with those of other royal tombs in the valley. Its design was certainly of the XVIIIth Dyn. Could it be the tomb of a noble, buried there by royal consent? Or was it a royal cache? As far as my investigations had gone there was absolutely nothing to tell me. Had I known that by digging a few inches deeper I would have exposed seal impressions showing Tût.ankh.Amen's insignia distinctly I ~~should~~ *would have fervently worked on and set my mind at rest, but as it was, it was getting late, the night had fast set in, the full moon had risen high in the eastern heavens, I refilled the excavation for protection, and with my men selected for the occasion – they like myself delighted beyond all expectation – I returned home and cabled to Ld. C. (then in England) the following message:-*

'At last have made wonderful discovery in Valley a magnificent tomb with seals intact recovered same for your arrival congratulations'

Refilling the excavation meant burying the steps under many tons of sand, rock and rubble, with large boulders rolled on top. This was an essential protection against thieves and the flash floods that had the potential to rush into the tomb and destroy everything; it would be done every time the excavation was closed down, and reversed every time it reopened.

Only when Carnarvon arrived in Luxor on 23 November 1922 was the work of emptying the stairwell and clearing the doorway completed. The stairway fill yielded an eclectic mix of artefacts, including broken pottery, a scarab of Tuthmosis III and fragments of boxes inscribed with the names of Amenhotep III, Akhenaten, Neferneferuaten and Meritaten, and Tutankhamun, and Carter was starting to believe that he had discovered a second late-18th Dynasty cache, a twin to KV55, when Tutankhamun's name was revealed, stamped into the plaster on the fully exposed doorway. He now knew that the door had been sealed by Tutankhamun's officials but, ominously, there were signs that the tomb had been opened and resealed before it had been lost beneath the floodwater.

Behind the blocked door a short descending passageway was packed to its ceiling with light-coloured limestone chips incorporating fragments of pottery, jar seals, broken and intact stone vessels and water skins abandoned by the ancient workmen. A tunnel cut through the upper-left corner of the fill had itself been filled with darker flint and chert gravel. By 26 November, this passageway had been emptied and Carter and Carnarvon once more stood before a blocked, plastered and sealed doorway. Again, there was unmistakable evidence of tampering and resealing.

It is only right that Carter should tell us what happened next. His words have often been quoted, but have never lost their magic:[10]

> With trembling hands I made a tiny breach in the upper left hand corner. Darkness and blank space, as far as an iron testing-rod could reach, showed that whatever lay beyond was empty, and not filled like the passage we had just cleared. Candle tests were applied as a precaution against possible foul gasses, and then, widening the hole a little, I inserted the candle and peered in. At first I could see nothing, the hot air escaping from the chamber causing

the candle flame to flicker, but presently, as my eyes grew accustomed to the light, details of the room within emerged slowly from the mist, strange animals, statues and gold – everywhere the glint of gold. For the moment – an eternity it must have seemed to the others standing by – I was struck dumb with amazement, and when Lord Carnarvon, unable to stand the suspense any longer, inquired anxiously, 'Can you see anything?' it was all I could do to get out the words 'Yes, wonderful things.' Then, widening the hole a little further, so that we both could see, we inserted an electric torch.

Although it had obviously been robbed on at least two occasions, it was clear, even from the doorway, that the tomb was substantially intact. Carter and Carnarvon had been proved right: the Valley of the Kings still had a secret to yield. It is perhaps nit-picking to question why the published account of this momentous occasion does not quite match either the account given in the excavation journal – 'Yes, it is wonderful' – or Carnarvon's remembered 'There are some marvellous objects here.'[11] This slight variation in the evidence is not in itself sinister or important. It does, however, serve as a useful reminder that our understanding of the discovery and emptying of Tutankhamun's tomb is dependent on information collated from several diverse sources. Archaeology by its very nature destroys the thing that it seeks, making accurate record keeping and prompt publication matters of vital importance. Alongside the object cards, photographs and excavation journals which form the official record of the tomb clearance, there are memoirs, letters and newspaper reports of varying accuracy, plus the three volumes published by Carter, which, as they are written for a general audience, lack the scientific rigour that we would hope to find in a full archaeological publication. Each of these sources tells the story from a slightly different angle, and it is only by combining them all that we are able to get something approaching a full understanding of the process. The 'Yes, wonderful things' reported in the first of these volumes is undoubtedly a more powerful, audience-friendly statement than the prosaic 'Yes, it is wonderful', but it leaves us wondering how often this slight tweaking of the facts to please the audience has occurred.

The newly fitted electric light confirmed Carter's first impression: the Antechamber had been so crammed with grave goods that it was difficult to enter without trampling a precious object. There were dismantled chariots, animal-headed beds and numerous, mysterious chests, bundles and boxes, each of which needed its own mini-excavation. The southern wall was living rock (we can assume that the cautious Carter checked this carefully), but an open hole in the west wall allowed sight of a smaller room, the Annexe, which was packed with a jumble of 'treasure', plus the stones that had fallen when the thieves breached the blocked doorway. As the floor of the Annexe was almost a metre below the floor of the Antechamber, the first objects would have to be removed by team members dangling head-first from the doorway. Back in the Antechamber the northern wall included the blocked, plastered and seal-stamped entrance to a room or rooms guarded by the two life-sized statues. Once again there was a very obvious robbers' hole that had been restored and resealed by the necropolis officials.

Did Tutankhamun still lie within his tomb, somewhere behind this northern wall? There was only one way to find out. Soon after the opening of the Antechamber, Carter, Carnarvon and Carnarvon's daughter, Lady Evelyn Herbert, reopened the robbers' hole and crawled into the Burial Chamber beyond. Curiosity satisfied, they then retreated, plastering over the hole and attempting to conceal it behind a basket lid, which, with the benefit of hindsight, appears very obvious in the official photographs. As we would expect, there is no official record of this adventure but it became a widely known 'secret' shared by, amongst others, the Egyptian workmen and the chemist Alfred Lucas, who, as an experienced archaeological conservator, immediately spotted the modern plaster lurking behind the basket lid. He thought this a matter of little significance: 'The question of the hole and its condition when found, whether open or closed, is a matter of no archaeological importance, and, by itself, is hardly worth mentioning . . .'[12] It was, however, a breach of Antiquities Service rules and it distorted the archaeology within the tomb. Carter, as an ex-Antiquities Service Inspector, would have understood this.

The Times told the story of the discovery on 30 November 1922, tempting readers with promises of hidden treasures to come:

> *There seems no doubt that this wonderful collection of objects formed part of the funeral paraphernalia of King Tutankhamun, whose cartouche is seen everywhere, in both its forms . . . What adds interest to this discovery is that there is still yet a third sealed chamber, which, significantly, the two figures of the king discovered are guarding, and which may possibly turn out to be the actual tomb of King Tutankhamun, with members of the heretic's family buried with him.*

No official exploring could be done, however, before the Antechamber had been cleared, and this was likely to be a long process. Every artefact would have to be numbered, photographed, recorded on the tomb plan, described and drawn. It would then have to be taken to the conservation lab – KV15, the repurposed tomb of Seti II – for treatment and further photography. Finally, it would be packed for the long and complicated journey to Cairo. Realising that he could not achieve this single-handed, Carter assembled a team of experts whose key members were a retired engineer, his friend Arthur Callender, the chemist Alfred Lucas, plus, on loan from the Metropolitan Museum of Art in New York, the archaeologist and conservator Arthur Mace and archaeological photographer Harry Burton. The addition of a pair of thick curtains converted KV55 into a darkroom, where Burton processed over 3,000 images of the tomb and its contents, some shot within the tomb and some more specific artefact portraits taken in the conservation lab. While the original team gradually dispersed – by all accounts the single-minded Carter was not an easy man to live and work with – Burton and Lucas stayed to the end, with Burton taking his last photograph inside the tomb in January 1933.

KV4, the tomb of Ramesses XI, became the 'luncheon tomb'; a place not only to eat and shelter from the noon sun, but also to store equipment and some finds. A photograph, not this time taken by Burton, shows a veritable galaxy of Egyptologists seated around the dining table; dressed formally in shirts, ties and jackets, they sport a formidable range of moustaches. Moving clockwise from the left, we see the eminent American linguist J. H. Breastead, Burton, Lucas, Callender, Mace, Carter and the equally eminent British linguist Alan Gardiner. The empty chair at the head of the table presumably belongs to Carnarvon, who, a keen photographer,

is busy taking the photograph. In the background two unidentified Egyptian servants stand ready to wait on the diners.

A low wall was built around the tomb entrance, providing
a cut-off point beyond which the uninvited could not pass.
With security a great concern, Callender's first job was to fit
a wooden gate at the tomb entrance. A few weeks later, this
was replaced by a steel security gate designed by Carter. A
tent and a wooden hut provided shelter and some privacy for
the soldiers and Antiquities Service guards who kept the site
secure.

Finally, the task of clearing the Antechamber could begin.
This was both difficult and time-consuming. There was no
space to manoeuvre; even to enter the room was difficult;
moving one artefact might seriously disturb the others. The
team worked their way around the room in an anticlockwise
direction, starting to the right of the doorway and ending
with the dismantled chariots that lay to its left. On the afternoon of Friday, 16 February 1923, the doorway to the Burial
Chamber was dismantled in the presence of an audience of
friends, archaeologists and government officials, listed in the
excavation journal as:

Abd El Halim Pasha Suleman, Under Sec. of State P.W.D;

Lacau. Dir. Gen. S. des. A.;

Engelbach. Chief Insp. Up. Eg. S. des A.;

Ibrahîm Effendi. Insp. Luxor S. des A. and Tewfik Effendi
Boulos;

Sir William Garstin;

Lythgoe and Winlock; Mace, Callender, Lucas, and Burton;

Ld. C. and Lady E.

and others.

The event started, naturally, with luncheon. The party then reassembled in the tomb, where they settled on chairs facing the wall to the Burial Chamber and waited for the performance to start. There were speeches – Carnarvon reportedly spoke well, Carter less so – then, standing on a wooden platform, Carter stripped to his trousers and vest and picked up a crowbar. It was hard, hot and dusty work. The wall had been built from substantial stone blocks that had to be passed from Carter to Mace to Callender, then along a chain of workmen, to be stacked outside the tomb. After about fifteen minutes there was a hole large enough to insert a torch; this revealed a wall of solid gold. Soon after, Carter was able to push a mattress through the hole, to protect the wall from falling masonry. After two hours the party was able to squeeze through the hole and drop down into the Burial Chamber, which was cut lower than the Antechamber.

The 'golden wall' was, as Carter and Carnarvon already knew, the side panel of the outermost of Tutankhamun's four concentric golden shrines. On the east side of the shrine there were double doors, closed and bolted but not sealed. Carter drew back the ebony bolts and swung open the doors to reveal the second golden shrine, shrouded by a delicate linen pall spangled with rosettes. Again, the shrine doors were bolted, but this time the seals – the necropolis seal and Tutankhamun's own seal – were intact. For the first time, the world could be certain that the ancient robbers had not reached the king's body. The quest for Tutankhamun had ended.

Years of hard physical work were to follow. The sarcophagus lid was raised, in front of an invited audience, on 12 February 1924. Mace, who helped Carter to roll back the delicate linen shroud covering the outermost coffin, recalled an audible gasp from the audience as the head of the anthropoid coffin was revealed.[13] The lid of the outermost coffin was raised on 13 October 1925, the middle coffin was opened on 23 October 1925, and the innermost coffin was opened on 28 October 1925 in a moment that Carter found quite moving:[14]

> *The pins removed the lid was raised. The penultimate scene was disclosed – a very neatly wrapped mummy of the young king, with golden mask of sad but tranquil expression, symbolizing Osiris. The similitude of the youthful Tut.Ankh. Amen, until now known only by name, amid that sepulchral silence, made us realize the past.*

On 31 December 1925, the innermost coffin and the funerary mask were sent to Cairo by train, escorted by Carter, Lucas and an armed guard. Attention then turned to clearing the Treasury and the Annexe. The final artefact was removed from the tomb in November 1930, when only the coffined king was left, still lying in his sarcophagus but now stripped of his grave goods. Conservation work continued in the tomb of Seti II and it was not until February 1932, almost ten years after the discovery of the tomb, that the final batch of grave goods was sent to Cairo.

Howard Carter died of Hodgkin's lymphoma in London on 2 March 1939. His own funeral was a simple, ill-attended affair; his grave in Putney Vale Cemetery was topped by a simple headstone commemorating 'Howard Carter, Archaeologist and Egyptologist, 1874–1939'. Today, thanks to a campaign led by the archaeologist Paul Bahn, his grave bears a more splendid headstone dedicated to 'Howard Carter, Egyptologist, Discoverer of the tomb of Tutankhamen 1922. Born 9 May 1874, Died, 2 March 1939'. The headstone bears a shortened form of the prayer from Tutankhamun's 'wishing cup':

May your spirit live, may you spend millions of years, you who love Thebes, sitting with your face to the north wind, your eyes beholding happiness.

Over the years since its discovery, Tutankhamun's tomb has effortlessly maintained its position as one of Egypt's most popular tourist destinations. This popularity has brought much-needed income to Luxor, but has caused serious conservation problems for the plastered and painted walls of the Burial Chamber. While it was buried beneath the Valley floor, the tomb maintained a static environment. The exposure of the tomb, followed by the influx of vast numbers of tourists, caused temperature fluctuations, introduced carbon dioxide, dust and lint, and raised relative humidity levels as high as 95 per cent. Further problems were caused by visitors – and on more than one occasion television crews – brushing against and deliberately touching the plastered walls; this mechanical problem was solved by the simple but effective measure of requiring visitors to stand behind a wooden barrier that allows them to look down on the Burial Chamber from the Antechamber. In 2009, working in conjunction with the American Getty Conservation Institute, Egypt's Supreme Council of Antiquities embarked on a five-year conservation and management project designed to restore the Burial Chamber walls to the state they were in – curious brown mould spots included – when Carter first entered the space.[15]

In 2014, an exact replica of Tutankhamun's Burial Chamber was opened close by Howard Carter's restored Luxor house. It is hoped that this alternative, high-quality visitor experience will considerably reduce the numbers visiting the genuine tomb, which can still be accessed for a far higher ticket price. Visitor reactions have so far been mainly positive.

As a preliminary to creating the replica tomb, Madrid-based art-replication specialists Factum Arte took a detailed series of high-resolution photographs and scans of the walls of the original Burial Chamber. These were published online in 2011, 'to help conservators and visitors monitor and understand the decay of the tomb'.[16]

Examining these images and observing what appeared to be irregularities in the walls, Nicholas Reeves has identified what he believes to be two sealed doors hidden beneath the plaster: one leading to a storage room, and one to an earlier burial, which he has identified as the burial of Nefertiti, whom he believes to have been the co-regent with and eventual successor to Akhenaten.[17] His theory would see King Nefertiti being buried by her successor, Tutankhamun, then, when Tutankhamun died before his own tomb was complete, her tomb being reopened and reconfigured to admit Tutankhamun's burial. The ancient robbers who attacked Tutankhamun's burial were either unaware of Nefertiti's presence, or did not have enough time to access her part of the tomb.

While the media have responded to it with great enthusiasm and occasional documentaries, few Egyptologists have accepted Reeves's theory in full. It would not be surprising to find 'shadow' doors – doors that had been started but never completed – hidden beneath the plaster of Tutankhamun's Burial Chamber. A similar unfinished door is very obvious as the 'niche' in the wall of the nearby KV55. But to deduce that Nefertiti lies surrounded by grave goods behind one of these doors seems a step too far. Although it would explain why Tutankhamun was buried in such a small tomb, the shared-tomb theory prompts us to ask why, if he did have to share a tomb, he was not added to the far more spacious tomb of his grandfather, Amenhotep III (WV22)? Or why was the nearby workshop tomb KV55 not emptied and repurposed for his burial? More importantly, Reeves's theory invites us to accept that Nefertiti ruled Egypt as an independent female king and, as we have already seen, there is no evidence to show that this is the case.

This would be an easy enough problem to solve if the plaster could be stripped from the Burial Chamber walls but that, of course, will never happen. Instead, we are left waiting for new, even more detailed scans which might make the situation clear. It seems appropriate to leave the last word on this matter to Dr Reeves:[18]

> *If I'm wrong, I'm wrong. But if I'm right, the prospects are frankly staggering. The world will have become a much more interesting place – at least for Egyptologists.*

8

The Journalist's Tale

Tutankhamun's Curse

The journalist and political activist Fikri Abaza reflects on Tutankhamun:[1]

My young king, are they going to transport you to the museum and set you next to the Qasr al-Nil barracks to add insult to injury? So that, my free king, you might look over your occupied country? So that you may see your enslaved people? So that you might learn that those who robbed your grave now dig another for your nation?

Once KV62 had been recognised as the substantially intact tomb of an Egyptian king, crowds of Egyptologists, journalists and tourists – both Egyptian and foreign – descended on Luxor. Such was the demand for accommodation, the hotels were forced to erect tents in their gardens to accommodate the overspill. When, in 1924, the Berlin Museum put a previously unseen portrait head of Queen Nefertiti on display, interest in the Amarna Period soared and the crowds around Tutankhamun's tomb increased. Western 'Egyptomania' was not a new phenomenon: the Romans had been so fascinated by ancient Egypt that they imported genuine obelisks to decorate their city, and the publication of the *Description* had inspired artists, architects and designers to create their own versions of Nile-style. But this was the first time that ancient Egypt had entered the lives of ordinary people via mass-circulation newspaper reports, photographs, wireless reports and even the occasional film reel shown in the cinema. Effectively, the tomb was being emptied before a fascinated Western audience: an audience who, after the grim years of the Great War, were eager to be distracted by exotic mysteries, strange religion and wonderful things.[2]

The Egyptomania experienced in Egypt itself was different and more intense: inspired by an increased longing for the glorious days when Egypt was free and greatly admired, Egyptology moved from an academic discipline to a subject of relevance to Egyptian artists and writers who were starting to regard ancient Egypt as the root of the modern Egyptian identity. The re-emergence of Tutankhamun was a parallel to the re-emergence of an independent Egypt.[3]

The Ottoman Antiquities Law of 1884 had specified that an excavator was entitled to a substantial proportion of any artefacts uncovered during a dig. At the end of every excavation season (a season would usually run from autumn to spring so that the heavy physical work occurred during the cooler months) the 'finds' would be divided and a share sent to Cairo, where they would either be displayed in the museum or, as often happened, be relegated to the basement. The remaining finds would be given to the excavator, to do with as he wished. Most used their share of the finds to reward the sponsors who had funded their fieldwork, so that, effectively, the fieldwork financed itself. This law has been gradually updated over the years, so that today everything found on an excavation remains the property of the Egyptian state and nothing – not even a soil sample or a broken sherd of pottery – may be exported or sold. But, in 1922, Lord Carnarvon expected to profit handsomely from the discovery of Tutankhamun's tomb.

However, with Howard Carter insistent that the tomb must be emptied slowly and methodically, and with the Antiquities Service in full agreement, it was likely to be many years before Carnarvon could claim his full share of the grave goods, and, in the meantime, he was committed to paying the wages of all those involved in the clearance of the tomb and the conservation of its artefacts. It therefore must have seemed a prudent move when, in January 1923, he sold the exclusive rights to the tomb and its contents to *The Times* newspaper and the *Illustrated London News*. The £5,000 fee plus an additional 75 per cent of any profits above that sum that *The Times* might make by selling on information and images would easily cover the costs of the fieldwork. Now *The Times* reporter Arthur Merton would be the only journalist allowed inside the tomb and, in an agreement reached without consulting the Metropolitan Museum of Art, the employer that had generously 'lent' Harry Burton to the excavation team, the newspaper would be allowed to publish Burton's atmospheric photographs.

The 1921 British Mount Everest Expedition had struck a similar deal with *The Times*, and all had gone well. But Luxor was not remote Everest, and events in the Valley of the Kings could not be kept hidden. The deal was deeply unpopular with the Western press, who felt that Tutankhamun's story belonged to everyone. It was even more unpopular with the Egyptian journalists, who, unsurprisingly, believed that Tutankhamun's story belonged to Egypt.

Tutankhamun had emerged from his tomb at a time of growing nationalism, with Sa'ad Zaghloul and his Wafd party challenging the years of British dominance that had followed centuries of Ottoman rule. In February 1922, Egypt had become a semi-independent kingdom ruled by Fuad, the younger son of the Khedive Ismail, with Britain retaining control of defence, communications and Sudan. In 1924, following Egypt's first elections, Zaghloul would become prime minister and archaeology would become the responsibility of an Egyptian government who saw Tutankhamun as a symbol of their country's new autonomy. The Antiquities Service was still run by a Frenchman, Pierre Lacau, but the politically astute Lacau was no longer prepared to be seen indulging foreign excavators in what many were beginning to regard as the exploitation of Egypt's heritage. Why should Egypt's journalists have to discover what was happening in the Valley of the Kings by reading *The Times*?[4]

Carnarvon – already wealthy beyond most people's wildest imaginings – was seen as both greedy and unscrupulous, a man prepared to gain at Egypt's expense. Carter's views of the deal are unrecorded, but as he continued the agreement following Carnarvon's death, we can assume that he was reasonably happy with it. His attempt to mend matters by offering Egyptian journalists the same press release as *The Times* but twelve hours later was not well received, and the journalists demanded that the government stop what appeared to be an unjustifiable Western monopoly. Meanwhile, Egypt's few professional Egyptologists found themselves excluded from the most important archaeological event of their lifetime. This was far from acceptable, and it met an angry response from the Egyptian public. At the start of the 1923–4 excavation season the journalists made an official complaint about *The Times* deal to the Ministry of Public Works, who now planned to issue their own press bulletins about events in the tomb.

From this point onwards, while *The Times* provided supportive and accurate accounts of events within the tomb, other newspapers, denied any form of official story, printed a mixture of truth (gained from *The Times*), speculation by self-appointed 'experts' and occasional misinformation deliberately supplied by the excavation team. The general flavour of their reports was unsupportive. It was into this atmosphere of anger and mistrust that the story of 'Tutankhamun's curse' was born. The curse is an entirely modern phenomenon that has no part to play in the story of Tutankhamun's life and death. However, for many non-specialists it has become the defining Tutankhamun tale, and so it deserves to be – albeit briefly – told.

Included amongst the angry journalists was Arthur Weigall, whom we last met in his former role as Antiquities Inspector for southern Egypt.[5] Weigall had left Egypt in 1914, retiring to England to become a successful stage-set designer, journalist and author. With the discovery of Tutankhamun's tomb he returned to Luxor as special correspondent for the *Daily Mail*, expecting to be welcomed by his former colleagues and invited into the tomb. When it became clear that this was not going to happen, he started to publish persuasive denunciations of Carnarvon's very obvious monopoly over one of the world's greatest assets. As an acknowledged Amarna expert – his 1910 book *The Life and Times of Akhnaton, Pharaoh of Egypt* had been a best-seller – his views carried a great deal of weight with his readers.

The tomb was Luxor's top tourist attraction. While it was true that there was little to be seen, a morning spent sitting by the wall around the tomb might be rewarded with a glimpse of a shrouded artefact being escorted to the conservation tomb. It might even be possible to bribe the workmen to disclose information about the grave goods: this is presumably how the rumours of eight mummies and an enormous cat statue started. Many, believing themselves to be people of importance, tried to cross the wall and enter the tomb. While large numbers were turned away, others – politicians, friends of politicians, royalty, friends of royalty, colleagues and friends and family of the team – were admitted on Tuesdays, the day that there was no work within the tomb. The list of distinguished guests was impressive – the commander of the Egyptian army and governor of Sudan, Sir Lee Stack; the governor of Qena province, 'Abd al-Aziz Yahya; the Director of the Indian Antiquities Service, Sir John Marshall; Sultana Malek, the widowed sister-in-law of King Fuad; Queen Elizabeth of the Belgians – but these visits were dreaded by the team, who simply wished to get on with their work.

There were plans afoot to make Tutankhamun a tourist attraction outside Egypt, too. On 23 April 1924, King George and Queen Mary would open the *British Empire Exhibition* at Wembley. A key attraction was the re-created 'Tomb of Tut-Ankh-Amen'. Entry cost 1s.3d., or 8d. for children, and for this price the visitor was able to experience the most famous archaeological site in the world.[6] The replica grave goods included the sarcophagus but not, of course, the coffins or mummy, as these had not yet been discovered. The artefacts were extremely good replicas; the hieroglyphs such faithful copies that they could be read by linguists. They had been created for the exhibition by a team of craftsmen employed by Messrs William Aumonier and Sons, with Weigall employed as the consultant Egyptologist. Carter was not amused. Assuming that the replicas were based on copyrighted plans and photographs, he attempted to stop the exhibition. As the *Daily Express* reported: 'Mr Carter's Wembley Bombshell – attempt to close the pharaoh's tomb – writ issued – replica said to be an infringement'. He only dropped his case when he received assurances that the information had come from the many non-copyrighted photographs taken by Weigall and others.

Back in Egypt, the team had grown weary and frustrated. When the unthinkable happened and Carnarvon and Carter started to quarrel, it became clear that they all needed a break. So, in late February 1923, the tomb was closed, the laboratories were shut and the team dispersed for a much-needed holiday. While Carter retreated to his Luxor house, Carnarvon and Lady Evelyn sailed southwards to enjoy a few days, rest and relaxation in Aswan. Here Carnarvon was bitten on the left cheek by a mosquito. Soon after his return to Luxor he sliced the scab off the bite while shaving. The wound became infected and Carnarvon started to feel unwell. He travelled to Cairo to discuss the division of finds with the Antiquities Service, but his condition deteriorated rapidly. Blood poisoning set in and pneumonia followed. At 1.45 a.m. on 5 April 1923, Carnarvon died, and with him died the concession to excavate in the Valley of the Kings. This would have been an ideal time for the Antiquities Service to take over the emptying of the tomb, but it lacked the funds to complete the work, while the Carnarvon estate was reluctant to abandon the project entirely, as it still had a vested interest in the grave goods. An agreement was therefore reached that Lady Carnarvon would finish her husband's work, but not conduct any further excavations in the Valley.

Lord Carnarvon's will left his private collection of antiquities to his wife, Almina. When, in 1926, she sold the collection to the Metropolitan Museum of Art in New York, Carter was asked to list and pack the artefacts. He listed 1,218 objects, or groups of objects, and added that 'A few unimportant antiquities not belonging to the above series I left at Highclere.'[7] This collection – forgotten until 1987 – included objects dating from the Middle Kingdom to the Ptolemaic Period. None of these pieces has any connection with Tutankhamun, and all were legally obtained. The circumstances of their rediscovery, however, have led to speculation that Carnarvon kept artefacts from Tutankhamun's tomb.

The press may have been thwarted in their attempts to report events within the tomb, but they could not be prevented from writing about the illness and sudden death of a British earl. As professional Egyptologists were on the whole disinclined to speak to the press, their reports were sprinkled with 'facts' obtained from the celebrities whom the public accepted as authorities on ancient Egypt. These experts – all authors of popular mummy stories, and all eager to give their opinions – included Sir Arthur Conan Doyle (author of the Egypt-themed *The Ring of Thoth* (1890) and *Lot No. 249* (1892), and a well-known believer in the supernatural), Sir Henry Rider Haggard (*She* (1887), *Cleopatra* (1889) and *Smith and the Pharaohs* (1910)), and Marie Corelli, the author of a series of immensely popular gothic tales.

On 24 March 1923, the *Daily Express* had reported Corelli's concerns:

> *I cannot but think that some risks are run by breaking into the last rest of a king of Egypt whose tomb is specially and solemnly guarded, and robbing him of possessions. According to a rare book I possess, which is not in the British Museum, entitled 'The Egyptian History of the Pyramids' (translated out of the original Arabic by Vortier, Arabic professor to Louis XVI of France) the most dire punishment follows any rash intruder into a sealed tomb. This book gives long and elaborate lists of the 'treasures' buried with several of the kings, and among these are named 'divers secret poisons enclosed in boxes in such wise that those who touch them shall not know how they come to suffer'. That is why I ask:*

'was it a mosquito bite that has so seriously infected Lord Carnarvon?'

Corelli was not the only clairvoyant to worry over Carnarvon's insensitive behaviour. Weigall, too, was widely credited with predicting his death. On observing the Earl's good mood as he entered the tomb for the opening of the Burial Chamber, he had apparently observed, 'If he goes down in that spirit, I give him six weeks to live.'[8] In contrast, Weigall's own writings specifically deny the existence of any curse within the tomb:[9]

> *Millions of people throughout the world have asked themselves whether the death of the excavator of this tomb was due to some malevolent influence which came from it, and the story has spread that there was a specific curse written upon the wall of the royal sepulchre. This, however, is not the case.*

Rumours spread like wildfire. At the very moment of Carnarvon's death, or so it was now told, all the lights in Cairo mysteriously failed, while, back at Highclere, Carnarvon's beloved dog, Susie, howled and died.[10] Soon it was widely accepted that a curse – 'death comes on swift wings to him that touches the tomb of the pharaoh' – was carved over the entrance to Tutankhamun's tomb, or carved above the entrance to the Burial Chamber, or inscribed on a mudbrick tablet found in either the Antechamber or the Burial Chamber. The fact that there was no trace of any such curse was easily explained by an elaborate conspiracy theory designed to reassure the Egyptian workmen:[11]

> *Neither Carter nor Gardiner [the linguist Sir Alan Gardiner] nor any of the other scholars present feared the curse then or took it seriously. But they worried that the Egyptian*

labourers would, and since they were dependent on native
helpers, mention of the clay tablet was wiped from the
written record of the tomb's discovery. Even the tablet itself
disappeared from the artefact collection – but not from the
memory of those who read it.

A second curse was apparently written on the back of a
statue discovered in the main chamber of the tomb:[12]

It is I who drive back the robbers of the tomb with the flames
of the desert. I am the protector of Tutankhamun's grave.

This is a mangled version of a genuine inscription discovered
on the threshold of the Treasury. A small reed torch, impreg-
nated in pine-resin, had been given a gold band and mounted
on a brick-like pottery pedestal incised with spell 151 from the
Book of the Dead, designed to protect the body of the king in
the embalming tent as he is prepared for burial and becoming
Osiris [no. 263]:[13]

I am the one who traps the sand at the wall of the secret
chamber,
the active fighter who repels him to the flame of the desert,
I have set the desert aflame, I have deflected the paths,
I am the protector of the Osiris [the deceased].

Many would come to believe that the last line of the inscription, 'I will call all those who cross this threshold into the
sacred precincts of the King who lives for ever', had been
erased by Carter once again to protect his workforce.

Carter's own position was clear. There was no ancient
curse, and Tutankhamun had not been able to use a superior
scientific knowledge – scientific 'rays', or microbes, or similar
– to somehow booby-trap his tomb:[14]

The Journalist's Tale

It is not my intention to repeat the ridiculous stories which have been invented about the dangers lurking in ambush, as it were, in the Tomb, to destroy the intruder . . . But there is another and a serious side to this question which calls for protest. It has been stated in various quarters that there are actual physical dangers hidden in Tut-ankh-Amen's tomb – mysterious forces, called into being by some malefic power, to take vengeance on whomsoever should dare pass its portals. There was probably no place in the world freer from risks than the Tomb. Scientific research had proved it to be sterile. Whatever foreign germs there may be within it today have been introduced from without, yet mischievous people have attributed many deaths, illnesses and disasters to alleged mysterious and noxious influences in the Tomb. Unpardonable and mendacious statements of this nature have been published and repeated in various quarters with a sort of malicious satisfaction. It is indeed difficult to speak of this form of 'ghostly' calumny with calm. If it be not actually libellous it points in that spiteful direction, and all sane people should dismiss such inventions with contempt. So far as the living are concerned curses of this nature have no part in the Egyptian Ritual.

This firm stance against the paranormal is, however, somewhat contradicted by his story 'The Tomb of the Bird': a tale that did much to reinforce the idea that Tutankhamun's tomb was under supernatural protection.[15] Having started by informing his readers that 'So many inaccurate accounts of the incident have been circulated that I thought it worth while to publish . . . the following account of the death of my canary', he goes on to explain how, at the start of the 1922 excavation, he was the proud owner of a caged bird which sang beautifully every day. The workmen believed the bird to be a good omen and, sure enough, the steps leading to Tutankhamun's tomb were soon discovered. The passageway had been cleared and the second doorway revealed when a cobra slithered into the cage and forever silenced the canary. Unable to accept the idea of supernatural intervention, Carter once again blamed his workmen for spreading rumours of malevolent spirits:

> [The workmen] saw in the death of the bird a portent of evil omen in spite of the treasures spread out before them. What did it threaten? Had the Jin which had protected the tomb for 3,000 years become enraged and hostile? 'May the evil omen be afar?' they muttered.

The workmen were not the only ones to interpret this as an ill omen. As everyone knew, Egypt's kings were protected by the uraeus snake: the fierce fire-spitting cobra rearing from the brow. Surely the appearance of a cobra at this precise moment must have been more than a coincidence? A basic account of the same event, told in a private letter written by Herbert Winlock, confirms the essence of the story while stripping it of any occult meaning.[16] Carter did indeed have a much-admired songbird, which he kept in a cage in his house. While Carter was away from home Arthur Callender found a cobra in the cage 'just in the act of gulping the canary down'.

Weigall included the tale of Carter's canary in *Tutankhamen and Other Essays*, published in 1923. This is not surprising: in 1923, Egyptologists knew very little about Tutankhamun's life and death, and the sinister tale would both bulk out what might otherwise have been a very thin book and attract readers keen to read about occult goings-on. The Western world had for years been reading mummy-based fiction, which stressed the potent nature of ancient Egyptian magic: now this fiction was fast becoming fact. Weigall went on to tell the equally eerie story of Carnarvon and the mummified cat (a cat mummy apparently comes to life), the tale of the earthenware lamp (a lamp brings bad luck to all who possess it), and the tale of the malevolent British Museum mummy (a mummy-board rather than a mummy which, as the story's title indicates, also brings bad luck). Throughout his writing he teases his readers with stories of supernatural happenings that might also be explained away in a rational manner and, in so doing, he continues the legend of Tutankhamun's curse, before finally, and mildly, denying its existence:[17]

> *The large number of visitors to Egypt and persons interested in Egyptian antiquities who believe in the malevolence of the spirits of the Pharaohs and their dead subjects, is always a matter of astonishment to me, in view of the fact that of all ancient people the Egyptians were the most kindly and, to me, the most loveable . . . I will therefore leave it to the reader's taste to find an explanation for the incidents which I will here relate.*

When Weigall died, on 2 January 1934, at just fifty-three years' of age, the *Daily Mail* used the headline: 'Death of Mr A. Weigall, Tut-ankh-Amen Curse Recalled'.

Initially confined to those who had attended the tomb opening, the curse quickly became a threat to anyone who could be deemed to have had any connection with the tomb, or with Tutankhamun more generally, or, in some cases, with Egypt. Even Jean-François Champollion (1790–1832), whose decoding of the hieroglyphic occurred a century before the discovery of Tutankhamun's tomb, was deemed to have been killed by a potent ancient curse. In 1934, Herbert Winlock, frustrated by the constant talk of supernatural death, collated information about those he deemed most vulnerable to the curse.[18] This showed that, of the twenty-six people present at the opening of the tomb, just six died within a decade; of the twenty-two people present at the sarcophagus opening, two died within a decade; and of the ten people present at Tutankhamun's autopsy, none died within a decade. By dying aged sixty-four, Carter managed to outlive Carnarvon by sixteen years. Lady Evelyn, who followed her father into the Burial Chamber and was with him when he was bitten by the fatal mosquito, died in 1980 at the age of seventy-eight. If Tutankhamun did indeed curse all who violated his tomb, we can only assume that his supernatural powers were remarkably ineffective.

9

The Waterboy's Tale

Seeing Tutankhamun Through Different Eyes

The Egyptologist and museum keeper I. E. S. Edwards, organiser of the British Museum's 1972 *Treasures of Tutankhamun* exhibition, re-thinks the discovery of the tomb:[1]

I used to think at one time that perhaps we had a special claim to have the exhibition, because the tomb had been discovered by a British archaeologist, but Magdi Wahba [Director of Foreign Relations, Ministry of Culture] soon disillusioned me. He said that was not the way the average Egyptian viewed it. The British had been allowed to excavate in what had always promised to be one of the richest sites in Egypt. They had made this marvellous discovery thanks to the generosity of the Egyptians in allowing them to excavate there, a sufficient reward in itself.

In life Tutankhamun had been surrounded by royal women. In death he was supported by powerful goddesses. In his resurrection he was excavated by men. We have become familiar with the core team responsible for the emptying of Tutankhamun's tomb: the patron Lord Carnarvon, the archaeologist Howard Carter, the conservator Arthur Mace, the engineer Arthur Callender, the chemist Alfred Lucas and, of course, the photographer Harry Burton. The Egyptian Antiquities Service was represented by its Director, the Frenchman Pierre Lacau, and the Chief Inspector of Antiquities for Southern

Egypt (Carter's old job), an Englishman, Rex Engelbach. Local inspectors assigned to work directly with the team were Ibrahim Habib, Mohamed Shaban and an inspector simply referred to as Abadir Effendi, who is now known to have been Abadir Effendi Michrqui Abadir.

As we might expect in the early twentieth century, there were no women admitted to this select group and any wives or daughters who accompanied their husbands to Luxor were expected to occupy themselves with feminine pursuits away from the Valley. Lady Evelyn Herbert, daughter of Lord Carnarvon, acted as hostess to high-ranking visitors and featured in several publicity photographs, but played no part in the excavation or emptying of the tomb. Minnie Burton, wife of Harry, kept a diary between 4 May 1922 and 20 October 1926 and this allows us to understand the limited routines of her daily life – a constant round of social engagements, shopping and domestic duties – while offering tantalising glimpses of the events hidden within the tomb:

30 November 1922: To Bank in morning. Then to Museum with wire from Mr Carter. Saying 'Discovery beyond the dreams of avarice'. Met Mme de Cramer. M^r & M^n & Lady Laird-Clowes to tea. Then to call on the Garrys. M^r & M^n Grant there. Caledonian Evening & great party with the Allans. Lady Bernard laid up with cold.

19 December 1922: Painting my furniture in morning & afternoon. Mr Carter sent over for me his donkey to ride over & see 'the' Tomb Tutankhamen. <u>Wonderful</u>. Mr Callendar there & later D^r & M^n Breasted & the little girl. Went over the hill both ways. Mr Hauser & Hall came back from Assuan. M^n W. & F. to the Davies' for tea.

24 January 1923: Went over to the Tombs of the Kings in morning to see the Couch being brought out. Harry with 'movie', & I took some snapshots. Crowds of people. The Wilsons, Mr Weigall, Mr Engelbach, Miss Forbes-Smith, Mrs Murray Graham, Mr Allan etc. Back in the car with Mr Hauser & Mr Hall. Very hot. Miss Hayward to lunch. Mr Carter to dinner. In no. 15 in morning & saw the glove, & the reconstructed sandals.

While no woman held an official position on the excavation team, there was no ban on their assisting with the conservation of the grave goods should they so wish. Burton's photographs show Essie Newberry, Vice-President of the Embroiderers' Guild (and wife to Carter's friend and mentor Percy Newberry), comfortably dressed in a flowing gown and sensible hat – a marked contrast to the formal dark suit worn by her husband – as she works to restore the linen pall which once shrouded the second shrine in the Burial Chamber (no. 209). The heavy rosettes had been cut from the cloth to allow its removal from the Burial Chamber, and she had agreed to stitch them back in place. But this was unusual, and it leaves us wondering whether more feminine input may have resulted in a different emphasis on the artefacts selected for conservation. This applies particularly to the linen, much of which was lost during the emptying of the tomb and unwrapping of the body.

As we have already seen, Tutankhamun was buried with a vast – and vastly expensive – amount of linen, ranging from his own bandages and clothes to the shrouds and cloaks wrapped around the divine and funerary figures. Carter's team – unthinkingly undervaluing the importance of the textiles, which were primarily seen as a female interest – interpreted the bandages as basic mummy-packaging, while the cloaks and shrouds were perhaps the ancient equivalent of dust sheets which could simply be discarded. Essie Newberry with her specialist knowledge might have argued differently, recognising both the quality of the textiles and, more importantly, the relevance of their placements.[2] Working from the University of Manchester at the heart of Britain's cotton industry, the Egyptologist Margaret Murray had already acknowledged the importance of mummy bandages as artefacts, while failing to recognise that the same bandages were an integral part of the mummy and not mere wrappings. In 1908, the bandages removed during the unwrapping of the 'Two Brothers' were recorded according to their different layers and the quality of their weave, and comparative samples were laundered, mounted and sent to other institutions. Less admirably, pieces of bandage were also given to the audience who watched the unwrapping of one of the 'Brothers', Khnum Nakht.[3]

While the women peripherally attached to the excavation occasionally appear in photographs, the self-proclaimed tomb guard, Acting Sergeant Richard Adamson of the Military Police, is stubbornly absent from the photographic record. In the late twentieth century Adamson became a familiar figure on the Egyptology lecture circuit – he himself estimated that he had given a surely exaggerated 1,500 presentations – giving an illustrated talk detailing the seven years that he spent guarding Tutankhamun's tomb. In 1981, aged eighty and wheelchair-bound following the amputation of both legs, Adamson returned to Luxor as the eponymous 'Last Survivor', accompanying a journalist, John Lawton.[4] Their stated aim was 'to defy – and therefore prove – the legendary "curse" of the exhumed Pharaoh, which has allegedly claimed the lives of 40 people'. The published account of their trip is filled with reminiscences. Here, for example, Lawton records Adamson's memories of the day when the tomb was discovered. His account is strikingly different to that recorded by Carter. Adamson was making his way along a steep path in the Valley of the Kings when he heard a shout:

> Attracted by the buzz of excitement, Adamson picked his way down the steep slope to where the Egyptians had unearthed several large boulders. But seeing no reason to get excited over a few boulders, the young soldier went back to his tent and the workmen covered them up.
>
> The next morning, though, when Carter arrived and found his men not working, he asked Adamson what had happened. 'Nothing, sir,' replied the sergeant. 'They did find some boulders but then they covered them up.' On hearing this, Carter ordered them to uncover the boulders again and found, beside one of them, a large stone step. Looking back, Adamson now says: 'The workmen knew they had found something. They also knew Carter was leaving and that they could come back and claim the credit themselves.'

There are, however, major problems with this tale. Adamson is not mentioned in any contemporary journal entry, diary or private writing and his memories only surfaced in 1966, following the deaths of his wife and the core team members, meaning that there was no one alive who could contradict them. There is, in fact, good evidence – including his marriage certificate and the birth certificates of his children – to suggest that he was not in Egypt at the times that he claimed. While some have interpreted this lack of evidence as a conspiracy – there is no record of Adamson's secondment to the Valley of the Kings because he was a spy in hiding – Egyptologists are agreed that Adamson did not guard Tutankhamun's tomb.[5] His story is, however, worth retelling as it highlights the fact that not every eyewitness account of events in the Valley of the Kings is true.

An equally unproven account, this time of the rediscovery of the tomb, is provided by an anonymous 'waterboy'.[6] His story emerged in the 1970s, at a time when a series of touring exhibitions had reignited interest in Tutankhamun. It tells how a young boy, having delivered a jar of water to the men toiling in the Valley of the Kings, conducted his own play-dig and uncovered a stone step. He ran to inform Carter of his find, and the rest was history. For some reason – colonialism, perhaps? – Carter excluded the waterboy from his diary, journal and published account of the discovery. However, during the 1926–7 excavation season, Burton photographed an Egyptian boy wearing one of Tutankhamun's elaborate necklaces (no. 267g). Many years later Hussein el-Rassul, a member of the family who discovered the Deir el-Bahri royal cache, identified himself as the boy in the photograph; later still, his family claimed that it was he who had discovered the tomb.

The waterboy's story is, like Adamson's account, unsupported by any evidence, and other Gurna families dispute the assertion that the el-Rassul family found the tomb. It seems unlikely that the foreman, Ahmed Gerigar, would have allowed a child to dig close to the official excavation area, and even more unlikely that Carter, who was always keen to appeal to a popular audience, would have missed the opportunity to promote such a heart-warming tale. The story does, however, serve as a useful reminder that Carter's specialist European and American team was supported by a team of skilled Egyptian workers, recruited and supervised by four experienced Egyptian foremen, or *reis*. The number of men working on site varied, but at times when there was digging or backfilling to be done there might be up to a hundred. These men would be recruited on a temporary basis, returning to their agricultural work when the excavation season ended or fewer labourers were required. The contribution of these men to the excavation and tomb clearance was gracefully (or patronisingly, depending on the viewpoint of the reader) acknowledged by Carter at the end of a surprisingly brief list of 'friends who have encouraged me with help and sympathy':[7]

> Last of all come my Egyptian staff and the Reises who have served me throughout the heat and burden of many a long day, whose loyal services will always be remembered by me with respect and gratitude, and whose names are herewith recorded: Ahmed Gerigar, Hussein Ahmed Saide, Gad Hassan and Hussein Abou Owad.

While we can glimpse some of these Egyptian workmen in Burton's photographs, they mainly go unnamed.[8] This is not an Egyptian phenomenon: the same thing happened in the Western-dominated archaeology of other countries and it happened in the United Kingdom too, where it was rare for an excavator to name the mere 'diggers' in his (lead excavators were almost always male) excavation publication. While this is often seen as a reflection of the colonialist nature of Egyptology, it is perhaps equally likely to stem from the elitist nature of archaeological excavation. Just as Gustave Eiffel would be credited with building his tower and, indeed, the 4th Dynasty pharaoh Khufu would be credited with building the Great Pyramid, so too Lord Carnarvon and then Howard Carter would be credited with finding and emptying Tutankhamun's tomb. The relationship between Carter and the Egyptian workforce could never be an equal one; no one would be able to forget that Carter was a member of the British ruling elite. But photographs showing Carter working alongside Egyptian workmen – all straining to carry the hippo-headed couch out of the tomb, for example – indicate that he at least did not see a firm division between the manual labour appropriate to the Egyptian workforce and the more cerebral archaeology conducted by the Europeans.

We can gain some insight into Carter's attitude to his Egyptian workforce by considering what has become known as the 'Sakkara Affair', an infamous event that occurred several years before he met Lord Carnarvon. On the afternoon of 8 January 1905, a group of drunken Frenchmen forced their way into the Sakkara Serapeum (the cemetery of the divine Apis bulls). They refused to buy tickets and, when challenged, assaulted first the site guards and then the Antiquities Inspectors. Carter, who was working as the Northern Antiquities Inspector, gave his men permission to defend themselves against the French. Arthur Weigall was an eyewitness to the fracas:[9]

> Fifteen French tourists had tried to get into one of the tombs with only 11 tickets, and had finally beaten the guards and burst the door open . . . Carter arrived on the scene, and after some words ordered the guards – now reinforced – to eject them. Result: a serious fight in which sticks and chairs were used and two guards and two tourists rendered unconscious. When I saw the place afterwards it was a pool of blood.

For an Englishman to encourage Egyptians to fight with Frenchmen was considered inexcusable. As the incident escalated into a diplomatic scandal the British Consul-General, Lord Cromer, ordered Carter to apologise to the French Consul. Carter, stubborn and defensive, refused. Today we might consider Carter to be taking a principled stand in support of the oppressed Egyptian workers; in 1905, he was seen as childish and unhelpful, the general feeling being that he should apologise even if he did not mean it. Gaston Maspero, then Director of the Antiquities Service, was able to resolve the matter without an apology, but he retaliated by restricting Carter's authority and, angered by what he saw as a lack of official support, Carter resigned his position with the Antiquities Service in October 1905. Several impecunious years followed, as Carter scraped a living working as an archaeological artist, a tourist guide, and a seller of art and antiquities. Only when Maspero introduced him to Lord Carnarvon did his life improve.

The workmen's view of Carter and his team goes unrecorded. However, it seems that they knew about the unauthorised first visit to the Burial Chamber – a visit that would have been very difficult to hide – yet chose to keep his secret rather than report him to the authorities. Others, those less closely connected to the excavation, were deeply suspicious of events in the Valley. There was a widespread assumption that the archaeologists were robbers who had been determined to steal Tutankhamun's treasure. Why else would they keep the grave goods hidden from view? When Weigall wrote to Carter in January 1923, he employed the language of his time and in so doing perfectly illustrated the social gulf that existed between the Egyptians and the Europeans in Luxor: 'the natives all say that you may therefore have had the opportunity of stealing some of the millions of pounds' worth of gold . . .'[10]

There was already a Tutankhamun rumour in circulation: three aeroplanes had, or so it was said, landed in the Valley and removed vast amounts of treasure to an unknown destination. The visitor days organised for prestigious guests were in part an attempt to counter these tales of inappropriate behaviour by demonstrating that all was indeed open and above board.

So, on 16 December 1922, we can read in the *Illustrated London News*:

> *The official opening of the tomb, or funeral chambers, of king Tutankhamun, found by the Earl of Carnarvon and Mr Howard Carter in the Valley of the Kings, near Luxor, took place on November 29. Before the opening, Lord Carnarvon's daughter, Lady Evelyn Herbert, entertained a large party for luncheon in the valley, among the guests being Lady Allenby and the governor of Kena Province, Abdel Aziz Bey Yehia, who had given invaluable assistance on guarding the treasures.*

While the Egyptians suspected Carter and his team of wishing to steal from Tutankhamun, Carter in turn suspected the Egyptians – outsiders, rather than his own trusted workmen – of having designs on the tomb. Three independent groups of watchmen, each answerable to a different authority, were employed to put his mind at rest.[11]

While Carter was comfortable in his dealings with his workmen, his relationship with his core team was less amicable: he quarrelled with his old friend Callender over money, he quarrelled with his patron, Carnarvon, over an unspecified matter and his friendship with Burton grew increasingly strained as the years went by. His relationships with the French-run Antiquities Service and the Egyptian-run Ministry of Public Works were even worse. Obstinate, single-minded and undiplomatic, and constantly aware of his own humble and ill-educated origins, Carter was unable to respond appropriately to anything that he deemed needless interference with the running of 'his' excavation. Already it had been announced that an Inspector of the Antiquities Service must always be present on site: a development that Carter did not take well. When, at the start of the 1923–4 excavation season, it was announced that the Antiquities Service was to approve all team members (and would therefore be able to exclude *The Times* journalist), he reacted badly. Today this is standard procedure; the Antiquities Service has the right to veto anyone whom it deems unfit to work on any archaeological site. But in the 1920s it was seen as gross interference. Carter attempted to argue, but there was no room for negotiations. Lacau stood firm: '. . . the Government no longer discusses, but informs you of its decision.'

Similarly, the raising of the sarcophagus lid in February 1924 was marred by quarrels over the numbers of visitors allowed to observe proceedings. Carter had invited seventeen guests; the Ministry of Public Works felt that this was too many. The matter was resolved amicably and, as planned, the granite lid was removed. The next day, however, the 'ladies' – the wives and family members of the archaeologists – were denied the visit that they had been promised because they did not have official permission to enter the tomb. The visit of the ladies was of course a symptom, not a cause. The underlying problem was the ownership of the tomb and its grave goods. Mace reported the rapidly escalating events in a lengthy diary entry dated 13 February 1924:

> *Early this morning Carter received a note from [the] Under Secretary, saying that he had received a wire from the Secretary absolutely prohibiting the ladies visit in the afternoon. He reported the matter to us and we felt that we must refuse to carry on any further work, as this was not only an insult to us, but a clear sign that the government were going to carry their policy of interference to even further lengths. Under such conditions scientific work became impossible . . .*

The directive had come from the Minister for Public Works, Morcos Hanna Bey; a man with absolutely no inclination to accommodate the British who, the previous year, had classified his political activism as treason and attempted to have him hanged. He, like many others, regarded Tutankhamun as a symbol of Egyptian independence: he did not feel that the British had any role to play in the Egyptian king's resurrection.

Mace's diary entry ends with some light relief:

> In this connection an account of the Marmur's [district chief's] movements will be of interest. He was ordered to the Valley some time in the morning. Meeting Carter on river bank he tried to obtain loan of car, camouflaging his movements by saying he only wanted it to take him to Mond's excavations. Failing in this he arbitrarily commandeered a cab which had been ordered by a party of tourists, and drove off in it, leaving the tourists stranded. At Mond's he left the carriage & borrowed M's car to drive him & his party to the Valley. There he told the chauffeur to come back for him at about 3 o'clock. Meanwhile Mond had found out what was up and refused to let his car go back. After waiting an hour or so he telephoned the Omdeh to go and ask Winlock to send our car for him. We got the message on our return at about six o'clock, and Winlock replied that as he was in the Valley for the express purpose of keeping our wives out of the tomb it was hardly up to us to fetch him away from it. Eventually he left the Valley by donkey at about 6.15 P.M.

The situation was, however, far from funny and the team found themselves locked out of the tomb as the government officials and the Egyptian press scrutinised the terms of Lady Carnarvon's permit in an attempt to have it withdrawn. So quickly had events worsened that the sarcophagus lid was left precariously suspended in mid-air while the spangled pall that had covered Tutankhamun's second shrine was left unattended, and rotted.

Things took a turn for the worse when Carter, most unwisely, turned to the courts to try to reclaim the excavation, with his lawyer, F. M. Maxwell (the lawyer who had previously prosecuted Morcos Bey Hanna for treason), tactlessly accusing the ministry of behaving like bandits. The suggestion that it was the Egyptian authorities who were doing the stealing did not go down well with the Egyptian press. Months of negotiations followed, complicated by the fact that Carter had a long-standing commitment to lecture in America and Canada. Then, on 19 November 1924, Sir Lee Stack, British commander-in-chief of the Egyptian army, was assassinated. The nationalist government fell, and Sa'ad Zaghlul Pasha was replaced as prime minister by Ahmed Ziwar Pasha, an old acquaintance of Carter. Finally, an agreement was reached. Lady Carnarvon, despite her lack of interest in ancient Egypt, would continue her husband's work and fund the tomb clearance. The Carnarvon estate would waive all rights to the grave goods and *The Times* deal would end. Carter would now work closely with the new Egyptian Chief Inspector for Southern Egypt, Tewfik Boulos, and the local inspector, Ibrahim Habib.

While Carter was occupied by his lecture tour – his accent astonishing audience members who believed that Tutankhamun had been an all-American discovery – the Antiquities Service took the opportunity to conduct a thorough survey of KV62 and the associated tombs used by the team. This revealed a near-life-sized wooden head of Tutankhamun as the young sun god Ra, packed in a wine box and stored in the luncheon tomb (KV4). As the head lacked an object number the Egyptian members of the committee felt that Carter must have stolen it. A telegram was sent to the prime minister, Saad Zaghlul, and the head was sent to Cairo. Carter's supporters pointed out that it made no sense for him to abandon a stolen item where anyone might find it. As the dispute rumbled on, Herbert Winlock, who was receiving daily reports from Reis Hussein, sent a coded telegram to Carter:[12]

> *Send all the information you can relating to origin STOP Advise us by letter if any inquiry is made we shall be pre- pared STOP Made a bad impression on Egyptian members it was announced by telegram to Zaghlool immediately and sent by express to Cairo STOP Lacau and Engelbach have suggested to them you have bought for account of Earl last year from Amarna do not know whether they believed that actually.*

Carter's reply provided an adequate explanation. The head had been recovered in the debris blocking the passageway. It had been conserved, and then put to one side at a time when KV4 was the only tomb available for storage. It had then been forgotten. This explanation was accepted without further question, and the matter was dropped.

The details of the original division of the finds had been set out in Lord Carnarvon's original permission to excavate. Article 8 made it clear that Tutankhamun's body would remain in Egypt: 'mummies of the Kings, of Princes, and of High Priests, together with their coffins and sarcophagi, shall remain the property of the Antiquities Service'. Articles 9 and 10 dealt with the grave goods:

> *9: Tombs which are discovered intact, together with all objects they may contain, shall be handed over to the Museum whole and without division.*

10: In the case of tombs which have already been searched, the Antiquities Service shall, over and above the mummies and sarcophagi intended in Article 8, reserve for themselves all objects of capital importance from the point of view of history and archaeology, and shall share the remainder with the Permittee.

Tutankhamun's tomb, with its evidence of at least two ancient robberies, would class as a tomb that had 'already been searched'; Carnarvon would therefore be able to claim a share of its contents. This has prompted some to suggest that perhaps the evidence for the ancient robberies – the damage to the doors, the tunnel through the chip-filled passageway, the disorder within the tomb and a collection of gold rings tied up in a linen cloth – is less clear-cut than Carter would have us believe.

Now, with all rights to the grave goods waived, Carter spent the winter of 1929–30 negotiating with the Egyptian authorities for a small percentage of the Tutankhamun finds. This was not a theoretical argument: Carter was not a man of independent means and he relied on the Carnarvons and their excavation (plus any spin-off fees raised from lecturing, writing and other freelance activities) for his own future. Initially the then prime minister, Ahmad Ziwar, had agreed that the Carnarvon estate would be offered duplicate artefacts, but by 1930, with Mustafa el-Nahhas in charge, the Egyptian government did not feel that they should give anything. Eventually Lady Carnarvon would receive the curious sum of £35,867.13s.8d. (roughly the equivalent purchasing power to £2,462,168.46 today), in compensation for the expense of clearing the tomb. Having paid death duties and taxes, she paid Carter £8,012 upfront, with a further £546.2s.9d. paid later that year. The Metropolitan Museum of Art, which had loaned staff, including Harry Burton, to work on site, received nothing.

From 1930 onwards, the right to work in the tomb passed to the Antiquities Service, and all Tutankhamun-related costs were met by the Egyptian government. This caused problems for Carter, who, as a foreigner with no official position, suddenly found himself locked out of the tomb and the lab that had been his domain for almost a decade. His initial, rather childish response – to argue that the steel gates, locks and keys actually belonged to Lady Carnarvon rather than the Antiquities Service – did little to help resolve the issue. Finally it was agreed that the keys would be held by a local Antiquities Inspector, who would arrive every day to unlock the tombs and allow Carter to enter.

Tutankhamun's tomb was both the highlight and the end of Carter's career as a field archaeologist. With the tomb empty, he returned to London to start writing up the official excavation report. This was never completed. When he died on 2 March 1939, he left a private collection of antiquities to be inherited by his niece, Phyllis Walker. Miss Walker consulted a trio of eminent Egyptologists – Burton, Newberry and Gardiner – and all three reached the same troublesome conclusion: the Carter collection included nineteen objects taken from Tutankhamun's tomb. While some of these items were of negligible value, some were inscribed with the king's name and one, a green-blue inscribed glass headrest, was unique. It was not clear how or when Carter obtained these artefacts, and it may be that some if not all had been taken from the Carnarvon collection in 1926 prior to its transfer to New York. The suspicion was, however, that he had brought them himself from Egypt. The grave goods were handed to the Egyptian Consulate in London, where they remained throughout the war. In 1946, they were returned to King Farouk, who presented some of them to Cairo Museum and retained others for his own collection. In 1960, the remaining objects were donated to the museum.

10

The Bishop's Tale

Investigating the Dead

The Bishop of Chelmsford writes to *The Times* newspaper in February 1923, expressing his concern over the fate of Tutankhamun's body:[1]

Sir – I wonder how many of us, born and brought up in the Victorian era, would like to think that in the year, say, 5923, the tomb of Queen Victoria would be invaded by a party of foreigners who rifled it of its contents, took the body of the great queen from the mausoleum in which it has been placed amid the grief of the whole people, and exhibited it to all and sundry who might wish to see it?

The question arises whether such treatment as we should count unseemly in the case of the great English Queen is not equally unseemly in the case of King Tutankhamen [sic]. I am not unmindful of the great historical value which may accrue from the examination of the collection of jewelry [sic], furniture and, above all, of papyri discovered within the tomb, and I realise that wide interests may justify their thorough investigation and even, in special cases, their temporary removal. But, in any case, I protest strongly against the removal of the body of the king from the place where it has rested for thousands of years. Such a removal borders on indecency, and traverses all Christian sentiment concerning the sacredness of the burial places of the dead.

*

Now that Tutankhamun had been discovered, what was to be done with him? The author Rider Haggard contributed to a vigorous debate in the letters section of *The Times* with the suggestion that all of Egypt's dead kings should be placed in the Great Pyramid 'and sealed there with concrete in such a fashion that only the destruction of the entire block of acres of solid stone could again reveal them to the eyes of man'.[2] General Sir John Maxwell disliked the idea of the pyramid but agreed that the bodies should not be put on public display:[3]

> *If public opinion in this matter is genuine, then, to be consistent, all bodies of the rich and poor alike should be recommitted to the earth, and all national museums should take steps to return their mummies to Egypt for reinterment. But it might be as well to remind good people at home that at all museums on a Bank Holiday the crowd dearly loves its mummy!*

Lord Carnarvon had already given his view: 'Tutankhamun's body will be treated with the utmost reverence and will be left lying in the sarcophagus unmoved from the spot where he has lain for three thousand years.'[4] The people of Luxor agreed. Tutankhamun's grave goods may have gone to Cairo, but his body should remain in his tomb, where it would draw tourists and generate income.

Traditionally, the modern world had not treated the ancient Egyptian dead with the respect accorded to the more recently deceased. In Egypt, where human and animal mummies were a seemingly infinite resource, the unscrupulous regarded them as a valuable commodity to be stripped or burned to retrieve their amulets, sold to wealthy tourists, or passed to the traders who would sell powdered mummy as either a medicine (*mumia*) or the eponymous ingredient in 'mummy brown paint'. Treasure seekers and archaeologists generally regarded human mummies as a nuisance, and Belzoni is entirely typical in showing no compassion for, or even interest in, the anonymous occupants of the tombs which so fascinated him:[5]

> *What a place of rest! Surrounded by bodies, by heaps of mummies in all directions; which, previous to my being accustomed to the sight, impressed me with horror . . . In such a situation I found myself several times, and often returned exhausted and fainting, till at last I became inured to it, and indifferent to what I suffered, except from the dust, which never failed to choke my throat and nose; and though, fortunately, I am destitute of the sense of smelling, I could taste that the mummies were rather unpleasant to swallow. After the exertion of entering into such a place, through a passage of fifty, a hundred, three hundred or perhaps six hundred yards, nearly overcome, I sought a resting place, found one, and contrived to sit; but when my weight bore on the body of an Egyptian, it crushed it like a band-box. I naturally had recourse to my hands to sustain my weight, but they found no better support; so that I sunk altogether among the broken mummies, with a crash of bones, rags and wooden cases, which raised such a dust as kept me motionless for quarter of an hour, waiting till it subsided again . . .*

This casual treatment of the dead, no matter how long deceased, makes modern readers wince. But Belzoni lived in an age when mummies were literally regarded as dead ends. An anonymous mummy was, to him, no more than a curiosity; an artefact with no beauty and little scientific value. Rather than a completed entity whose every layer had meaning and significance for its creators, the mummy was seen as a treasure-filled parcel waiting to be unwrapped.[6]

Outside Egypt, mummies had become public entertainment. Whole and unwrapped, they could be the highlight of a private cabinet of curiosities or a public museum collection. Better still, they could be performance art. 'Unrollings' were hugely popular ticketed events, and Belzoni himself had opened his London exhibition by unwrapping a mummy to the horrified delight of his audience. It is a mark of the separation between the long-dead mummy and the recently dead corpse that the Christian audiences, who hoped to be resurrected whole, and whose fear of autopsy made it almost impossible for the medical schools to obtain bodies for their dissecting rooms, were more than happy to watch this desecration, although, as this was a time of public hangings, we should perhaps not be too surprised by their lack of sensitivity. Unwrapping, like archaeology, was a destructive process that might, or might not, yield a valuable crop of amulets and other precious items. A competent anatomist might then record information about height, gender and the presence or absence of teeth and hair. He might even speculate about age at death and cause of death. But that was it: no further information could be obtained. The mummy had told its tale.

The decoding of hieroglyphs and the discovery of the two royal caches challenged this view. Suddenly Egyptologists were faced with a collection of named individuals from a known historical context. The royal mummies, at least, deserved to be treated with respect. This did not, however, save them from destruction. Gaston Maspero and Émile Brugsch, men with no medical training, felt confident that they should be the ones to perform the royal autopsies, which they did in front of an invited audience of dignitaries. While there is an argument for conducting unwrappings in public to show that nothing is being 'hidden', this was a strong reminder of unrolling as public entertainment. The royal mummies were then put on display in the museum, prompting Sir Edward Poynter to write to *The Times* in May 1890, expressing his feeling of regret over this undignified end. Foreshadowing the Tutankhamun debate, the Egyptologist Édouard Naville suggested, again via the letters page of *The Times*, that they should be reburied in the pyramids.

Tutankhamun was an entirely different case. He had a name, a tomb and a history, and the public had, over the past few years, become as familiar with him as it was possible to be with a 3,000-year-old Egyptian king. Furthermore, he had been discovered immediately after the Great War and the subsequent influenza pandemic, at a time when many were mourning their own dead and seeking reassurance that their bodies had been treated with proper respect. Carter, the man who had dedicated much of his working life to painstakingly conserving the artefacts from Tutankhamun's tomb, clearly saw the mummy as belonging to the medical rather than the archaeological world. The unwrapping, and unavoidable destruction, of the mummy was, to him, the final, logical stage in his quest for the king. When Douglas Derry suggested that an X-ray might make it unnecessary to unwrap Tutankhamun he agreed to the procedure, although he still felt that the mummy should be unwrapped to extract the jewellery and other precious items, which would otherwise make it a target for thieves. This is an argument that would have been familiar to the Third Intermediate Period priests of Amun, but it made little sense in twentieth-century Egypt.

Derry, unlike Carter, was aware of the need to justify the unwrapping:[7]

The Bishop's Tale

A word may fittingly be said here in defence of the unwrapping and examination of Tut-ankh-Amen. Many persons regard such an investigation as in the nature of sacrilege, and consider that the king should have been left undisturbed . . . It will be understood that once such a discovery as that of the tomb of Tut-ankh-Amen has been made, and news of the wealth of objects contained in it has become known, to leave anything whatsoever of value in the tomb is to court trouble . . . The same argument applies to the unwrapping of the king, whose person is thus spared the rude handling of thieves, greedy to obtain the jewels massed in profusion on his body. History is further enriched by the information which the anatomical examination may supply, which in this case . . . was of considerable importance.

Unfortunately, the chosen radiographer, Sir Archibald Douglas Reid, died in Switzerland in 1924. His untimely death at just fifty-three years old would later spark rumours that he had passed away on the train to Luxor, yet another victim of Tutankhamun's curse (although a curious one: surely Tutankhamun would have preferred to be X-rayed rather than unwrapped?). With no immediate possibility of finding a new radiographer Carter decided not to wait, but asked Derry to perform the unwrapping. It soon became clear that it would not, in fact, have been possible to X-ray the mummy, as it could not be extracted whole from its innermost coffin.

We met Tutankhamun's medical team in Chapter 1. Professor Douglas Derry, Professor of Anatomy in the Kasr el-Ainy Medical School at Cairo University, was assisted by Dr Saleh Bey Hamdi of Alexandria, the ex-director of the same medical school and current director of sanitation in Alexandria. Harry Burton, the photographer, worked alongside the anatomists, documenting their work, and the chemist Alfred Lucas was present to analyse any samples taken from the mummy. Pierre Lacau, Director General of the Antiquities Service, attended in his official capacity as an observer, and there was a small group of Egyptian and European guests. The autopsy began on the morning of 11 November 1925 in the outer corridor of the tomb of Seti II.[8] It was scheduled to take a week.

The resin-based unguents had not only left an unsightly mess: they had glued the bandaged face into the funerary mask, and both the mask and the mummy had been glued into the innermost coffin, whose base was glued into the base of the middle coffin. Derry therefore had to work within the confines of the innermost coffin base. Ideally, the shrouded mummy would have been revealed by first untying the outer sheet, which was bound to the body by bandages passing around the ankles, knees, hips and shoulders, and then unrolling the individual bandages in the reverse order to their application. However, the linen was too badly decayed to be removed in this way. This was a surprise. The bandages wrapping the mummies recovered from the two royal caches had retained their strength, but those mummies, of course, had been unwrapped, washed and rewrapped in antiquity. Tutankhamun had lain in his unguent-soaked bandages for 3,000 years, and his linen had suffered from the combined effects of a damp tomb, proximity to a decaying body and the chemical action of the unguents that had caused them to char.

Derry started his work by applying a generous amount of melted paraffin wax to stiffen the crumbling outer sheet. He then cut down the middle of the sheet, from the lower edge of the mask to the feet. He had hoped that this would allow him to lift the bandaged body clear of its shroud, but this was not possible as the bandages beneath the sheet were in an even worse state of decomposition. Instead he was forced to work on the body from the legs upwards. After five days the torso and limbs had been exposed, measured and strengthened with paraffin wax, and the clothing, amulets and jewellery dotted about the various layers had been removed, photographed and numbered. Derry had reached the head and shoulders, which were still covered by the helmet-like funerary mask. Tutankhamun's head was eventually extracted from the mask using 'hot knives'. Carter later used the heat generated by several primus stoves to separate the coffin bases and the mask. The heat caused the glass inlays to separate from the mask, which underwent restoration before being taken, with the solid gold inner coffin, to Cairo. With the world's attention now focused on these astonishing funerary artefacts, far less attention was directed towards Tutankhamun himself.

Tutankhamun emerged from his autopsy a fleshless skeleton. His head had been cut off, his arms separated at the shoulders, elbows and hands, his legs at the hips, knees and ankles, and his torso cut from the pelvis at the iliac crest. With the scientific investigation complete he was reassembled on a sand-covered tray that had once been used to store sugar, and some sections were glued together with resin to give the appearance of an intact body. This decision to hide the extent of the autopsy damage had unintended consequences when it led to the suggestion that Tutankhamun must have suffered from the rare Klippel–Feil syndrome, a condition which would have fused his spine and made it impossible for him to move his head. In fact, his skull had simply been glued to his spine to hide the fact that he had been decapitated.

His autopsy had proved what the archaeologists had long suspected: Tutankhamun had not been an elderly courtier who became king by marrying a royal princess. He had been a young man, closely related to the Amarna royal family. Almost overnight, Tutankhamun had lost his reputation as a traditional New Kingdom pharaoh and restorer – a reputation that he had worked hard to create – and been reinvented as the 'boy-king', a damaged Amarna orphan to be pitied rather than admired. This view of the weak Tutankhamun remains popular today, enhanced by widely publicised reconstructions of his physical appearance which focus on his perceived (but far from proven) disabilities: his damaged foot, wide hips, gynaecomastia and abnormally large head.[9]

An entry in Carter's journal, dated 1 October 1925, makes it clear that he always intended to rewrap Tutankhamun:

> Saw Edgar [Campbell Cowan Edgar, Museum Keeper] at the Cairo Museum. Arranged with him for the electric light at the tombs of the Kings to start from Oct. 11th. I also conveyed to him my programme for this season's work, and the necessity of making the examination of the royal mummy as early as possible, mentioning that the arrangement was for it to take place on or about the 25th of Oct., when Prof. Douglas Derry and Saleh Bey Hamdi would assist. That this scientific examination should be carried out as quietly and conveniently as possible, but that I should delay rewrapping the mummy until I knew whether the Ministers would like to inspect the royal remains.

On 23 October 1926, he confirmed that: 'The first outermost coffin containing the King's mummy, finally re-wrapped, was lowered into the sarcophagus this morning.' Lucas would later remember that Tutankhamun had been wrapped in linen. The king, still lying on his sand tray, was placed in the outermost (now the sole) coffin base, and the lid was closed. Finally, the open sarcophagus was covered with a glass lid that would allow visitors to see the golden Tutankhamun–Osiris. The glass lid remained in place until it was removed, and broken, by Harrison's team in 1968. It was replaced, free of charge, by a sheet of Pilkington's armour-plated glass. As the coffin lid was raised it became obvious that Tutankhamun had been dismembered, a discovery which sparked outrage amongst the watching press. Tutankhamun was tucked beneath a blanket of cotton wool tied in place by bandages, but his body parts were scattered around the sand tray and his beaded skullcap and chest cover, which Carter had considered too fragile to remove, had vanished. It is impossible to know if this disruption occurred accidentally or whether, as seems more likely, it is a sign that the sarcophagus and coffin were unofficially opened and superficially 'restored' at least once between 1926 and 1968.

The new glass lid was raised in 1978, when Tutankhamun's head was examined by Harris's team, and raised again in 2005, when Tutankhamun left his tomb to visit a mobile CT scanner. Finally, on 4 November 2007, exactly eighty-five years after the discovery of the steps leading to his tomb, Tutankhamun took up residence in a new, state-of-the-art, nitrogen-filled glass coffin with integral light and accurate temperature and humidity control. As his Burial Chamber is almost entirely filled by his stone sarcophagus, his new coffin was placed in a corner of the Antechamber while his outer-most coffin was sent to Cairo, to join the other two. The trio will be displayed alongside the funerary mask in designated Tutankhamun galleries in the new Grand Egyptian Museum.

Tutankhamun has not made the long and complicated journey to Cairo. He remains on permanent display in his tomb, still lying on his sand tray but now covered by a simple linen sheet which leaves his face and feet exposed and his battered body hidden from view. He has been stripped of his carefully chosen grave goods, and divested of the bandages which formed an essential part of his transformation into the god Osiris. We are left to reflect whether this is the image of himself that Tutankhamun would have wished to present to the world.

Epilogue
Tutankhamun's Family

Traditionally, new students – here I use the term loosely to cover anyone with an interest in learning more – would be attracted to ancient Egypt through a combination of museum visits, public lectures and extensive reading. Today the same students are more likely to be drawn to ancient Egypt through broadcast documentaries, Internet resources and, increasingly, games. In many ways this is a good thing: a subject that was once the preserve of academics has opened up to a far wider audience. But it does cause a big problem. While it is generally recognised that games present a fantasy world and the Internet provides a mass of diverse information of variable accuracy, expensively produced documentaries tend to be unquestioningly accepted as the 'truth'. It is therefore unfortunate that documentary makers are prone to simplifying the past and identifying just one of many possible sequences of events as the correct one. Too often, their desire to tell a story with a positive and ideally spectacular ending within severe budgetary and timetable constraints overrides any desire to tell a complete or well-rounded tale. The underlying belief is that viewers – the same viewers who will happily sort through the intricate clues and red herrings presented in forensic-based crime fiction – cannot cope with a complicated storyline. Many students arrive at university convinced that they already have a good understanding of Tutankhamun and his world because they have (best-case scenario) watched a few persuasive documentaries or (worst-case scenario) watched an 'imaginative' mini-series.

The reluctance to tell a full tale becomes more significant as documentary makers move from observing and reporting to actually financing archaeological work. This in itself is not a bad thing. Archaeology can be hugely expensive and Egyptologists rarely have access to infinite resources. However, there are drawbacks. Broadcasters are rarely interested in the full, scientific publication of results. Nor, as we have just noted, are they interested in the subtleties and intricacies that are a fundamental part of ancient world studies. Finally, they inflict a ruthless schedule on those who work with them. The pressure to come up with spectacular results by a given deadline can be severe. Meanwhile, with no evidence of anyone questioning or contradicting the spectacular results, viewers are conditioned to accept the broadcast story, particularly when it is narrated by a reassuringly familiar voice.

Those of us who enjoy fictional crime know that uncontaminated scientific evidence is beyond challenge. We watch, enthralled, as television pathologists crouch over the recently dead, collecting the blood and tissue samples that, within an hour or two of viewing, will lead to an arrest and a conviction. DNA evidence in particular is accepted without question; no one ever stands up in a television court scene to argue that the science is wrong, even though, behind the scenes, there are different methods of analysing different forms of DNA and different methods of interpreting the evidence, some recognised as more reliable than others.[1]

Unfortunately, ancient DNA, the evidence that is increasingly being sought from Egypt's royal mummies, is not beyond challenge. This has become a highly divisive subject, with some experts accepting mummy DNA analysis as a viable scientific tool and others arguing quite vehemently that it is not. There are certainly many problems associated with the process. It is this uncertainty over the accuracy of the method which has caused me to relegate the DNA 'evidence' to a separate Epilogue, where it can be considered alongside yet apart from the archaeological evidence and medical evidence obtained by old-fashioned observation and deduction.

DNA is known to degrade over time, with higher temperatures leading to increased rates of degradation. This means that frozen tissue recovered from an icy mountain will preserve DNA far better than mummified tissue recovered from the hot Egyptian desert. At the same time, contamination is a huge problem. The minute amounts of degraded ancient DNA that can be recovered from the long dead are liable to be overwhelmed by modern DNA picked up from airborne bacteria and, of course, from the scientists themselves. This may not be a problem if the scientists are looking for animal DNA, but when they are dealing with humans there is an awful lot of potential contamination around.

We have seen how, over the past 150 years, Egyptologists have been able to recover most of Egypt's 18th Dynasty monarchs from the Valley of the Kings. These kings now lie peacefully in their coffins in Cairo, showing little evidence of disturbance. A visitor to the mummy room might be forgiven for thinking that they have simply been lifted from their sarcophagi and then transported northwards for their own protection. But we know that this is far from the case. None of these mummies was recovered from anything resembling an uncontaminated 'crime scene', and some have undergone repeated interference over the centuries. They were all eviscerated, dissociated, oiled and wrapped, in a lengthy embalming house ritual occurring soon after death. They were then attacked and at least part-stripped by tomb robbers. Many years later they (or their surviving parts) were taken from their tombs, cleaned and rewrapped by the Third Intermediate Period priests. Some had to be reconstructed: Tuthmosis III, for example, was so badly damaged, he had to be stiffened by four oar-shaped paddles hidden within the bandages. Three thousand years later he was attacked again when the el-Rassul brothers burrowed through his neat, new bandages in search of his nonexistent heart scarab. Finally, in Cairo, he was unofficially unwrapped by Émile Brugsch (1881) and officially unwrapped by Gaston Maspero (1886). Both Egyptologists worked in front of an audience who crowded round the autopsy table.

Tutankhamun experienced the same extended mummification process. He was spared the indignity of ancient robberies and restorations, but in modern times was examined by Derry, Harrison, Harris, Hawass and their teams. He may also have been robbed one or more times between 1926 and 1968. Crucially, his body suffered chemical damage and charring caused by the unguents poured over his body, which had seeped into his bones. His most recent removal from his glass-protected sarcophagus saw the team, without the benefit of protective clothing, hovering inches away from his body.

Added to the general problem of human contamination must be the specific problems of chemical damage caused during the embalming process.[2] Here, luckily, Egyptologists have a modern mummified body to provide a control. In 1994, Professor Bob Brier mummified a seventy-year-old man using techniques, tools and drying salts as closely aligned to the ancient ones as possible.[3] His mummy is subjected to regular inspection, and this has shown that the skin cells are already showing signs of damage. This makes it clear that bone (ideally flat bone) or teeth are the best source of mummy DNA. This has to be collected in a tiny sample using a biopsy needle so that the mummy is left undamaged.

Finally, we have the problem of identity. Tutankhamun and Tiy's parents, Yuya and Thuya, are the only members of the later 18th Dynasty royal family to have been found in their own, near-intact tombs. All others are identified either by archaeological deduction (KV55) or by the labels applied by the Third Intermediate Period priests. In at least one case it is likely that these labels are incorrect. The body identified as Amenhotep III has been mummified using a technique unusual for the later 18th Dynasty. Although it has been suggested that this may be Ay, the mummy should probably be regarded as belonging to the 20th Dynasty.

In 2004, *National Geographic* gave the Supreme Council of Antiquities (the former Egyptian Antiquities Service) the generous donation of a state-of-the-art Siemens CT scanner. This became the basis of an ambitious project to study mummies throughout Egypt. In January 2005, Tutankhamun became the first mummy to be examined. The results of the CT scan would later be combined with a project to use DNA analysis to identify Tutankhamun's birth family and solve the riddle of the Amarna succession. Tissue samples would be taken from eleven mummies to develop genetic fingerprints of the DNA inherited from their parents. The scientists would also search from mitochondrial DNA (passed down the female line) and Y chromosome DNA. The mummies involved in the study were:

Tutankhamun

KV55

Amenhotep III

Epilogue

Yuya

Thuya

Foetus 1

Foetus 2

KV35EL (The Elder Lady)

KV35YL (The Younger Lady)

KV21a

KV21b

We have already met all of the above apart from the two female mummies recovered from tomb KV21. Pottery from their tomb suggests that they date to the earlier 18th Dynasty, but, as both were mummified with the bent left arm that is often accepted as a sign of royalty, the investigators felt that they, too, could be related to Tutankhamun.

In 2007, the Discovery Channel broadcast *Secrets of Egypt's Lost Queen*, the gripping story of the forensic quest to identify the missing mummy of the female pharaoh Hatshepsut. The programme proved immensely popular with the viewing public, paving the way for a major deal with the Discovery Channel that would fund the establishment of a dedicated ancient-DNA laboratory in the basement of Cairo Museum and a second laboratory in Cairo University, where the results from the primary lab could undergo independent testing. To reduce contamination, the film crew would be banned from the labs, and any laboratory scenes subsequently aired would be reconstructions. The project would eventually be broadcast as the 2010 two-part four-hour-long documentary *King Tut Unwrapped*. Not everyone was happy with this Egyptian–American collaboration; it seemed to some that non-Egyptians were once again interfering with Tutankhamun.

Epilogue

The scientific results of the project were announced on 17 February 2010 via a press release issued by the Supreme Council of Antiquities, a press conference held at Cairo Museum and a paper published in the *Journal of the American Medical Association*.[4] The conclusions were impressive, with every mummy providing DNA, some more than others. The highlights of the report were:

— KV35EL (The Elder Lady) is the daughter of Yuya and Thuya and therefore Queen Tiy.

— KV55 is the son of Amenhotep III and KV35EL. He is therefore Akhenaten, his elder brother, Tuthmosis, or a previously unidentified brother who might be Smenkhkare. The conclusion was that he is 'most probably Akhenaten'.

— KV55 is the father of Tutankhamun.

— KV35YL (The Younger Lady) is both Tutankhamun's mother and a full sister to KV55. She is therefore a daughter of KV35EL and Amenhotep III.

— The foetuses did not provide enough DNA to allow a full identification, but there was nothing to suggest that they were not Tutankhamun's daughters.

— KV21A was identified as the probable mother of the foetuses, suggesting that she was Ankhesenamun.

While the world's press celebrated this scientific triumph – 'Riddle of King Tut: DNA Unlocks Secrets' – Egyptologists and scientists were not so sure.[5] The Egyptologists were cautious in their response, reluctant, perhaps, to prejudice their relationship with the Supreme Council of Antiquities. When Jo Merchant, a science-trained journalist, attempted to obtain quotable responses to the study, she found that 'Although no one comes out and says the data on Tutankhamun and his family are definitely wrong, I have trouble finding anyone who believes them.'[6]

The identification of KV35EL as Tiy was generally accepted. The identification of KV55 as a close relative of Tutankhamun also seemed reasonable: anatomy had already suggested that this was the case. However, as we have previously seen, many experts are agreed that KV55 was barely twenty years old when he died and this makes it difficult for him to be Akhenaten.

The identification of the KV21A mummy as Ankhesenamun caused more surprise, as there is nothing to indicate that KV21 is a royal tomb, and it is difficult to imagine how her body ended up there. It is not entirely clear why this mummy, which was generally believed to date to the earlier 18th Dynasty, was included in the testing.

The identification of KV35YL as Tutankhamun's mother and Akhenaten's full sister was equally surprising. Amenhotep III and Tiy show their daughters on their official art; we can name them and, to a limited extent, trace their lives. There is no indication that any of them married their brother. Could Nefertiti have been a sister to Akhenaten who once bore a different name? Or, if KV55 is, as the present writer believes, Akhenaten's son Smenkhkare, could KV35YL be either Meritaten (suggesting that Smenkhkare and Meritaten may have been Tutankhamun's parents) or Ankhesenamun if she is not KV21A? A member of the investigating team has been quoted in the German press as stating that KV35YL may be the granddaughter rather than the daughter of KV35EL. If this is the case, it is indeed possible that KV35YL may be one of the lost Amarna princesses. However, further examination of the genetic data published by the Egyptian team indicates that the foetuses could not be the children of Tutankhamun plus any daughter fathered by KV55.[7] This leaves three possibilities: Tutankhamun had one or more unknown wives who were the mother(s) of the foetuses; KV55 is not Akhenaten, father of Ankhesenamun, who is herself the mother of the foetuses; or the foetuses are not immediate family members.

Scientists, more direct in their approach, have criticised the methodology underpinning the DNA gathering and analysis, and have highlighted the discrepancies between the information provided in the press release and the information in the published article. In particular, they have expressed surprise that it proved possible to retrieve so much useful DNA from ancient Egyptian remains.[8] They have also expressed concerns about the analytical techniques used. While mummy studies normally look for mitrochondrial DNA – the DNA passed from mother to child – Tutankhamun's family team had looked for nuclear DNA, which they analysed using DNA fingerprinting. This is a less reliable method, more prone to errors caused by contamination. Finally, it has been argued that the testing should have been done blind to rule out the possibility of influence and unconscious bias, and that the raw data should have been fully published which, so far, it has not been.

It is, of course, very easy to criticise a brave attempt to use a new technique to untangle the mysteries of the past. Mummy DNA analysis is a relatively new science and we will have to wait for more sophisticated testing, more effective contamination control and more rigorous data analysis, to be certain that the results obtained are valid. In the meantime, we are

Epilogue

left with the strong possibility that Akhenaten, Smenkhkare and Ankhesenamun have still to be identified. Have the scientists succeeded in identifying Tutankhamun's family? As on so many Tutankhamun-related issues the experts are divided, with some saying a firm 'yes' and others an equally firm 'no'.

Glossary of Key Terms

Amarna: The modern name for the acient city of Akhetaten, purpose-built by Akhenaten to serve his god, the Aten.

Amarna Age: The reigns of Akhenaten and Smenkhkare, when Egypt was ruled from Amarna and dedicated to the solar deity known as the Aten.

Aten, the: A solar god; the focus of state worship during the Amarna Age.

Cartouche: The loop surrounding the king's throne name and personal name.

Dynastic Age: The period when Egypt was an independent land ruled by a king known today as the 'pharaoh'. The Dynastic Age started in approximately 3100 BCE with the unification of the independent city states of the Nile Delta and Valley, and ended in 30 BCE with the death of Cleopatra VI.

Dynasty: A modern term for a line of kings who were connected but not necessarily related by blood. Tutankhamun ruled during the 18th Dynasty.

Field of Reeds: The land of the dead, ruled by the god Osiris.

Hieratic: The cursive, everyday writing of New Kingdom Egypt.

Hieroglyphs: The 'picture writing' used in monumental and significant texts.

Hypostyle Hall: A hall whose roof is supported by many columns, often found in Egyptian temples.

Ka: The spirit or soul which would be released from the body at death.

King List: A record of royal names and reign lengths maintained by the Egyptian priests.

New Kingdom: A modern term for Dynasties 18–20 (1550–1069 BCE).

Lower Egypt (or Northern Egypt): The moist, wide and flat Nile Delta.

Mortuary temple (or memorial temple): The place where the cult of the dead would be eternally maintained.

Mummy-board: A decorated cover placed on top of a mummy within its coffin.

Ostracon (plural ostraca): A broken piece of pottery or limestone flake, used to record informal writings and images. Pylon: A monumental temple gateway.

Side-lock: An elaborate plait worn by elite children on the side of their shaven head.

Stela (plural stelae): A carved or painted stone or wooden slab, used to convey an important text or image. The Amarna 'Boundary Stelae' surrounded the city, and told the story of its founding.

Upper Egypt (or Southern Egypt): The hot, long and narrow Nile Valley.

Uraeus: The rearing snake depicted on the king's brow.

Resources and Sources

Online resources

Tutankhamun: Anatomy of an Excavation allows free access to the excavation records, photographs, journals and diaries which record the discovery and emptying of Tutankhamun's tomb from various viewpoints: http://www.griffith.ox.ac.uk/discoveringtut/.

The Amarna Project website allows visitors to explore the city of Tutankhamun's early years: www.amarnaproject.com.

The Theban Mapping Project provides a digital passport to the Valley of the Kings: https://thebanmappingproject.com/.

Published sources

Agnew, N. and Wong, L. (2019), Conserving and Managing the Tomb of Tutankhamen, *Getty Magazine*, Winter 2019: 8–11.

Aldred, C. (1973*)*, *Akhenaten and Nefertiti*. London: Viking Press.

Aldred, C. (1988), *Akhenaten: King of Egypt*, London: Thames and Hudson.

Allen, J. P. (1988), Two Altered Inscriptions of the Late Amarna Period, *Journal of the American Research Center in Egypt* 25: 117–26.

Allen, J. P. (2009), The Amarna Succession, in P. J. Brand and L. Cooper, eds., *Causing his Name to Live: Studies in Egyptian Epigraphy and History in Memory of William J. Murnane*. Leiden: Brill: 9–20.

Allen, J. P. (2010), The Original Owner of Tutankhamun's Canopic
    Coffins, in Z. Hawass and J. Houser Wenger, eds., *Millions of
    Jubilees: Studies in Honour of David P. Silverman*. Cairo: American
    University in Cairo Press: 27–41.

Allen, S. J. (2002), Tutankhamun's Embalming Cache Reconsidered,
    in Z. Hawass, ed., *Egyptology at the Dawn of the 21st Century:
    Proceedings of the Eighth International Congress of Egyptologists,
    Cairo, Egypt. 2000*. Cairo: American University in Cairo Press:
    23–9.

Arnold, D. (1996), Aspects of the Royal Female Image during the
    Amarna Period, in D. Arnold, ed., *The Royal Women of Amarna:
    Images of Beauty from Ancient Egypt*, New York: The Metropolitan
    Museum of Art: 85–120.

Beinlich, H. (2006), Zwischen Tod und Grab: Tutanchamun und das
    Begräbnisritual, *Studien zur altägyptischen Kultur* 34: 17–31.

Belekdanian, A. O. (2015), *The Coronation Ceremony during the
    Eighteenth Dynasty of Egypt: An Analysis of Three 'Coronation'
    Inscriptions*. Unpublished D.Phil. thesis, University of Oxford.

Bell, M. A. (1990), An Armchair Excavation of KV 55, *Journal of the
    American Research Center* 27: 97–137.

Belzoni, G. B. (1820), *Narrative of the Operations and Recent
    Discoveries in Egypt and Nubia*, Verona. New edition 2001, edited
    by Alberto Siliotti. London: British Museum Press.

Berman, L. M. (1998), Overview of Amenhotep III and his Reign, in
    D. O'Connor and E. H. Cline, eds, *Amenhitep III: Perspectives on
    his Reign*. Ann Arbor: University of Michigan Press: 1–25.

Bickerstaffe, D. (2005), The Royal Cache Revisited, *Journal of the
    Ancient Chronology Forum* 10: 9–25.

Bickerstaffe, D. (2009), *Identifying the Royal Mummies: The Royal
    Mummies of Thebes*. Chippenham: Canopus Press.

Bosse-Griffiths, K. (1973), The Great Enchantress in the Little Golden
    Shrine of Tutankhamun, *Journal of Egyptian Archaeology* 59:
    100–8.

Boyer, R. S., Rodin, E. A., Grey, T. C. and Connolly, R. C. (2003),

The Skull and Cervical Spine Radiographs of Tutankhamen: A Critical Appraisal, *American Journal of Neuroradiology* 24: 1142–7.

Brier, B. and Wade, R. S. (2001), Surgical Procedures during Ancient Egyptian Mummification, *Chungará* 33: 1.

Bruce, J. (1790), *Travels to Discover the Source of the Nile*, Vol. 1. Edinburgh.

Bryan, B. (2006), Administration in the Reign of Thutmose III, in E. H. Cline and D. O'Connor, eds, *Tuthmose III: A New Biography*, Ann Arbor: University of Michigan Press: 69–122.

Carnarvon, F. (2007), *Carnarvon and Carter: The Story of the Two Englishmen Who Discovered the Tomb of Tutankhamun*. Newbury: Highclere Enterprises.

Carter, H. (1927), *The Tomb of Tut.ankh.Amen: The Burial Chamber*. London: Cassell and Company Limited. Reprinted 2001 with a foreword by Nicholas Reeves, London: Gerald Duckworth and Co. Ltd.

Carter, H. (1933), *The Tomb of Tut·ankh·Amen: The Annexe and Treasury*. London: Cassell and Company Limited. Reprinted 2000 with a foreword by Nicholas Reeves, London: Gerald Duckworth and Co. Ltd.

Carter, H. and Mace, A. C. (1923), *The Tomb of Tut·ankh·Amen: Search, Discovery and Clearance of the Antechamber*. London: Cassell and Company Limited. Reprinted 2003 with a foreword by Nicholas Reeves, London: Gerald Duckworth and Co. Ltd.

Carter, H. and White, P. (1923), The Tomb of the Bird, *Pearson's Magazine* 56 (November): 433–7.

Cerny, J. (1929), Papyrus Salt 124, *Journal of Egyptian Archaeology* 15: 243–58.

Chamberlain, G. (2001), Two Babies That Could Have Changed World History, *The Historian* 72: 6–10.

Colla, E. (2007), *Conflicted Antiquities: Egyptology, Egyptomania, Egyptian Modernity*. Durham, NC, and London: Duke University Press.

Connolly, R. C. et al. (1980), An Analysis of the Interrelationship between Pharaohs of the 18th Dynasty, *Museum Applied Science Centre for Archaeology Journal* 1(6): 178–81.

Cross, S. W. (2008), The Hydrology of the Valley of the Kings, *Journal of Egyptian Archaeology* 94: 303–10.

Crowfoot, G. M. and Davies, N. de G. (1941), The Tunic of Tut'ankhamūn, *Journal of Egyptian Archaeology* 27: 113–30.

Curl, J. S. (1994), *Egyptomania. The Egyptian Revival: A Recurring Theme in the History of Time*. Manchester: Manchester University Press.

Darnell, J. C. and Manassa, C. (2007), *Tutankhamun's Armies: Battle and Conquest during Egypt's Late Eighteenth Dynasty*. Hoboken: John Wiley & Sons, Inc.

Davies, B. G. (1992), *Egyptian Historical Records of the Later Eighteenth Dynasty, Fascicle IV*, Warminster: Aris & Phillips.

Davies, B. G. (1995), *Egyptian Historical Records of the Later Eighteenth Dynasty, Fascicle VI*, Warminster: Aris & Phillips.

Davies, N. de G. (1905), *The Rock Tombs of el-Amarna*, Part II: *The Tombs of Panehesy and Meryra II*. London: Egypt Exploration Society.

Davies, N. de. G. (1906), *The Rock Tombs of El Amarna*, Part IV: *The Tombs of Penthu, Mahu and Others*. London: Egypt Exploration Society.

Davies, N. de G. (1923), Akhenaten at Thebes, *Journal of Egyptian Archaeology* 9: 132–52.

Davies, Nina de G. and Gardiner, A. H. (1926), *The Tomb of Huy: Viceroy of Nubia in the Reign of Tut'ankhamun*. London: Egypt Exploration Society.

Davis, T. M. (1910), *The Tomb of Queen Tiyi*. London: Archibald Constable and Co. Reprinted 2001 with a foreword by Nicholas Reeves. London: Gerald Duckworth and Co. Ltd.

Davis, T. M. (1912), *The Tombs of Harmhabi and Touatânkhamanou*. London: Archibald Constable and Co. Reprinted 2001 with a foreword by Nicholas Reeves. London: Gerald Duckworth and Co. Ltd.

Derry, D. E. (1927), Appendix I: Report upon the Examination of Tut-Ank-Amen's Mummy, in H. Carter, *The Tomb of Tut·ankh·Amen: The Burial Chamber*. London: Cassell and Company Limited: 143–61.

Derry, D. E. (1931), in R. Engelbach, The So-Called Coffin of Akhenaten, *Annales du Service des Antiquités* 31: 98–114.

Derry, D. E. (1972), The Anatomical Report on the Royal Mummy, in F. F. Leek, *The Human Remains from the Tomb of Tut'ankhamūn*. Oxford: Griffith Institute: 11–20.

Diodorus Siculus, *Library of History*, Book I. Translated by C. H. Oldfather (1933), Vol. I, Loeb Classical Library. Harvard University Press: Cambridge, Mass.; and Heinemann: London.

Dodson, A. (1990), Crown Prince Djhutmose and the Royal Sons of the Eighteenth Dynasty, *Journal of Egyptian Archaeology* 76: 87–96.

Dodson, A. (1999), The Canopic Equipment from the Serapeum of Memphis, in A. Leahy and J. Tait, eds, *Studies on Ancient Egypt in Honour of H. S. Smith*. London: Egypt Exploration Society: 59–75.

Dodson, A. (2009a), Amarna Sunset: The Late-Amarna Succession Revisted, in S. Ikram and A. Dodson, eds, *Beyond the Horizon: Studies in Egyptian Art, Archaeology and History in Honour of Barry J. Kemp*. Cairo: Supreme Council of Antiquities: 29–43.

Dodson. A. (2009b), *Amarna Sunset: Nefertiti, Tutankhamun, Ay, Horemheb and the Egyptian Counter-Reformation*. Cairo: American University in Cairo Press.

Eaton-Krauss, M. (1993), *The Sarcophagus in the Tomb of Tutankhamen*. Oxford: Griffith Institute.

Eaton-Krauss, M. (2000), Restorations and Erasures in the Post-Amarna Period, in Z. Hawass, ed., *Egyptology at the Dawn of the Twenty-First Century: Proceedings of the Eighth International Conference of Egyptologists*, Vol. 2: 194–202.

Eaton-Krauss, M. (2015), *The Unknown Tutankhamun*. London: Bloomsbury Academic.

Edgerton, W. F. (1951), The Strikes in Ramses III's Twenty-Ninth Year, *Journal of Near Eastern Archaeology* 10:3: 137–45.

Edwards, I. E. S. (2000), *From the Pyramids to Tutankhamen: Memoirs of an Egyptologist*. Oxford: Oxbow Books.

El-Khouly, A. and Martin, G. T. (1984), *Excavations in the Royal Necropolis at El-Amarna*. Cairo: Supplément aux Annales du Service des Antiquités de l'Égypte, Cahier 33.

Engelbach, R (1915), *Riqqeh and Memphis VI*. London: British School of Archaeology in Egypt.

Engelbach, R. (1931), The So-Called Coffin of Akhenaten, *Annales du Service des Antiquités de l'Égypte* 31: 98–114.

Faulkner, R. O. (1994), *The Egyptian Book of the Dead*. San Francisco: Chronicle Books.

Fletcher, J. (2004), *The Search for Nefertiti; The True Story of a Remarkable Discovery*, London: Hodder and Stoughton.

Forbes, D. C. (2014), New 'Virtual Autopsy' Creates a Grotesque Tutankhamen, *KMT* 25:4: 24–5.

Frayling, C. (1992), *The Face of Tutankhamun*. London: Faber and Faber.

Gardiner, A. (1946), Davies's Copy of the Great Speos Artemidos Inscription, *Journal of Egyptian Archaeology* 32: 43–56.

Gardiner, A. (1953), The Coronation of King Haremhab, *Journal of Egyptian Archaeology* 39: 13–31.

Gardiner, A. (1957), The So-Called Tomb of Queen Tiye, *Journal of Egyptian Archaeology* 43:1: 10–25.

Geddes, L. (2010), Fallible DNA Evidence Can Mean Prison or Freedom, *New Scientist Online*, 11 August.

Germer, R. (1984), Die angebliche Mumie der Teje: Probleme interdisziplinärer Arbeiten, *Studien zur altägyptischen Kultur* 11: 85–90.

Giménez, J. (2017), Integration of Foreigners in Egypt: The Relief of Amenhotep II Shooting Arrows at a Copper Ingot and Related Scenes, *Journal of Egyptian History* 10: 109–23.

Graefe, E. (2004), Final Reclearance of the Royal Mummies Cache DB320, *KMT* 15(3): 48–57 and 62–3.

Green, L. (1996), The Royal Women of Amarna: Who Was Who, in D. Arnold, ed., *The Royal Women of Amarna: Images of Beauty from Ancient Egypt*, New York: The Metropolitan Museum of Art: 7–15.

Grimm, A. (2001), Goldsarg ohne Geheimnis, in S. Schoske and A. Grimm, eds, *Das Geheimnis des goldenen Sarges: Echnaton und das Ende der Amarnazeit*. Munich: Staatliches Museum Ägyptischer Kunst: 101–20.

Güterbock, H. G. (1959), The Deeds of Suppiluliuma as Told by his Son, Mursili II, *Journal of Cuneiform Studies* 10: 41–68, 75–98, 107–30.

Haikal, F. (2010), Egypt's Past Regenerated by its Own People, in S. MacDonald and M. Rice, eds, *Consuming Ancient Egypt*. London: UCL Press.

Hankey, J. (2001), *A Passion for Egypt: Arthur Weigall, Tutankhamun and the 'Curse of the Pharaoh'*. London and New York: I. B. Tauris.

Harer, W. B. (2007), Chariots, Horses or Hippos: What Killed Tutankhamun? *Minerva* 18: 8–10.

Harer, W. B. (2011), New Evidence for King Tutankhamun's Death: His Bizarre Embalming, *Journal of Egyptian Archaeology* 97: 228–33.

Harris, J. (1973a), Nefernefruaten, *Göttinger Miszellen* 4: 15–17.

Harris, J. (1973b), Nefertiti Rediviva, *Acta Orientalia* 35: 5–13.

Harris, J. (1974), Nefernefruaten Regnans, *Acta Orientalia* 36: 11–21.

Harris, J. E. et al. (1978), Mummy of the 'Elder Lady' in the Tomb of Amenhotep II: Egyptian Museum Catalogue Number 61070, *Science* 200: 1149–51.

Harris, J. E. and Wente, E. F. (1980), *An X-Ray Atlas of the Royal Mummies*. Chicago: University of Chicago Press.

Harrison, R. G. (1966), An Anatomical Examination of the Pharaonic Remains Purported to Be Akhenaten, *Journal of Egyptian Archaeology* 52: 95–119.

Harrison, R. G. (1971), Post Mortem on Two Pharaohs: Was
 Tutankhamen's Skull Fractured? *Buried History* 4: 114–29.

Harrison, R. G., Connolly, R. C. and Abdalla A. 1969), Kinship
 of Smenkhkare and Tutankhamen Affirmed by Serological
 Micromethod: Kinship of Smenkhkare and Tutankhamen
 Demonstrated Serologically, *Nature* 224: 325–6.

Harrison, R. G., Connolly, R. C., Ahmed, S. et al. (1979), A
 Mummified Foetus from the Tomb of Tutankhamun, *Antiquity*
 53(207): 19–21.

Hawass, Z. et al. (2009), Computed Tomographic Evaluation of
 Pharaoh Tutankhamun, ca. 1300 BC, *Annales du Service des
 Antiquités de l'Égypte* 81: 159–74.

Hawass, Z. et al. (2010), Ancestry and Pathology in King
 Tutankhamun's Family, *Journal of the American Medical Association*
 303(7): 638–47.

Hellier, C. A. and Connolly, R. C. (2009), A Re-assessment of the
 Larger Fetus Found in Tutankhamen's Tomb, *Antiquity* 83:
 165–73.

Herodotus, *The Histories*. Translated by A. de Sélincourt (1954),
 revised with introduction and notes by J. Marincola (1996).
 London: Penguin Books.

Hohneck, H. (2014), Alles für die Katz'? Nochmals zum
 „Katzensarkophag" des Prinzen Thutmosis, *Zeitschrift für
 Ägyptische Sprache und Altertumskunde* 141(2): 112–31.

Hoving, T. (1978), *Tutankhamun: The Untold Story*. New York: Simon
 and Schuster.

Ikram, S. (2013), Some Thoughts on the Mummification of King
 Tutankhamun, *Institut des Cultures Méditerranéennes et Orientales
 de l'Académie Polonaise des Sciences*. Etudes et Travaux 26: 292–301.

James, T. G. H. (1992), *Howard Carter: The Path to Tutankhamun*.
 London: Kegan Paul International.

Johnson, W. R. (2009), Tutankhamen-Period Battle Narratives at
 Luxor, *KMT* 20(4): 20–33.

Johnson, W. R. (2010), Warrior Tut. *Archaeology* 63(2): 26–8.

Krauss, R. (1986), Kija – ursprüngliche Besitzerin der Kanopen aus KV 55, *Mitteilungen des Deutschen Archäologischen Instituts Abteilung Kairo* 42: 67–80.

Kurth, D. (2012), Die Inschriften auf den Stöcken und Stäben des Tutanchamun, in H. Beinlich, ed., *'Die Männer hinter dem König': 6. Symposium zur ägyptischen Königsideologie*. Wiesbaden: Harrassowitz: 67–88.

Lansing, A. (1951), A Head of Tut'ankhamūn, *Journal of Egyptian Archaeology* 37: 3–4.

Lawton, J. (1981), The Last Survivor, *Saudi Aramco World* 32(6): 10–21.

Leek, F. F. (1972), *The Human Remains from the Tomb of Tut'ankhamūn*. Oxford: Griffith Institute.

Leek, F. F. (1977), How Old Was Tut'ankhamūn?, *Journal of Egyptian Archaeology* 63: 112–15.

Lichtheim, M. (1973), *Ancient Egyptian Literature, I: The Old and Middle Kingdoms*. Berkeley: University of California Press.

Lichtheim, M. (1976), *Ancient Egyptian Literature, II: The New Kingdom*. Berkeley: University of California Press.

Loeben, C. E. (1986), Eine Bestattung der grossen königlichen Gemahlin Nofretete in Amarna? – die Totenfigur der Nofretete, *Mitteilungen des Deutschen Archäologischen Instituts Abteilung Kairo* 42: 99–107.

Loeben, C. E. (1994), No Evidence of a Coregency: Two Erased Inscriptions from Tutankhamun's Tomb, *Amarna Letters* 3: 105–9.

Loret, V. (1899), Les Tombeaux de Thoutmès III et d'Aménophis II, *Bulletin de l'Institut Égyptien, Cairo*.

Lucas, A. (1931), The Canopic Vases from the 'Tomb of Queen Tiyi', *Annales du Service des Antiquités* 31: 120–22.

Lucas, A. (1942), Notes on Some Objects from the Tomb of Tut-Ankhamun, *Annales du Service des Antiquités de l'Égypte* 41: 135–47.

Mace, A. C. (1923), The Egyptian Expedition 1922–23, *The Metropolitan Museum of Art Bulletin* 18(2): 5–11.

Mallinson, M. (1989), Investigation of the Small Aten Temple, in B. J. Kemp, ed., *Amarna Reports 5*. London: Egypt Exploration Society.

Martin, G. T. (1985), Notes on a Canopic Jar from Kings' Valley Tomb 22, in P. Posener-Kriéger, ed., *Mélanges Gamal Eddin Mokhtar II*. Cairo: Institut Français d'Archéologie Orientale: 111–24.

Martin, G. T. (1989a), *The Memphite Tomb of Horemheb, Commander-in-Chief of Tutankhamun. I: The Reliefs, Inscriptions and Commentary*. London: Egypt Exploration Society.

Martin, G. T. (1989b), *The Royal Tomb at el-Amarna 2*. London: Egypt Exploration Society.

Martin, G. T. (1991), *A Bibliography of the Amarna Period and its Aftermath*. London: Kegan Paul International.

Mayes, S. (1959), *The Great Belzoni: The Circus Strongman Who Discovered Egypt's Ancient Treasures*. London: Bloomsbury.

McDowell, A. G (1999), *Village Life in Ancient Egypt: Laundry Lists and Love Songs*. Oxford: Oxford University Press.

Merchant, J. (2011), New Twist in the Tale of Tutankhamun's Club Foot, *New Scientist* 212(2833): 10.

Merchant, J. (2013), *The Shadow King: The Bizarre Afterlife of King Tut's Mummy*. Philadelphia: Da Capo Press.

Moran, W. L. (1992), *The Amarna Letters*. Baltimore: Johns Hopkins University Press.

Moser, S. (2006), *Wondrous Curiosities: Ancient Egypt at the British Museum*. Chicago and London: University of Chicago Press.

Murnane, W. J. (1977), *Ancient Egyptian Coregencies*. Chicago: Oriental Institute Studies in Ancient Oriental Civilization: 40.

Murnane, W. J. (1995), *Texts from the Amarna Period in Egypt*. Atlanta: Society of Biblical Literature.

Murnane, W. J. and Van Sicklen, C. C. (1993), *The Boundary Stelae of Akhenaten*. London and New York: Kegan Paul International.

Navratilova, H. (2012), *Visitors' Graffiti of Dynasties 18 and 19 in Abusir and Northern Saqqara*. Liverpool: Abercromby Press.

Newberry, P. E. (1927), Appendix III: Report on the Floral Wreaths Found in the Coffins of Tut-ank-Amen, in H. Carter, *The Tomb of Tut·ankh·Amen: The Burial Chamber*. London: Cassell and Company Limited: 189–96.

Newberry, P. E. (1928), Akhenaten's Eldest Son-in-Law 'Ankhkheperure, *Journal of Egyptian Archaeology* 14: 3–9.

Newberry, P. E. (1932), King Ay, the Successor of Tut'ankhamūn, *Journal of Egyptian Archaeology* 18(1): 50–52.

Ockinga, B. (1997), *A Tomb from the Reign of Tutankhamun*. Warminster: Aris & Phillips.

Peden, A. J. (1994), *Egyptian Historical Inscriptions of the Twentieth Dynasty*, Jonsered: Paul Åstroms förlag.

Pendlebury, J. D. S. (1935), *Tell el-Amarna*. London: Lovat Dickson & Thompson.

Pendlebury, J. D. S. (1951), *The City of Akhenaten*, Part III: *The Central City and the Official Quarters*. London: Egypt Exploration Society.

Perlin, M. W., Belrose, J. L. and Duceman, B. W. (2013), New York State TrueAllele® Casework Variation Study, *Journal of Forensic Sciences* 58: 6: 1458–66.

Pfluger, K. (1946), The Edict of King Haremhab, *Journal of Near Eastern Studies* 5(1): 260–76.

Phizackerley, K. (2010), *DNA Shows the KV55 Mummy Probably Not Akhenaten*, https://katephizackerley.wordpress.com/2010/03/03/dna-shows-that-kv55-mummy-probably-not-akhenaten/ (2 March 2010).

Pococke, R. (1743), *A Description of the East and Some Other Countries*, Vol. 1: *Observations on Egypt*. London.

Porter, B and Moss, R. L. B. (1972), *Topographical Bibliography of Ancient Egyptian Hieroglyphic Texts, Reliefs, and Paintings II: Theban Temples*, 2nd edn, revised and augmented. Oxford: Clarendon Press.

Price, C. (forthcoming), Interpreting the 'Two Brothers' at Manchester Museum; Science, Knowledge and Display. *Archaeologies: The Journal of World Archaeology*.

Ray, J. (1975), The Parentage of Tutankhamūn, *Antiquity* 49: 45–7.

Redford, D. B. (1975), Studies on Akhenaten at Thebes II: A Report on the Work of the Akhenaten Temple Project of the University Museum, The University of Pennsylvania, for the Year 1973–4, *Journal of the American Research Center in Egypt* 12: 9–14.

Reeves, C. N. (1981), A Reappraisal of Tomb 55 in the Valley of the Kings, *Journal of Egyptian Archaeology* 67: 48–55.

Reeves, C. N. and Wilkinson, R. H. (1996), *The Complete Valley of the Kings: Tombs and Treasures of Egypt's Greatest Pharaohs*. London: Thames and Hudson.

Reeves, N. (1990), *The Complete Tutankhamun: The King, the Tomb, the Royal Treasure*. London: Thames and Hudson.

Reeves, N. (2015a), *The Burial of Nefertiti?* Amarna Royal Tombs Project: Valley of the Kings, *Occasional Paper* 1.

Reeves, N. (2015b), Tutankhamun's Mask Reconsidered, in A. Oppenheim and O. Goelet, eds, *The Art and Culture of Ancient Egypt: Studies in Honor of Dorothea Arnold*. Bulletin of the Egyptological Seminar 19: 511–26.

Reid, D. M. (2015), *Contesting Antiquity in Egypt: Archaeologies, Museums, and the Struggle for Identities from World War I to Nasser*. Cairo and New York: American University in Cairo Press.

Riggs, C. (2014), *Unwrapping Ancient Egypt*. London: Bloomsbury.

Riggs, C. (2018), *Photographing Tutankhamun: Archaeology, Ancient Egypt, and the Archive*. London: Routledge.

Riggs, C. (2020), Water Boys and Wishful Thinking. Photographing Tutankhamun blog 20 June: https://photographing-tutankhamun.com/2020/06/20/the-water-boy-who-wasn't/.

Riggs, C. (2021), *Treasured: How Tutankhamun Shaped a Century*. London: Atlantic Books.

Robins, G. (1981), Hmt nsw wrt Meritaten, *Gottinger Miszellen* 52: 75–81.

Robins, G. (1984), Isis, Nephthys, Selket and Neith Represented on the Sarcophagus of Tutankhamun and in Four Free-Standing Statues Found in KV 62, *Göttinger Miszellen* 72: 21–5.

Romer, J. (1988), *Valley of the Kings*. London: Michael O'Mara Books.

Rühli, F. J. and Ikram, S (2014), Purported medical diagnoses of
    Pharaoh Tutankhamun, c. 1325 BC, *HOMO: Journal of
    Comparative Human Biology* 65(1): 51-63.

Schulman, A. R. (1978), Ankhesenamun, Nofretity and the Amka
    Affair, *Journal of the American Research Center in Egypt* 15: 43–8.

Seele, K. C. (1955), King Ay and the Close of the Amarna Age, *Journal
    of Near Eastern Studies* 14: 168–80.

Siculus, Diodorus (1933), *Library of History* Book I, trans. by C. H.
    Oldfather. Vol I, Loeb Classical Library, Cambridge, Mass.:
    Harvard University Press and London: Heinemann.

Smith, G. E. (1910), A Note on the Estimate of the Age Attained by the
    Person Whose Skeleton Was Found in the Tomb, in T. M. Davis,
    The Tomb of Queen Tiyi. London: Archibald Constable and Co.:
    xxiii–xxiv,

Smith, G. E. (1912), *The Royal Mummies*. Cairo: Service des Antiquités
    de l'Égypte.

Snape, S. (2011), *Ancient Egyptian Tombs: The Culture of Life and
    Death*. Oxford: Wiley–Blackwell.

Stevens, A. (2017), Death and the City: The Cemeteries of Amarna
    in their Urban Context, *Cambridge Archaeological Journal* 28:1:
    103–26.

Strouhal, E. (2010), Biological Age of Skeletonized Mummy from
    Tomb KV 55 at Thebes, *Anthropologie* XLVIII(2): 97–112.

Strudwick, N. (2005), *Texts from the Pyramid Age*. Atlanta: Society of
    Biblical Literature.

Troy, L. (1986), *Patterns of Queenship in Ancient Egyptian Myth and
    History*. Uppsala: Acta Universitatis Upsaliensis.

Tyldesley, J. A. (1998), *Nefertiti: Egypt's Sun Queen*. London: Viking.

Tyldesley, J. A. (2012), *Tutankhamun's Curse: The Developing History of
    an Egyptian King*. London: Profile Books.

Tyldesley, J. A. (2018), *Nefertiti's Face: The Creation of an Icon*.
    London: Profile Books.

Tyndale, W. (1907), *Below the Cataracts*. London: Heinemann.

Van der Perre, A. (2012), Nefertiti's Last Documented Reference (for

Now), in F. Seyfried, ed., *In the Light of Amarna: 100 Years of the Nefertiti Discovery*. Berlin: Michael Imhof Verlag: 195–7.

Van Dijk, J. (1993), The New Kingdom Necropolis of Memphis: Historical and Iconographical Studies. Thesis: University of Groningen.

Van Dijk, J. and Eaton-Krauss, M. (1986), Tutankhamun at Memphis, *Mitteilungen des Deutschen Archäologischen Instituts Abteilung Kairo* 42: 35–41.

Vandenberg, P. (1975), *The Curse of the Pharaohs,* trans. T. Weyr. London: Book Club Associates.

Vogelsang-Eastwood, G. M. (1999), *Tutankhamun's Wardrobe: Garments from the Tomb of Tutankhamun*. Leiden: Van Doorn & Co.

Weigall, A. E. P. B (1922), The Mummy of Akhenaten, *Journal of Egyptian Archaeology* 8: 193–200.

Weigall, A. E. P. B. (1923), *Tutankhamen and Other Essays*. London: Thornton Butterworth.

Wente, E. F. (1990), *Letters from Ancient Egypt*. Atlanta: Society of Biblical Literature.

Willerslev, E. and Lorenzen, E. (2010), King Tutankhamun's Family and Demise, *Journal of the American Medical Association* 303(24): 2471.

Winlock, H. E. (1941), *Materials Used at the Embalming of King Tutankhamun: The Metropolitan Museum of Art Papers 10*. Reprinted 2010 with a foreword by D. Arnold as *Tutankhamun's Funeral*. New York: The Metropolitan Museum of Art/Yale University Press, New Haven and London.

Zivie, A. (2009), *La Tombe de Maïa: mère nourricière du roi Toutânkhamon et grande du harem*. Toulouse: Caracara Edition.

Zivie, A. (2013), *La Tombe de Thoutmès: Directeur des Peintres dans la Place de Maât*. Toulouse: Caracara Edition.

Zivie, A. (2018), Pharaoh's Man: 'Abdiel: The Vizier with a Semitic Name, *Biblical Archaeology Review* 44(4): 22–31.

Zwar, D. (2007), Tutankhamun's Last Guardian, *History Today* 57:11.

References

Prologue

1 Anatomy of an Excavation: www.griffith.ox.ac.uk/gri/4tut.html.
2 *National Geographic* online, 8 November 2017.
3 *Egypt Today* online, 31 March 2020.

1. The Prince's Tale

1 Extract from the *Great Hymn to the Aten*, inscribed on the wall of Ay's Amarna tomb. Translation by Steven Snape. For a translation of the full text see Lichtheim (1976: 96–100).
2 Priest statuette, Louvre Museum, Paris E2749 N792, and Dodson (1990); cat sarcophagus, Cairo Museum CG5003, but see Hohneck (2014); mummy statuette, Ägyptisches Museum Berlin VAGM1997/117.
3 Allen (2009: 13 and Fig. 5).
4 Extract from Amarna Boundary Stela S. Translation by Steven Snape. For a translation of the full text see Lichtheim (1976: 48–51).
5 For details of Tutankhamun's wine jars see Reeves (1990: 202–3).
6 Derry (1972: 15). Derry's investigation was itself investigated by Leek (1977).
7 Pendlebury (1951, Vol. 2: pl. 95: no. 279).
8 Carter and Mace (1923: 171).
9 Carter and Mace (1923: 172).

References

10 Reeves (1990: 158).

11 Oriental Institute Museum, Chicago E12144.

12 British Museum, London EA2; Ray (1975).

13 Tyldesley (2018: 9).

14 Extract from Amarna Boundary Stela K. Translation by Steven Snape. For a translation of the full text see Murnane and Van Siclen (1993: 33–47).

15 Martin (1989b: 37–41).

16 Discussed in Arnold (1996: 115).

17 Metropolitan Museum of Art, New York 1991.237.70.

18 Tomb Bubasteion 1.20: Zivie (2009).

19 Bryan (2006: 97–9).

20 Zivie (2018).

21 Ockinga (1997).

22 *The Satire of the Trades*. For a full translation see Lichtheim (1973: 184–92).

23 Reeves (1990: 166–7).

24 TT109. Discussed in Giménez (2017).

25 Extract from the Sphinx Stela of Amenhotep II. Translation by Steven Snape. For a translation of the full text see Lichtheim (1976: 41–2).

26 Extract from the *Great Hymn to the Aten*. Translation by Steven Snape. For a translation of the full text see Lichtheim (1976: 96–100).

27 Stevens (2017).

28 Mallinson (1989: 138).

29 Davies, N. de. G. (1906: 16 and Plate XXXII).

30 Davies, N. de G. (1905: 38–43 and Plate XXXVII).

31 Tyldesley (1998: 151).

32 See, for example, Davies (1923: 133); Pendlebury (1935: 28–9); Seele (1955: 168–80).

33 Van der Perre (2012).

34 Extract from the Seti Abydos temple inscription. Translated by

Steven Snape. For a translation of the full text see Murnane (1977: 58).

35 Extract from the Kuban Stela. Translation by Steven Snape. For a translation of the full text see Murnane (1977: 59).

36 Harris (1973a, 1973b, 1974).

37 Davies (1905: 43–4).

38 Reeves (1990: 199); Loeben (1994).

39 Allen (2009: 9).

40 EA10: British Museum, London EA 029786. Translated by Moran (1992: 19).

2. The King's Tale

1 Extract from Tutankhamun's Restoration Stela. Translated by Steven Snape. For a translation of the full text see Murnane (1995: 212–14).

2 Turin Museum 1379. Translation by Steven Snape. For a translation of the full text see Gardiner (1953).

3 Belekdanian (2015).

4 Lansing (1951) and Eaton-Krauss (2015: 55–6). Metropolitan Museum of Art, New York 50.6.

5 Reeves (1990: 153–4). A third flail is uninscribed and missing its crook (no. 44u).

6 Translation by Steven Snape.

7 Ägyptisches Museum Berlin ÄM 37391 and ÄM 34701.

8 Tomb Bubasteion 1.19: Zivie (2013).

9 Tyldesley (2018).

10 Murnane (1995: 211[97]).

11 Navratilova (2015: 122–5).

12 The separate *shabti* pieces are housed in the Louvre Museum, Paris, and the Brooklyn Museum. See Loeben (1986) and Aldred (1988: 229).

13 Translation by Steven Snape. For a translation of the full text see Davies, B. G. (1995: 30–33). Part of a duplicate text was

discovered in the foundations of the temple of Montu. Cairo Museum JE 41504 and 41565.

14 Extract from the Speos Artemidos inscription. For a translation of the full text see Gardiner (1946: 47–8).

15 Translation by Steven Snape. To read more of Horemheb's decrees see Pfluger (1946).

16 EA64: British Museum, London EA29816. For a translation of the full letter see Moran (1992: 135–6).

17 EA170: Staatliche Museen, Berlin VAT327. For a translation of the full letter see Moran (1992: 257–8).

18 Johnson (2009) and (2010).

19 Reeves (1990: 170–73).

20 Hawass et al. (2010).

21 Merchant (2011).

22 Kurth (2012).

23 Lichtheim (1973: 61–80).

24 Extract from Maya's stela: Garstang Museum, University of Liverpool E583. Translation by Steven Snape. For a translation of the full text see Murnane (1995: 215–16).

25 Cairo Museum JE57 195; Van Dijk and Eaton-Krauss (1986: 39–41).

26 Discussed in Eaton-Krauss (2015: 49).

27 Murnane (1995: 219).

28 Tutankhamun's Nubian projects are discussed in Eaton-Krauss (2015: 70–71).

29 Eaton-Krauss (2000).

30 Egyptian Museum, Cairo CG 42091.

31 Carter (1927: 41).

32 Vogelsang-Eastwood (1999: 17–19).

33 Figures given in the *Independent*, 3 August 2000.

34 Carter, diary, 16 November 1925.

35 Zahi Hawass: press release, Supreme Council of Antiquities, 10 May 2005.

36 Martin (1989b: plates 110–12).

37 Dodson (1999: 62).

38 Nina de G. Davies and Gardiner (1926: plates IV–VIII and XXII–XXXI).

39 Newberry (1927).

40 Carter (1927: 86).

41 Mace (1923: 6).

42 Harrison (1971).

43 Boyer, Rodin, Grey and Connolly (2003:1146–7); Hawass et al. (2010).

44 Zahi Hawass: press release, Supreme Council of Antiquities, 10 May 2005.

45 Harer (2007).

3. The Undertaker's Tale

1 Translation by Steven Snape. For a translation and discussion of the complete set of texts on Tutankhamun's sarcophagus see Eaton-Krauss (1993).

2 Translation by Steven Snape. For a translation of the full text see Gardiner (1953, 14).

3 Discussed in Van Dijk (1993: 10–64).

4 Darnell and Manassa (2007: 178–84).

5 Snape (2011: 242) discusses the mechanism of buying a coffin in a land with no currency.

6 Herodotus, *Histories* 2: 86. Translated by de Sélincourt (1954: 127–8).

7 Brier and Wade (2001).

8 Porter and Moss (1972: 454–9).

9 Cairo Museum JE 59869; Oriental Institute, Chicago 14088; Ägyptisches Museum Berlin 1479/1.

10 Herodotus, *Histories* 2: 89. Translated by de Sélincourt (1954: 128).

11 Diodorus Siculus, *Library of History* 1: 91. Translated by Oldfather (1933: 309, 311).

References

12 Harer (2011).

13 Brier and Wade (2001).

14 Allen (2010).

15 Carter and Mace (1923: 184).

16 Robins (1984).

17 Papyrus Vindob 3873: Österreichische Nationalbibliothek, Vienna.

18 Carter, journal, 18 November 1925.

19 The mask is made of gold sheets beaten together, the surface being 18.4 carat gold, the headdress 22.5 carats and the underlying mask 23 carats.

20 Extract from *Book of the Dead*, Spell 151. Translation by Steven Snape. For a full translation of this spell see Faulkner (1994: 123).

21 Reeves (2015b).

22 Winlock (1941: 21–3).

23 Winlock (1941).

24 Discussed in S. J. Allen (2002).

25 Discussed by Arnold in Winlock (1941: 16–17).

26 The others being KV55 and KV63.

27 Eaton-Krauss (2015: 106); all measurements are taken from Reeves (1990: 70–71).

28 Translation by Steven Snape.

29 Reeves (2015b: 514–15).

30 Beinlich (2006).

31 Carter (1927: 41).

4. The Queen's Tale

1 Güterbock (1959: 94).

2 Neues Museum, Berlin 14145.

3 Translated by Steven Snape. For a translation of the full text see Lichtheim (1976: 96–100).

4 Redford (1975); Robins (1981).

5 Extract from the *New Kingdom Instructions of Ani*. Translation by Steven Snape. For a translation see Lichtheim (1976: 135–46).
6 Discussed with further references in Eaton-Krauss (2015: 3–6).
7 Carter and Mace (1923: 119). The scenes decorating the Little Golden Shrine are discussed in Troy (1986: 100ff). See also Bosse-Griffiths (1973).
8 Carter and Mace (1923: 117).
9 Arnold (1996: 107).
10 Eaton-Krauss (1993); Robins (1984).
11 Derry quoted in Leek (1972: 21–3).
12 Cairo Museum JE 39711; Reeves (1990: 123).
13 Harrison et al. (1979).
14 Chamberlain (2001); Hellier and Connolly (2009).
15 Carter (1933: 28).
16 Newberry (1932).
17 'Marriage Scarab' of Amenhotep III: Davies, B. G. (1992: 38).
18 Güterbock (1959: 94–5). See also Schulman (1978).
19 EA4: Staatlichen Museen, Berlin VAT1657. For a translation of the full letter see Moran (1992: 8–9).
20 Güterbock (1959: 96–7).

5. The Thief's Tale

1 Extract from the hieratic Papyrus Mayer B. Reeves and Wilkinson (1996: 192).
2 Engelbach (1915: 12).
3 Warning inscription in the Giza tomb of Peteti. Strudwick (2005: 437).
4 Ineni tomb: TT81.
5 Ostracon OIC 16991 (McDowell (1999: 218)) and Ostracon Deir el-Medina 317 (Wente (1990: 154)).
6 Cross (2008) and personal communication.
7 Translation based on Edgerton (1951: 141).
8 Peden (1994: 245–57).

6. The Lawyer's Tale

1 Davis (1912: 3).

2 Diodorus Siculus, *Library of History* I: 46, translated by Oldfather (1933).

3 Homer, *The Iliad*, translated by Alexander Pope, with notes by the Rev. Theodore Alois Buckley, M.A, F.S.A. and Flaxman Designs, 1899, Book IX: 381–2.

4 Pococke (1743: 97–8).

5 Bruce (1790: 126–8).

6 Moser (2006: 34).

7 The British Museum refused to pay £2,000 for the sarcophagus, which is today displayed in Sir John Soane's Museum, London.

8 British Museum, London EA24.

9 For a reappraisal of the DB320 cache see Bickerstaffe (2005). For details of the most recent survey see Graefe (2004).

10 Loret (1899).

11 Loret (1899), translated by Romer (1988: 161–2).

12 Smith (1912: 38).

13 Harris et al. (1978).

14 Germer (1984).

15 Connolly et al. (1980).

16 Bickerstaffe (2009: 105–12).

17 Hawass et al. (2010).

18 Weigall (1922: 193).

19 Davis (1910). Davis's publication should be read in conjunction with Bell (1990) and Reeves (1981).

20 Cross (2008: 305) and personal communication 2011.

21 Martin (1985: 112).

22 Krauss (1986).

23 Lucas (1931).

24 Quoted in Gardiner (1957: 25).

25 Davis (1910: 9 and 2). The inscribed gold sheets are housed in the Cairo Museum. Six uninscribed sheets were given to Davis; today

these are in the collections of the Metropolitan Museum of Art, New York.

26 Engelbach (1931: 98ff).

27 Translation by Steven Snape. See J. P. Allen (1988), and Gardiner (1957: 19–20).

28 Davis (1910: 2).

29 Weigall (1922:196).

30 Hankey (2001: 93).

31 Derry (1972: 14); Connolly, Harrison and Ahmed (1976).

32 Smith (1910: xxiv).

33 Smith (1912: 52, 54).

34 Derry (1931: 116).

35 Harrison (1966: 111).

36 Harris and Wente (1992).

37 Discussed by Eaton-Krauss (2015: 8, fn. 28).

38 Hawass et al. (2010: 640).

39 Gardiner (1957: 10).

40 Quoted in the *Manchester Guardian*, 27 January 1923.

41 Davis (1912: 3).

42 Maspero's contribution to Davis's publication (1912: 111–23) more or less ignores his 'discovery of Tutankhamun's tomb'.

7. The Archaeologist's Tale

1 Carter and Mace (1923: 76).

2 *The Times*, 30 November 1922.

3 Carnarvon (2007: 14).

4 Introduction to Carter and Mace (1923: 25).

5 Quoted in James (1992: 413–15).

6 Carter and Mace (1923: 82).

7 Carnarvon writing for *The Times*, 11 December 1922.

8 Carter and Mace (1923: 86).

9 Carter and Mace (1923: 87); Carter, diary, 1 November 1922; Cross (2008: 308, Fig. 4).

10 Carter and Mace (1923: 95–6).

11 James (1992: 253).

12 Lucas (1942: 136).

13 Mace diary entry dated 12 February 1924.

14 Carter journal entry dated 28 October 1925.

15 Agnew and Wong (2019); details of this project are given on the Getty website: https://www.getty.edu/conservation/our_projects/field_projects/tut/index.html.

16 https://www.factumfoundation.org/pag/207/recording-the-tomb-of-tutankhamun.

17 Reeves (2015a).

18 Quoted in BBC online article Nefertiti Was Buried inside King Tut's Tomb, 11 August 2015.

8. The Journalist's Tale

1 Abaza (1924) quoted in Colla (2007: 172).

2 Curl (1994: 211–20).

3 Colla (2007: 13); Haikal (2010).

4 Discussed in Reid (2015: 64).

5 Hankey (2001).

6 Frayling (1992: 33).

7 James (1992: 326).

8 See, for example, Hoving (1978: 194).

9 Weigall (1923: 136).

10 That all the lights in Cairo should have failed is far from remarkable. Susie apparently died shortly before 4 a.m. London time. In 1923, English time was two hours behind Egypt. Susie actually died four hours after her master.

11 Vandenberg (1975: 20).

12 Vandenberg (1975: 20).

13 Translation by Steven Snape. See Carter (1933: 33, 40–41).

14 Unpublished article quoted in James (1992: 371).

15 Carter and White (1923).

References

16 Letter Written to Edward Robinson, Director of the Metropolitan Museum of Art, 28 March 1923. Quoted in Hoving (1978: 82).

17 Weigall (1923: 138).

18 Winlock, *The New York Times* (26 January 1934: 19–20).

9. The Waterboy's Tale

1 Edwards (2000: 271–2).

2 See Riggs (2014) for the importance of textiles as wrappings.

3 Discussed in Price (forthcoming).

4 Lawton (1981).

5 Zwar (2007).

6 Hoving tells this tale (1978: 76–7), quoting an unpublished memoir by Carter's American agent, Lee Keedick. It is discussed by Riggs (2020).

7 Carter (1927: XXIV).

8 Discussed by Riggs (2018: 5). Burton himself was supported in his photographic work by adult Egyptian 'camera boys'.

9 Letter written to his wife, Hortense; cited in Hankey (2001: 51).

10 Quoted in Hankey (2001: 265).

11 Carter and Mace (1923: 125–6).

12 James (1992: 315).

10. The Bishop's Tale

1 *The Times*, 3 February 1923.

2 *The Times*, 13 February 1923.

3 *The Times*, 20 March 1923.

4 *The New York Times*, 24 February 1923.

5 Belzoni, *Narrative* (1820/2001: 168–9).

6 Riggs (2014) discusses the importance of regarding the wrapped mummy as a whole entity, rather than a wrapped parcel.

7 Derry (1927: 145).

8 Derry published a brief summary of his work as an appendix to Carter's second popular Tutankhamun book (1927), but

his scientific report remained unpublished until Leek (1972) reconstructed the results of the autopsy.

9 Forbes (2014).

Epilogue

1 See, for example, Geddes (2010); Perlin et al. (2013).
2 An alternative argument, that the rapid desiccation process and, in particular, the resin may have actually helped to preserve the DNA, is discussed by Merchant (2013: 206).
3 Brier and Wade (2001).
4 Hawass et al. (2010).
5 Headline in the *Sydney Morning Herald*, 18 February 2010.
6 Merchant (2013: 198).
7 Phizackerley (2010).
8 For example, Willerslev and Lorenzen (2010) point out that in most ancient Egyptian remains ancient DNA does not survive at a level that is currently retrievable.

Index

Index

Index

Index

Index

Index

Index

Picture Credits

1 Painted Box © Roger Wood/CORBIS/VCG via Getty Images
Amarna Stela © Heritage Image Partnership Ltd./Alamy

2 Blue Crown Head, Metropolitan Museum of Art, Rogers Fund, 1950
Statue © The Trustees of The British Museum
Crooks and Flails by Harry Burton © Griffith Institute, University of
Oxford

3 Dyad © Steven Snape

4 KV55 Coffin © Steven Snape
Tomb East Wall © Iberfoto/Bridgeman Images

5 Guardian statues © *Illustrated London News*/Bridgeman Images
Little Golden Shrine © Heritage Image Partnership Ltd./Alamy

6 Canopic Shrine © NPL – DeA Picture Library/S. Vannini/Bridgeman
Images
Canopic Chest © Heritage Image Partnership Ltd./Alamy
Sarcophagus © robertharding/Alamy

7 Inner Coffin © NPL – DeA Picture Library/S. Vannini/Bridgeman Images
Mask, DeA Picture Library/A. Jemolo/Getty Images

8 Autopsy © *Illustrated London News*/Bridgeman Images
Lotus Head © Luisa Ricciarini/Bridgeman Images